FORD CAPRI
'The Car You Always Promised Yourself'

Other Titles in the Crowood AutoClassics Series

AC Cobra	Brian Laban
Alfa Romeo: Spider, Alfasud and Alfetta GT	David G. Styles
Aston Martin and Lagonda	David G. Styles
Aston Martin: DB4, DB5 and DB6	Jonathan Wood
Austin-Healey 100 and 3000 Series	Graham Robson
BMW M-Series	Alan Henry
Ferrari Dino	Anthony Curtis
Jaguar E-type	Jonathan Wood
Jaguar XJ Series	Graham Robson
Jensen Interceptor	John Tipler
Lamborghini Countach	Peter Dron
Lotus Elan	Mike Taylor
Lotus Esprit	Jeremy Walton
Mercedes SL Series	Brian Laban
MGB	Brian Laban
Morgan: The Cars and the Factory	John Tipler
Porsche 911	David Vivian
Porsche 924/928/944/968	David Vivian
Sporting Fords: Cortina to Cosworth	Mike Taylor
Sprites and Midgets	Anders Ditlev Clausager
Triumph TRs	Graham Robson
Triumph 2000 and 2.5PI	Graham Robson
TVR: The Complete Story	John Tipler

Ford Capri
'The Car You Always Promised Yourself'

Mike Taylor

CROWOOD
AutoClassic

First published in 1995 by
The Crowood Press Ltd
Ramsbury, Marlborough
Wiltshire SN8 2HR

British Library Cataloguing-in-Publication Data
A catalogue record for this book is available from the British Library

ISBN 1 85223 798 8

Picture Credits
All photographs supplied by Ford UK; Stephen Young; Richard Rycraft and the author. The photograph on page 8 is reproduced by courtesy of Mrs Henry Ford II. The bottom photograph on page 157 is reproduced by courtesy of Walter Hayes. All line-drawings by Bob Constant

Typeset by Footnote Graphics, Warminster, Wiltshire
Printed and bound in Great Britain by The Bath Press

Contents

Acknowledgements

In my research for this book I have had to draw on a multitude of sources, including the authoritative writings of fellow journalists (whose works I have listed separately in the Bibliography) and people whose lives have revolved around cars – and Ford in particular. I have also had to call upon the good offices of people who have allowed me to interrupt their ever-busy working lives, including the team at Boreham, who cheerfully took time out to discuss the Capri with me.

To the people in Ford's Public Affairs Department, I say a big thank you for allowing me the use of a Probe, which features in these pages. A special thanks must also go to Walter Hayes, who kindly talked to me at length about his life and the importance of the Capri in his long and fascinating career, and to Rod Mansfield, the man whose name is associated with so many exciting Ford products and who also discussed the Capri with me in detail.

As ever, I am grateful to the team at *Classic Cars*, *Autocar & Motor* and *Ford Heritage* magazines, who kindly allowed me to reproduce their informative text and tables within these pages.

As for photographs – upon which a publication such as this relies so strongly – I must say a special thanks to Barry Reynolds, who happily threw open the doors of Ford's extensive photographic library at South Ockenden, and to Sheila and Fran, whose unstinting help routed out the majority of the pictures that appear in these pages. I must also mention the considerable help and support given so agreeably by the charismatic John Hill and Capri Club International, and thank them for allowing me to join them at their Windsor Castle venue where I enjoyed a memorable day among club enthusiasts. I was given total freedom to poke my camera into impressively clean wheelarches and under highly polished bonnets.

Additionally, I would like to thank the following people: Roy Bishop; the management of Buxted Place Hotel; Heather Chatfield; Terry Coomber; Glen Butler; Don Hilton; Don Hume; Bill Meade; Charlie Meade; Richard Rycraft; Simon Sproule; Harry Warrall; and Stephen Young.

Finally, I would like to salute Capri enthusiasts everywhere. Despite traffic jams and road works it is still possible to enjoy owning and driving something rather special. Long may you derive pleasure from your cars.

Foreword

J Walter Thompson suggested that the Capri should be introduced as 'The car you always promised yourself' and, as car-advertising slogans go, this seemed to be more accurate than most.

Car ownership in Britain did not become widespread until 1955, and inevitably the first offerings by post-war British manufacturers were predominantly functional; it was something of an adventure to own a car at all. As the market matured it became evident that there was an unsatisfied demand for a genuinely affordable sports coupé that would, in particular, capture the hearts of young buyers, those extrovert post-war baby boomers who had invented the 'Swinging Sixties'. No company was better placed than Ford to take up this challenge: the sporting derivatives of its Escorts and Cortinas had made friends all over the world and the company had also established a remarkable sporting pedigree which the Capri could inherit to the full.

There were obviously many more baby boomers in the United States than in Britain, and it was the Mustang that had for them become a cult car. The ambitions for the Capri were much smaller, but it was the first European Ford to be manufactured in both Britain and Germany, this fact giving it additional significance within the company. No matter what claims are made with hindsight, nobody knows what makes a car popular, or why one captures a special place in the estimation of its owners more than another; it is something that is only evident with the passage of the years.

The Capri, however, soon established itself as special because it was accessible to the young; as much fun could be had in the 1.6-litre version as in the later and more powerful 3-litre performance derivatives. And nobody, certainly not within Ford, anticipated its successes in motor sport, beginning with private owners and, some say, culminating in the dazzling victory in the 24-hour race at Spa in Belgium and the unprecedented class victory at Le Mans by the German team.

Ford of Britain took its introductory Capris to Cyprus, and I saw three of them there recently, all in spanking condition even though one had 109,000 miles on its clock. Cars such as these are also always evident at the growing number of classic car events held throughout Britain. Not every car has what it takes to become a classic in its own lifetime, but the Ford Capri truly deserves that honour. It has kept its promise.

Walter Hayes CBE
August 1994

Introduction

So much has been written about Ford cars in all their forms over the years that when the Crowood Press asked me to consider writing a book on sporting Fords, I was worried that there would be nothing new to say. In the event, the reviews were positive, sufficient in fact for the publisher to suggest a follow-up. 'Write a second book on Ford,' I was commanded. 'Something on the Capri.'

For a volume manufacturer like Ford, the Capri really was something rather special. First introduced as the RB60 Consul Capri 109E in 1961, it pre-dated the American Mustang by some three years, totally destroying the theory that the British Capri coupé concept followed in the Mustang's footsteps.

It was, however, never intended that the first Capri would have sports-car-like speed or handling; rather, it was what Americans call a boulevard car, its shape and style making a profound statement in the heady days of the early 1960s. But the real surprise for car buffs was that Ford of Britain should build such a car at all; after all, it offered neither value for money nor would it be a volume seller. Indeed, when Ford's Product Planning team began considering the next

Henry Ford II changing a wheel on his Capri – it can happen to anyone!

generation of Capri – the Mk I, introduced in 1969 – it was only with the support and market potential of Ford Europe that the programme was approved. The Capri of the 1970s and 1980s was a very different motor car to the early versions, sales markedly outstripping expectations and the model often figuring in the UK's sales top twenty. The Capri also established an enviable reputation for itself in world motor sport.

For me, the delight in writing this second book on Ford has been to meet the people behind the Capri, by both renewing old friendships and making new ones. Believe me, the Capri would not have been the car it was without the help of some very special people, many of whom you will meet in the following pages. Car enthusiasts all, the Capri was their kind of car. But, as we gallop through the 1990s, I also write with a degree of sadness as I have found that Ford's people are changing, people such as the Capri champions, Walter Hayes and Rod Mansfield, both of whom have now retired. Today, Ford is a very different firm with very different objectives; it's a tough world out there, with no room for sentiment.

Could the Capri happen today? I doubt it. The Probe, which some people say is the Capri's natural successor, is essentially a Japanese design and is built in the United States. That said, the press demonstrator kindly lent to me by Ford's Public Affairs team turned many heads in the short time it was 'mine' – although this may have been because the Probe is still a rarity on British roads. Only time will tell if it achieves the Capri's level of notoriety.

The Capri was built to be driven and enjoyed. I very much hope the words and pictures in this book will give Capri-owners a little insight into the cars they drive, helping them to gain more pleasure from them and to preserve them for the future.

Mike Taylor
December 1994

1 Sporting Chances

YOUTH MARKET

In November 1960 John Fitzgerald Kennedy emerged as the new President of the United States, scraping home to victory with just 120,000 more votes than his Republican opponent, Richard Nixon. Upon accepting his title as leader of the world's foremost superpower, 43-year-old Kennedy grinned, looked at his pregnant wife Jacqueline and said, 'Now my wife and I prepare for a new administration and a new baby.' The son of a self-made millionaire, JFK, the Princeton- and Harvard-educated Roman Catholic, had become America's youngest President, an event that was to mark the beginning of a remarkable assertiveness in youth culture which would affect the entire world.

'In 1960 the whole country was optimistic. With Kennedy in the White House, a fresh breeze was blowing across the land. It carried an unspoken message that anything was possible. The striking contrast between the new decade and the 1950s, between John Kennedy and Dwight Eisenhower, could be summed up in one single word – youth,' was how the Italian-bred Lee Iaccoca, known as 'Mr Mustang' and Ford's Vice-President, painted the picture in his book, *Iaccoca*. 'Lee Iaccoca was spellbinding,' remarked Walter Hayes, ex-Vice-President of Ford Europe. 'He would make speeches off the cuff and people would sit and listen, open-mouthed. He built up an extraordinary loyalty.'

Research by Ford's marketing men in the States revealed some startling facts when they highlighted the likely effect the post-war baby-boom years would have on consumer spending. The research predicted that during the 1960s the 20–25-year-old age group would double, and that half the predicted increase in car sales would be brought about by people in the 18–34-year-old category. It also indicated that the better educated post-war adults would no longer simply think of cars as a mere means of transport. Instead, the younger generation would begin to demand sportiness and style in their cars, which, incidentally, they would replace more frequently than the older, less well-educated car-buying population.

In addition to this demand for sleek, sporty models, there was also a call for true sports cars in the best European tradition. Popular magazines such as *Road & Track* promoted 'foreign' models through even-handed reporting, with the result that manufacturers such as Austin Healey, MG, Jaguar and even the little Malvern Link firm of Morgan found the American market insatiable. European sports cars were also popular on American race-tracks such as Watkins Glenn, Willow Springs and Riverside Raceway, where the maxim 'win on Sunday, sell on Monday' proved particularly appropriate. In 1960, over 80 per cent of all British sports cars were exported to the United States.

Indeed, the youth market in the States brought a whole new culture to automotive design, promotion and sales, which over the next decade would permeate its way across Europe. And while it is true to say that the average British youth may not have shared the same potential affluence as his American counterpart, the sheer energy and lust for creating a new lifestyle in Britain out-

The Ford Pilot, flagship of the company's post-war range. Powered by a 30hp side-valve engine – despite petrol rationing – the Pilot proved the most successful of all British V8s.

stripped anything seen either before or since. Ford was eager to be part of this trend, and its manufacturing and marketing base was geared up to accept the challenge. This, however, had not always been the case.

EARLY YEARS

In the immediate post-war years, Ford UK was, as most motoring historians would agree, a somewhat old-fashioned organization with few professionally talented people in its management structure and a creakingly ancient model range. At the bottom of the range were the E493A Prefect and E494A Anglia models, direct descendents of the first cheap English Fords of 1932 vintage which, perhaps surprisingly, were designed in the studios of Ford Detroit. The later cars boasted the same simple pre-war side-valve engines, three-speed gearboxes and rod/cable brakes. At the top of the range was the flagship 30hp four-door Pilot, with its side-valve V8 engine and column gear-change; not an inspiring beginning. During a visit by Henry Ford II to Ford's Dagenham headquarters, the path was paved for Ford UK to establish a more autonomous approach to its operations, and an agreement was struck which allowed styling and engineering managers to be appointed in-house. The deal also set Ford in Britain free to pursue a vigorous sales drive world-wide, a campaign so successful that by 1957 Ford UK was the largest exporter of cars to the States!

The late 1940s also saw Ford UK embark on a huge expansion programme that was centred on expanding its manufacturing facilities and output capacity. Pivotal to this programme was the purchase of the Dagenham-based wheel-making firm of Kelsey-Hayes in 1947, and also of the American-owned firm of Briggs Motor Bodies in 1953, who had supplied Ford with bodyshells since 1932. Ford UK perceived, quite rightly as it turned out, that Chrysler would buy Briggs' American operations, the UK-based deal resulting in factories being established at Dagenham, Romford,

Doncaster and Southampton. A year after this, Ford embarked on a huge £75 million investment scheme which increased Dagenham's output markedly. Indeed, the yardstick by which we can measure the success of this programme today is that Ford's output increased from just 2,324 cars in 1945 to a record 284,081 units thirteen years on. The stage was set for a range of technically advanced new models.

The lifting of petrol rationing in Britain on 26 May 1950, after a seemingly lifelong ten years, laid the foundation for a dramatic increase in the use of the motor car for pleasure, this giving the UK motor industry a much-needed boost in demand for both new and used cars. In October of that year, Ford's post-war collection got off to a promising start with the launch, to much acclaim, of the Consul and Zephyr four-door saloons. Retrospectively called Five Star cars because of the design of their grille-mounted badges, these models utilized unitary bodies with MacPherson strut front-suspension units developed by Earle MacPherson, Ford America's Vice-President of Engineering. They were powered by ohv four- and six-cylinder 79 × 76mm engines of 1,508cc and 2,262cc capacity, which shared many common components for easy, cheap assembly.

The up-market Zodiac model appeared three years later, with white-wall tyres, a distinctive duotone paint finish and a slightly more powerful six-cylinder engine. With their column gear-changes and bench-style front seats, the Five Star cars were full six-seaters. At the same time, their handling, performance, road-holding and general rugged construction made them ideal contenders in the growing field of international motor sport, this creating good press coverage in the daily newspapers and motoring journals. Moreover, the Consul, Zephyr and Zodiac illustrated beyond doubt the wisdom of allowing the British Ford team its independence, and the team members' engineering talent and styling skills were soon established.

By 1959, the Consul, Zephyr and Zodiac range, with their drophead and estate vari-

With the launch of the Five Star cars in 1950, Ford made a huge leap forward in technology; the cars boasted unitary body construction, independent MacPherson strut front suspension and a new range of ohv engines. (This is a top-of-the-range Zodiac.)

In 1953 the features of the Five Star cars permeated through to the smaller Anglia and Prefect, although the legacy of the pre-war side-valve engine still lingered on.

ants, had progressed to the larger, albeit sleeker Mk IIs, and were joined by the 105E Anglia ('E', incidentally, standing for English Ford) in the same year. With its charismatic reverse sheer rear window, tapering front bonnet line and lack of bulbous curves, the Anglia looked elegantly chic; inside, the well-shaped seats, good ventilation system, short gearstick and electric (as opposed to vacuum) wipers were a great improvement over its predecessor. However, it was under the bonnet that the greatest change had

The introduction of the 105E Anglia in 1959 (this is a 1964 Super) brought family motoring to a new sector of the public. Cheap to buy and run, the Anglia offered an alternative to BMC's front-wheel-drive Mini.

The 997cc 105E Anglia engine laid the foundation for a new generation of drivetrains. Its 80.97 × 45.62mm dimensions made it an ideal base for tuning, while the drivetrain/suspension layout was further developed for the Cortina GT and much-loved Lotus version.

been made. Gone was the side-valve 100E engine of the cheap English Ford, and in its place was the beautifully neat ohv unit of 80.97 × 48.41mm and 997cc developed by Alan Worters. The oversquare engine developed 39bhp at 5,000rpm, sufficient to give the new Anglia a 0–50mph (0–80km/h) time of 15 seconds and a maximum speed of 76mph (122km/h). Better still, the engine's improved efficiency gave the Anglia an overall fuel consumption of around 40mpg (7l/100km), a 30 per cent increase over the old sv-driven Anglia. And although Ford's marketing people stressed that the sloping rear screen gave rear-seat Anglia passengers improved headroom, the real reason for this design was that it was simply cheaper to manufacture!

THE COMPETITION

The Anglia was launched at the 1959 London Motor Show and immediately drew keen interest, even though there had been considerable anxiety at Dagenham during the early days of its development. It was at these early stages that Ford had learned that BMC was planning to introduce an all-new 'baby' car at the very same show. This car would feature diminutive proportions, yet still provide full four-seat capacity and be driven by a revolutionary front-wheel-drive engine/transmission package. Terrence Beckett, Ford's product planning supremo, was not impressed by the news. Beckett had joined Ford in 1950 and was both an economist and an engineer, having studied at South Staf-

SIR TERRENCE BECKETT CBE

Sir Terrence Beckett

Born in 1923, Terry Beckett was educated at Wolverhampton Municipal Secondary School, after which he took an engineering course at the Wolverhampton and South Stafford Technical College. During World War II Beckett saw service in India and Malaya as a captain in the REME. After completing an Honours degree at the London School of Economics, he joined Ford's graduate training programme, as did so many who became key men in the company.

Beckett joined in 1950, at the age of twenty-seven, whereupon he began a management training course. Promotion followed soon after, and within twelve months he was made personal assistant to Deputy Chairman and Managing Director, Sir Patrick Hennessy. The job required Beckett to keep an eye on product and engineering aspects of the business. At the age of thirty-one he was made manager of the company's styling studios at a time when Ford in Detroit was giving more freedom to the British-based design team. In 1955 Beckett was given his big break, being made Divisional Manager of the American-orientated Product Planning Team, some of whose staff were almost twice his age.

It was during this time that Beckett played such a major role in the Cortina programme, the car proving to be a bench-mark in British automotive design, combining as it did low cost, reliability, durability and the capacity for high-volume production. Crucial to the success of Cortina was Beckett's Red Book sign-off process, which kept cost, weight and design under strict control. Beckett was also responsible for planning the Transit van and D-Series truck ranges.

In the early 1960s, Beckett was appointed Marketing Staff Director and, later, Director of Sales, Car Division. In late 1969 Beckett was made Vice-President European and Overseas Sales Operations for Ford Europe, and in January 1974 he succeeded Sir William Batty as Managing Director and Chief Executive Ford of Britain, being honoured with a CBE in the same month.

ford Technical College before completing his National Service and at the London School of Economics. Beckett joined Ford as a trainee manager, becoming assistant to Sir Patrick Hennessy, Ford's Chairman, after just twelve months. In 1954 he was made Styling Manager and the following year became head of Ford's Product Planning Department. Product planning was a wholly new concept to the British motor industry, and one which Hennessy himself had imported from the States two years before against stiff opposition from many senior Ford managers. Beckett took over from Martin Tustin (who had left to join Standard), and immediately set up separate departments responsible for small, medium and large cars, their purpose being to take responsibility for the creation of model ranges. The product planning concept was one of the better innovations introduced by Ford US as a way of ensuring against any new model being the 'brainchild' of, perhaps, a single executive. In the event, product planning in Ford UK would not really take effect until the Cortina programme was born some seven years on.

Faced with news that BMC's 'baby' car could severely impinge on Ford's policy of selling value-for-money products, Beckett argued that the manufacturing costs for a new transmission system using the technology available at that time would not be viable for a bottom-of-the-range car, while the installation of new and complex manufacturing equipment would be vast and could not be recouped in the retail price.

The official press launch for the Mini took place in August 1959, and there was no doubt that the car's diminutive size – just 10ft (3m) long, 4ft 7in (1.4m) wide and 4ft 5in (1.3m) high – had most motoring journalists quickly readjusting their values, such was the interior accommodation of the car and performance of its transversely mounted 37bhp 62.92 × 68.26mm 848cc four-cylinder 'A' series engine. The Mini's top speed was a little over 70mph (113km/h), and its list price? Just £496.

The buying public were equally amazed and forgave the car its austere interior – early Minis, remember, had washing-line-type interior door handles, sliding side-windows, a single instrument pod centrally mounted on the dashboard that housed a large speedometer, and a very upright driving position. Indeed, it was for these very reasons that Ford UK would never have contemplated making such a car.

Interestingly, when the Mini was introduced Ford got hold of one of the first to come off the production line and had stripped it down for inspection in one of its research workshops. After an exhaustive component- and assembly-cost interrogation, Ford arrived at the conclusion that the car could not be built for the list price, and the product analysts calculated that BMC was losing around £30 for each Mini it built! Even so, while Ford's executives convinced their masters that there really was no cause for alarm as 'baby' cars with slim profit margins could not sell in large quantities and hence BMC's profits would be proportionally low, during one month in 1960 the Mini achieved a 19 per cent market penetration – and that was with just the one model!

Meanwhile, Ford UK expanded still further by purchasing more sites, including the 329-acre (133ha) Halewood location on Merseyside and an old Pressed Steel factory in Swansea for the manufacture of rear axles. Halewood's capacity alone would, in time, increase Ford's output by 200,000 cars per year. In this respect the Anglia was a fundamental first step, for its engine, gearbox and final drive would provide the mechanical components that would be developed for future models. The Anglia itself achieved 191,752 sales in 1960, its first full year of manufacture.

The Anglia was also in immediate demand by leading racing experts such as Keith Duckworth, who extracted almost indecent amounts of power from the car's highly revvable engine and who found its severely undersquare dimensions ideal for race development. Within months, Duckworth had an engine producing 80bhp (used in single-seater racing cars), while concentrated effort created 100bhp; it was the first normally aspirated 1-litre engine to achieve the magic figure. Out on the tracks, Anglias could be seen 'doorhandling' with Minis and even Austin A40s, much to the delight of the applauding crowds. 'The point was Ford's ability in those days to design and build almost unburstable engines,' recalled Walter Hayes recently. 'Formula Junior was invented by my old friend, Count Johnnie Lorannie, which used the Anglia 105E engine, gaining a huge reputation in motor sport.'

AMERICAN INFLUENCE

The next model to come from Ford during this period was the less-than-popular Consul Classic 315 109E, which was styled at the same time Fred Hart, Executive Engineer Light Car Design, and his team at South Ockenden were working on the Anglia 105E. In fact, in the grand scheme of things Ford had planned to introduce the Classic in advance of the Anglia, and it was only a shortage of 1,172cc side-valve engines fitted in the earlier Anglia 100E that brought about the abrupt change in the model-release programme.

The shape and style of the Classic was clearly strongly influenced by American trends, with many Detroit touches such as twin front headlamps and rather obvious rear fins. Other questionable ornamental details were chromed stars set into the grille aperture and twin circular rear lamps. The Classic also shared the Anglia's reverse sloping rear window treatment, although this feature never looked right on the larger car. Heavy swage crease lines were added to many of the Classic's body panels to increase structural rigidity, creating a major fold that ran from the top of the front headlamps to meet up with the rear fins. Overall, weight was also a Classic shortfall, the car turning the scales at a shade over 2,000lb (900kg).

Two years after the launch of the 105E Anglia came the Consul Classic in 1961, with its distinctly US-influenced styling: twin headlamps; heavy swage-line body creases; and tail fins.

The Classic shared the same reverse sheer rear-window style as the Anglia, although it never looked right on the larger car. Heavy use of chrome was another American styling trend.

Introduced in 1961, the Classic was fitted with the newly launched 1,340cc 80.97 × 65.07mm version of the 997cc Kent engine, which utilized a longer (by 2.56in/5.1cm) crankshaft to create the increase in capacity. Regrettably, the longer crankshaft, with only three main bearings for support, made this version of the legendary Kent engine family the least smooth, especially when revved. And as this heavy car produced only 54bhp at 4,900rpm, performance was not its strong point – it took 14 seconds to reach 60mph (97km/h) and had a maximum speed of just 78mph (126km/h).

The Classic range was manufactured on soft metal dies and included a two-door and a four-door saloon, as well as what Ford had clearly hoped would be the showroom stopper its range so obviously cried out for – a two-door coupé called the Consul Capri 335. Introduced in July 1961, and initially for export only, the Capri shared the saloon's floorpan and body pressings below the waistline. The car featured a fixed hard top more than 2in (5cm) lower than the roof-line of the saloon, and a sleekly raked rear screen. Moreover, since the Capri shared the same overall dimensions as the Classic, the boot area was huge, with an additional 6in (15cm) in length over the trunk found in four-seater models.

Inside the Consul Capri, accommodation was strictly 2 + occasional 2, the rear shelf intended primarily to seat small people on very short journeys! Front-seat comfort was immeasurably better, with contoured seats (which, incidentally, could be ordered in leather as an optional extra) that were lowered correspondingly to retain adequate headroom. Emulating the design of Detroit-built 1950s cruisers were the frameless door windows which, together with the rear side windows, could be rolled down to give an open aspect – very Californian! 'I remember when I first saw the RV60 Consul Capri not long after I'd joined Ford as a young development engineer,' recalled Rod Mansfield, ex-boss of SVE. 'I looked through the window at Boreham and saw a prototype and thought, "Wow, what a terrific-looking car".'

Sadly, the Capri's performance just did not live up to its pretentiously sporting appearance, the 1,340cc engine struggling to produce a maximum speed of little over

FORD CONSUL CAPRI (1962)

LAYOUT AND CHASSIS
Two-door coupé/monocoque construction

ENGINE

Type	Kent
Block material	Cast iron
Head material	Cast iron
Cylinders	4
Cooling	Water
Bore and stroke	80.96 × 65.07mm
Capacity	1,340cc
Valves	ohv
Compression ratio	8.5:1
Carburettor	Ford
Max. power	54bhp @ 4,900rpm
Max. torque	74lb/ft @ 2,500rpm
Fuel capacity	9 gallons (41 litres)

TRANSMISSION

Gearbox	4-speed
Ratios	4.12:1, 5.83:1, 9.88:1, 16.99:1
Final drive	16.5mph/1,000rpm

SUSPENSION AND STEERING

Front	MacPherson strut
Rear	Semi-elliptic springs
Steering	Recirculatory ball
Tyres	5.60 × 13
Wheels	Steel
Rim width	4.5in

BRAKES

Type	Girling hydraulic disc/drum
Size	9.5in disc, 9 × 1.75in drum

DIMENSIONS (in/mm)

Track: front	49.5/1,257
rear	49.5/1,257
Wheelbase	99/2,515
Overall length	170.8/4,338
Overall width	65.2/1,656
Overall height	54/1,372
Unladen weight	2,017lb/915kg

PERFORMANCE

Top speed	82.5mph (132.7km/h)
0–60mph	21.3sec

A typical 1960s publicity shot showing the Capri plus admiring couple. Using the two-door Classic body tub as a basis, the boot space on the coupé was truly huge, although rear seat room was very limited.

80mph (129km/h) (though the car was thankful if you cruised around 65mph, or 105km/h) and a 0–60mph (0–97km/h) acceleration of 21 seconds.

In July 1962 the 1,340cc engine gave way to the altogether improved 1,498cc five-bearing 80.97 × 72.75mm engine. To produce the increase in capacity, the 7.25in-deep (18.42cm-deep) cylinder block was increased in height by 0.66in (1.68cm) to accommodate the 72.75mm crankshaft stroke. To overcome the marked roughness of the 1.34-litre engine, Ford added two further crankshaft bearings, while the opportunity was taken to relocate the cylinder-bore centres. In this form, the engine produced 60bhp at 4,600rpm. Classics and Capris became designated 116E accordingly.

In February the following year the Capri GT was launched, powered by an uprated version of the 1.5-litre engine that was tuned to produce 78bhp at 5,200rpm by the addition of a high-lift camshaft, a twin-choke Weber carburettor and a tubular exhaust manifold designed by Keith Duckworth. Performance was improved as a result, the Capri's abilities finally reflecting its shape if not its 'GT' badging. Maximum speed was now up to 92mph (148km/h), with a 0–50mph (0–80km/h) time of around 10 seconds. Inside, the GT was given a remote-control gear-change and a rev counter. Unfortunately, the retail price had jumped to a serious £900, which looked decidedly expensive when compared to other models in Ford's line-up. However, the Capri GT's handling qualities generally found favour with the motor-noters of the day, the impression given being of a boulevard tourer rather than a sports coupé.

THE END OF THE CLASSIC

The Classic saloon, meanwhile, did not align itself with Ford's model strategy; its performance was poor and it was costly to make. Worst of all, it flew in the face of Ford's marketing image since it clearly did not offer value for money. In sales terms,

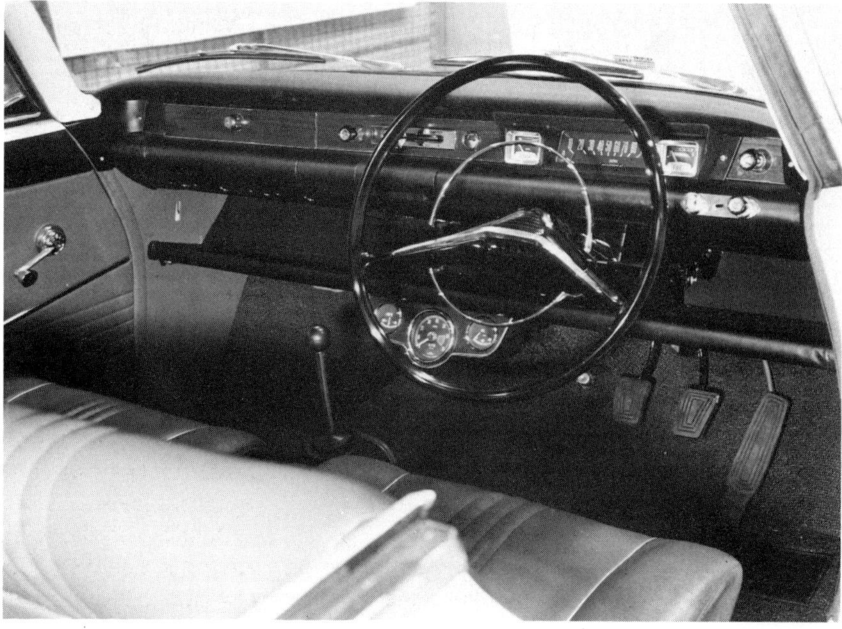

The Capri GT was powered by the 80.97 × 72.75mm 1.5-litre engine, which it shared with the Cortina GT. There was extra instrumentation (oil-pressure gauge, ammeter and rev counter), all located below the parcel shelf. Top speed was over 90mph (145km/h).

CAPRI SB60 CHASSIS/DATE IDENTIFICATION DETAILS

Engine	Date	Type	Number	Details
4-cy ohv 80.96 × 65.07 1,340cc	Sep 61	109E	5733	Two-seater two-door FH coupé introduced based on Classic
	Oct 61		38521	Final eng. no. of old numbering scheme
	Nov 61		37A	Column change model } new eng. nos.
			38A	Floor change model } new eng. nos.
	Jan 62		B005556	Model continued
	Jly 62		B148386	1,340cc engine discontinued
4-cy ohv 80.96 × 72.7 1,498cc	Jly 62	116E	B148496	1,500cc engine. Five-Bearing crank-shaft. All synchromesh box
	Jan 63		C000001	Steering and suspension greased for life
	Feb 63		39C026120	Capri GT. 78bhp. Weber carb
	Jan 64			Improved interior trim and instrument cluster
			37D002098	Column change model
			38D001182	Floor change model continued
	Jly 64		39D000246	GT model
			H38D204160	FH coupé discontinued
			H39D207161	GT discontinued

SB60 CAPRI PERFORMANCE FIGURES

Model	Performance (0 to 50 mph)	Max speed	Fuel consumption
Consul Capri 109E 1,340cc	13.7 sec	80mph (129km/h)	36.7mpg (7.7l/100km)
116E 1,498cc GT	9.9 sec	93mph (150km/h)	29.5mpg (9.6l/100km)

SB60 CAPRI PRODUCTION DETAILS

Consul Capri 109E 1,340cc: July 1961 to Sep 1962	11,143 units
Consul Capri 115E 1,498cc + GT: July 1962 to July 1964	7,573 units

1962, the first full year of Classic production, saw only 58,622 units sold, while total production of Classics and Capris of all versions amounted to a miserable 130,000 units. (Compare this to the Cortina, the Classic's successor, which reached over 1 million sales during its four-year life.)

Production of the Classic 116E ceased in September 1963, leaving the Capri to continue until July 1964. Without doubt the Capri was important in Ford's model evolution, demonstrating the company's willingness to introduce a car whose appearance took precedence over passenger space and which had limited sales appeal in the mass-volume market. As a sleek two-door coupé, it predated the next generation of Ford Capris by some eight years.

Another contributing factor to the Classic's early demise was that news began to leak out that BMC were about to launch another

The British Capri Coupé predated America's Mustang by some three years, thus showing that Dagenham was prepared to enter the low-volume market. Questionable styling and a high price-tag – especially in Capri GT form – ensured poor sales.

front-wheel-drive car, a four-door family-sized model called the 1100, badge-engineered in the memory of once-famous names like Wolsely, Riley, and MG, long since absorbed into BMC's history. Immediately, there was cause for concern in the Dagenham headquarters. The Mini was selling well at a cut-rate price. If BMC applied the same policy to a bigger, technically advanced four-door saloon, Ford desperately needed a new model to meet it head on. The midnight oil began to burn.

The story of Archbishop, Ford's code-name for the Cortina programme, could be said to have begun in 1957 when Ford America, disturbed by the volume of sales in the US of Volkswagen Beetles, looked at ways of meeting the threat. The solution was to consider a compact model suitable for international manufacture in Ford's factories all over the world, volume sales making the project viable. For this model, code-named Cardinal Ford, Detroit sought design proposals from both Britain and Germany for consideration. The studies that emerged were quite different in concept, the German design utilizing a new V4 engine with front-wheel-drive transmission, the Dagenham package relying on straightforward engineering with a conventional drive train. Curiously, it was the German design that won the day, although the situation was not without irony. When Lee Iaccoca visited Cologne to inspect what was on offer as part of his job of being responsible for the overall project, he immediately vetoed the proposal and recommended to Henry Ford that the Americans should distance themselves from the German plan. This they did, and Ford Detroit instead introduced its own 'compact' in the shape of the Ford Falcon in 1960. Ford America did, however, invite Dagenham to become involved with the Cardinal programme, an offer that was politely turned down by the British team, which jealously guarded its independence.

Significantly, fundamental to Cardinal's assembly process was a new building philosophy masterminded by Ford's engineers in Detroit. This policy employed strict control over the amount of metal used in the construction of the unitary body structures; less metal meant less weight and hence reduced manufacturing costs, while less weight also meant reduced running costs. It was to be a policy which would pay enormous dividends in the Archbishop programme later on.

With the knowledge that BMC was working on the four-door 1100, project Archbishop moved into high gear in the spring of 1960. It all started when Sir Patrick Hennessy returned from one of his regular trips to Detroit. Hennessy, an Irishman by birth, had joined Ford in 1920, quickly establishing himself on the managerial ladder and building an enviable rapport with Henry Ford I and II. Knighted in 1941, Hennessy had masterminded the dealings behind the Briggs buy-out (which incidentally reduced the holding of Ford US in Ford UK from 59 per cent to 54 per cent) and the large-scale post-war programme of Ford UK's manufacturing expansion.

ARCHBISHOP

At a briefing in Hennessy's office, Engineering Designer Fred Hart and Product Planning supremo Terrence Beckett were made privy to the plot: design, develop and introduce an all-new car whose launch programme was scheduled to coincide with that of the Cardinal and BMC's larger front-wheel-drive model, both due for release in a little over two years. Such a project would put enormous pressures on everyone involved at Ford as normal development time for a new model from drawing-board to production line was three years. Hennessy was talking about doing it in two and a half years!

Of course, the rewards for being able to pull off such an audacious stunt would be enormous. Grasping the enormity of what was being proposed, Hart replied that to meet these time-scales the car would need to have a conventional drive train, utilizing many parts already in use on existing Ford models. Yet, by rigorous cost control and weight-conscious body engineering, manufacturing costs could be kept within strict guide-lines, the retail price undercutting the opposition and thereby maintaining Ford's value-for-money policy.

Using the Classic bodyshell as a starting point, the aim was to remove around 150lb (91kg) from its structure, the all-up target weight for Archbishop being under 1,700lb (1,036kg). Don Ward, Ford's Chief Body Engineer, gave the task to Dennis Roberts, ex-employee of Bristol Aeroplane Company and a stress/structure expert. As Colin Chapman had proved already, the trick was to reduce weight without dangerously forfeiting strength.

A key ingredient in manufacturing cost control was to be the management of component technology. This was achieved by focusing on 500 chosen parts from the Anglia, and comparing them to the weight and cost of similar items on competitors' models: the Hillman Minx and the Volkswagen Beetle. A team of five product planning executives were then given a list of components for which they were responsible. Each component was entered into the 'Red Book' for sign-off, to show that the component's specification had been agreed and delivery time-scales could be met. Working in collaboration with the product planners were some 200 cost estimators, whose responsibility was to enforce tough component-costing schedules. Where parts could not be priced within their guide-lines, savings had to be achieved elsewhere to redress the balance.

The man in charge of Ford's styling studios was Canadian Roy Brown, who had joined Ford in 1953 and was responsible for the shape of the Edsel in the States. The styling parameters for Archbishop were documented on eight pages of manuscript, and by November 1960 the clay model was

Code-named Archbishop, the Cortina entered the market as a direct competitor to BMC's 1100 range, and offered simple, reliable engineering allied to 4–5 seat accommodation. The car proved to be the UK's fastest selling model.

approved and ready for transposition into the full-size product. The whole programme had taken just eighteen months of concentrated effort.

Initially, the car was to be called Consul, an already familiar Ford name for middle-of-the-road models; 225 for the 1.2-litre version and 335 for the 1.5-litre version. Then Terrence Beckett came up with the name Cortina, after the Italian ski resort of Cortina d'Ampezzo, which not only had a sporting ring to it but also acknowledged Britain's desire to join the Common Market.

That the Red Book sign-off process was a success can be gauged by the project investment costs and the Cortina's retail price-tag. The project had cost Ford some £50,000 less than the £13 million allocated to it, while the 1.2-litre four-door Cortina saloon was priced at just £591, £1 cheaper than the technically advanced Morris 1100 which was launched at the same time.

In June 1962, some nineteen months after approval had been given for the Cortina clay model, cars began rolling off the Dagenham production line. The Cortina was to overshadow the German Ford Taunus 12M (Cardinal) completely, some 1,010,090 of the former being built in all its various forms, including the Estate, GT and Lotus Cortina, before the Mark I range was finally phased out in 1966. The Cortina was also the fastest-selling model in the history of the British motor industry.

As they had done with the Mini, Ford took one of the first Morris 1100s off the production line for cost analysis. And, like the Mini, Ford's engineers concluded that the car was being built at a loss. Ford then carried out a thorough investigation of BMC's finances since the retail price of BMC's products affected those coming out of Dagenham. The result indicated that the Longbridge-based company was heading for bankruptcy, and Sir Patrick Hennessy took the unusual step of telephoning George Harriman at BMC to reveal the news. Hennessy's outstretched hand was met with disinterest, as was an offer from Ford of a Cortina for appraisal. BMC's prices remained unaltered, and within a few short years the company was to become British Leyland Motor Holdings, signalling the beginning of a painful decline which is all too graphically described in Jonathan Wood's excellent book, *Wheels of Misfortune*.

In sharp contrast to the impressive story of Cortina's goal to reach fruition, Ford UK did not lead an entirely problem-free life during this period. For, in addition to the

Rugged reliability was to prove the Cortina's strength when competing in international rallies. Much of this reliability can be traced back to continuous development, such as this, at MIRA.

Classic of 1961, just two years later came the equally lamentable (from Ford's point of view at least) Corsair which, in production terms, was intended to share many parts with the Cortina, using a lengthened floor-pan. In reality, the project involved horrendous development costs. Initially utilizing the Cortina engine before going on to be powered by 1,663cc and 1,996cc versions of Ford's new V4 engines, early units suffered badly from in-balance vibration. In fact, it wasn't until after the mid-1960s that the range became fully established, with the 2000E flagship model at its helm.

The Fred Hart-styled Mark IV Zephyr/Zodiac range also suffered, though for different reasons. It replaced the Ernie Page-designed Mark III cars too soon (in five years just 149,247 units were built), although by far the strongest gripe was the sheer size and inelegance of the Mark IVs which followed the American 'big is beautiful' policy of the time.

For sporting Ford fans however, the Cortina range will best be remembered for the GT and Lotus versions, which gained so much publicity.

THE LOTUS POSITION

January 1962 saw Walter Hayes joining Ford, a man who was to make a fundamental mark on the company's attitudes to marketing. With a journalistic rather than motoring background, Hayes' *raison d'être* was as a communicator. He began talking to people in motor sport and soon realized that while the youth market in the States was all about young people who wanted stylish cars for cruising, in the UK a small, energetic race-team beavered away in a draughty lock-up garage down every side-street (or so it seemed).

In his role as editor of the *Sunday Dispatch* newspaper, Hayes had hired Colin Chapman to write the occasional column on motor sport. Hayes was to relate much later that while Chapman would never have made a journalist, he just happened to be the right person for developing Hayes' ideas once he had joined Ford. Hayes' directive at Ford was to set up an all-new public affairs department that would report direct to Sir Patrick Hennessy. Having formulated his plans, he contacted Chapman once more to discuss matters of mutual interest, describing the new 1,498cc Kent engine and Cortina programmes, and outlining the possibility for a high-performance version. As so often happens, Hayes' timing could not have been better judged, for at the time Chapman was looking for a suitable engine to power his new sports car – the Elan.

The story of how Chapman enlisted the help of Harry Mundy, Technical Editor of *The Autocar*, is legendary. Suffice it to say that Mundy, who had had a distinguished career with ERA, BRM and Coventry Climax, accepted the task of sketching out the design for a new toch cylinder head, suitable for mounting on the 80.97mm Ford cylinder block.

Initial tests were carried out using three-bearing 997cc, 1,100cc and even 1,477cc cylinder blocks. Then, with the launch of the 1,498cc five-bearing engine, development got into its stride and a prototype was fitted into a Lotus 23 single-seater and taken to the Nürburgring. Driven by Jim Clark, it quite simply outstripped the opposition.

Throughout 1962 the Lotus team struggled with the seemingly impossible task of

WALTER HAYES CBE

When it comes to 'fast' Fords most people immediately think of one man, Walter Hayes, for it was he who engineered the company into thinking 'competition' as a very dynamic way of publicizing its products. Born in Harrow, Middlesex, in 1924, Hayes was educated at Hampton School before joining the Royal Air Force as a Cadet Pilot.

However, it was to be in the media world where Hayes was to make his career, rising to the rank of Associate Editor of the *Daily Mail* and on to become Editor-in-Chief of *The Sunday Dispatch* at the age of only thirty-two, making him one of the youngest editors in British newspaper history.

Looking for new fields to conquer, he joined the Ford Motor Company in 1962 as Public Relations Manager (soon after that memorable meeting with 'Edgy' Fabris, Publications and Competitions Manager, who remarked that hitherto each year they finished publications early so they could compete in the Monte Carlo Rally).

Meanwhile, Ford realized that the future lay in a corporate identity and policy, Hayes being instrumental in helping Henry Ford II to bring together fifteen countries, forty-one major factories and 135,000 people speaking fourteen different languages. By June 1967 all the arrangements had been completed to establish Ford of Europe, and the following year Hayes was appointed as Vice-President, Public Affairs. He was then appointed Vice-Chairman of Ford Europe and in 1976 became a member of the Board of Directors, being elected to Vice-President of the parent company the following year. Between 1980 and 1984 he was assigned to the US as Vice-President, Public Affairs, as well as serving on the boards of Ford Switzerland, Ford Belgium and Ford Germany during his long and impressive career.

However, it was as the man instrumental in setting up the deal with Colin Chapman over the Lotus engine and Lotus Cortina deals, the GT40 programme (which proved so successful during the period Hayes was in charge of Ford's racing programme) and the relations with Cosworth for which Walter Hayes is most readily recognized.

In 1979 Hayes was awarded the CBE for his contribution to Britain's industry and trade. In May 1989 Walter Hayes retired from Ford and is now a director of Aston Martin Lagonda Ltd.

COLIN CHAPMAN

Born in 1928, the son of a North London publican, Anthony Colin Bruce Chapman and Lotus – the company he created – matured to become world renowned as manufacturers of sports and racing cars: the Elite, the Seven, the Elan, not to mention a whole list of successful, even controversial, racing cars. The list goes on and on.

Chapman built his first 'kit' car for what might loosely be called production in 1953, its great attributes being that it was light and impressively engineered, a Chapman hallmark. Four years later came the first GRP monocoque-bodied car, the Elite, with its classic lines and Coventry Climax engine. In 1960 Chapman won his first Grand Prix.

Next came his deal with Walter Hayes which resulted in the Ford-based twin cam engine which first appeared in the Elan in 1962, and the Lotus Cortina, a car which gave both Lotus and Ford tremendous publicity. Meanwhile, Lotus itself was growing and in 1966 moved to its present location at Hethel, near Norwich, and with it Chapman's desire to move his company up-market as manufacturers of prestigious GT cars.

The first stage in this master plan was the design of an all-new, wholly Lotus-based engine – the sixteen-valve all-alloy 907. But the period 1973 to 1976 saw Chapman struggling to keep his company afloat as the effects of the energy crisis hit home. But, with an almost reckless disregard for the consequences, he launched his new model range: the Elite, followed by the Eclat and, later still, the dramatic Esprit.

However, it was for his dynamism that Chapman is chiefly remembered, running at first hand his car company *and* his racing team – not to mention having a fundamental effect on designs for both. He also diversified, albeit temporarily, into boat-building and, just before his untimely death in 1982, into light aircraft too. Without doubt, his alter ego was Enzo Ferrari (he always harboured a desire to be the British equivalent). Today, Chapman remains an enigma: sometimes loved; sometimes hated; but almost always admired. Life was never boring when 'ACBC' was around.

making the tohc 1,500cc engine sufficiently powerful *and* reliable. Problems with casting processes (production heads were sand-casted by William Mills) and cylinder-head gaskets were just two of the difficulties to be overcome. Also, a change in the rules for international events raised the engine size from 1,500cc to 1,600cc, whereupon Ford agreed to deliver cylinder blocks whose wall thickness was sufficient to allow overboring to 82.5mm, giving a capacity of 1,558cc. In this version, when fitted with twin 40DCOEZ carburettors, the engine developed 105bhp at 5,500rpm.

As time went on relations between Ford and Lotus became strained as delivery dates were missed. After all, Lotus was a race-car-design company and was happy to change patterns on a whim without recourse to volume-production considerations. Reliability for Lotus was largely a factor of lasting the duration of the race, policies hardly applicable to Ford's Product Planning Department. 'I met Chapman once or twice in those early days,' Rod recalled recently. 'He'd walk into Lotus's Cheshunt workshops and stand talking, sometimes accompanied by John Whitmore – who was God to me, then. Next, he'd walk out in a typical Chapman flurry.'

In true Lotus brinkmanship, however, the 125E Lotus Cortina made its début in January 1963. At the front, the MacPherson struts were changed to zero wheel camber, while a stiffer anti-roll bar was added. At the rear, more radical changes were made, the Ford leaf springs being discarded in favour of coil springs located by large 'A'

Early Lotus Cortinas such as this had a modified rear-axle location which utilized an A frame. The frame caused differential-casing leaks and cracks over rough rally stages and hence was dispensed with on later models.

brackets that pivoted on the differential casing (this design would later cause severe headaches on rough rally stages when torsional stresses resulted in cracked casings and oil leaks). The brakes were uprated to handle the additional power and 5.5in (14cm) road wheels were added. The transmission was also uprated to include new gearbox ratios, first gear being extremely 'tall' and calling for a degree of clutch slip by the driver if jerky take-offs were to be avoided.

Inside, there were remodelled seats, a special three-dial dashboard and a wood-rim steering-wheel, while outside, the doors, bonnet and boot panels were re-skinned in alloy to save weight. And, of course, we mustn't forget that the cars were available in white only, with a green side-flash. On the road the Lotus Cortina could complete a 0–60mph (0–97km/h) sprint in 10 seconds and peak out at 110mph. 'I would drool over the Lotus Cortina and drive one whenever I could,' laughed Mansfield at the memory of Ford's all-white flyer. 'The man who had it really sewn up was George Baggs, who was Ford's Lotus Liaison Manager. But I would get involved whenever the opportunity presented itself, driving over to see Hugh Gaskell, who was Baggs' equivalent at Lotus.'

At the outset of the Lotus Cortina programme, Ford had no plans to introduce an in-house sporting version of the Cortina saloon. However, it appears that Fred Hart and his team, miffed by the Lotus programme, set to work themselves and developed the Cortina GT. The prototype was fitted with the engine that also powered the Capri GT with Weber carburation and sporty camshaft, and was shown to Henry Ford II, who happened to be at Monthlery for a marketing conference in September 1962. After a quick demonstration the Cortina GT was given an enthusiastic seal of approval.

The GT was not as extensively modified as the Lotus Cortina, and was available in two- and four-door body styles which, incidentally, the Lotus version was not. The suspension was lowered and disc brakes were added to the front. Inside was the obligatory rev counter and remote-control gear-change. The GT's maximum speed was a healthy

A Lotus Cortina undergoing adjustment at Lotus's Cheshunt factory. Productionizing the car caused many harsh words between Ford and Lotus; Chapman's team was not used to volume manufacture!

94mph (151km/h), and it could gallop to 50mph (80km/h) in 9.9 seconds. The Cortina GT was a very acceptable compromise, midway between the temperamental Lotus version and the standard 1.5-litre model, though its rugged reliability proved its worth in rough rallies such as the East African Safari.

LOOKING TO THE FUTURE

During 1965 Sir Patrick Hennessy held the office of President of the Society of Motor Manufacturers and Traders, and in keeping with tradition wrote an article in an October issue of *The Autocar* magazine as an introduction to the 50th London Motor Show. Viewed almost forty years on his comments make for interesting reading. During the first eight months of the year, he explained, Britain had earned over £520 million in currency from exports, up £7 million on the previous year even though production and export quantities had been reduced due to industrial disputes in factories and docks. Demand on the home market had, however, dropped, partially because of a tough credit-squeeze programme imposed by Harold Wilson's Labour government of the day and masterminded by Chancellor George Brown. Sir Patrick also sighted a cause of poor performance as a lack of motorway construction, highlighting the fact that just 8.25 miles (13.28km) of motorway had been opened in 1964 and an equally derisory 60 miles (97km) during the first ten months of 1965, a further 20-odd miles (30km) due for completion 'soon'.

Naturally, Ford's Chairman saved his brightest comments for the export market, saying that it was towards Europe that motor manufacturers were looking (including Ford themselves), though Britain's lack of membership of the Common Market – vetoed by France – was causing a severe setback in tariff credentials. It was still America and Canada, he concluded, which represented the best potential overseas market, although

Perturbed by the news that Lotus was developing a 'hot' version of the bread-and-butter Cortina, Ford's development team produced the GT model. Cheaper and less temperamental than the all-white Cheshunt car, the GT triggered off the trend for sports family saloons.

As with the Capri GT, additional instrumentation in early versions of the Cortina GT were fitted using 'add-on' panels. Later versions incorporated the dials into improved fascia layouts.

as we shall see this was an opportunity largely missed.

Meanwhile, Ford was busily involved in developing a new family of engines and the Competitions Department (based at Boreham, near Chelmsford) was notching up more victories in motor sport. 'I said to Alan Bark, who was Ford's Managing Director at the time, I felt we needed a competitions centre,' Hayes explained, recalling the beginnings of Ford's Motor Sport Department recently. 'Alan Platt, who was involved with Ford's Marketing Department, said he knew of accommodation at Boreham. And I got £50,000 to build the centre and £75,000 for the first season.' In the States, the Total Performance marketing programme was gaining momentum, helped, of course, by the GT40 programme. In the fifteen years since the introduction of the MK I Consul, Zephyr and Zodiac range, Ford had become a formidable leader in the British motor industry. Meanwhile, in the background work was starting on a sleek new coupé, code-named Colt.

2 Better Things

When Harold Macmillan made his memorable remark in 1959, 'you've never had it so good', he might well have been referring to the British sports-car buyer, for at that time there was an almost bewildering array of products to suit most pockets, from the budget-priced Austin Healey Sprite through to the MGA and TR3, and on to the elegant Jaguar XK150. There was also, lest we should forget, a good number of 'specialist' manufacturers – Lotus, Turner, Faithorpe, Rochdale – to fill in the gaps. All, in their own way, provided what the enthusiast perceived as the key ingredients for a sports car: bucket seats, short gearshifts, a throaty exhaust and a tuned engine, all wrapped up in a sleek body. Some were open with a soft top for poor-weather protection while others had fixed roofs, but all managed to look the part.

Within just a few short years, however, the traditional sports-car market was beginning to change. An increase in traffic density on the roads was creating a less-than-pleasant environment for open-topped motoring while, in truth, there were fewer opportunities for using the extra performance anyway. Buyers still demanded that their sporting cars looked sleek and racy, but a growing number of people wanted the comfort of a sports coupé rather than the irritation of flapping side-screens and a canvas 'lid'. To satisfy this demand, MG launched the MGB GT in late 1965, Triumph answering back a year later with the GT6 and its beautifully smooth straight-six engine and unpredictable rear suspension. Meanwhile, as we have seen, the Cortina GT, the Lotus variant and the evergreen Mini Coopers bridged the gap between family responsibilities and demand for good performance and handling.

In the States, Iaccoca's youth market had responded magnificently to the introduction of the Mustang in 1964, with 680,992 cars being sold by the end of 1965 (its first full production year) and the millionth of the marque produced in March of the following year. The Mustang was small by American standards, *Road & Track* referring to it as 'A 4-passenger Cobra'. One of the car's great attractions, however, was that it was available in so many forms: drophead; hard top and 2 + 2 body shapes; and a variety of engine sizes from the 2,786cc six-cylinder unit and the standard 4.2-litre V8, to the 4.7-litre V8 which reputedly produced 210bhp in off-the-shelf form. In addition, a catalogue full of styling and performance options was available which allowed the proud new owner to customize the car, personalizing it to his or her own choice. Indeed, Mustang's whole marketing ethos was watched very closely by the men in Dagenham, who would apply it to the next generation of the Capri when it was unveiled five years later.

The fastback four-seater was another variation on the sports coupé theme; one example was the Sunbeam Rapier introduced by Chrysler UK in 1967, which utilized some mechanical parts from the Arrow saloon yet had unique body panels. In H120 form, when it was powered by a Holbay-tuned engine fitted with twin Weber carburettors and an alloy cylinder head, the unit produced 106bhp at 5,200rpm, giving a maximum speed of 107mph (172km/h) and a 0–50mph time (0–80km/h) time of under 8

Ford Dearborn's Pony car, the Mustang. Intended to promote Ford's Total Performance image and aimed at the youth market, the Mustang sold strongly in its early years, although the car's V8 engine options did not make it very attractive to UK buyers.

Compare this photograph with the interior of the Capri GT shown on page 20. Mustangs could be bought with manual transmission – unusual for American cars of the period and clearly an acknowledgement of the car's sporting pretensions.

seconds. Sadly, style was not the Rapier's strong point (some even said the body shape was 'bizarre'), although it was comfortable and reasonably spacious.

Another slant on the four-seater two-door sporty theme was served up by the small Tamworth-based factory of Reliant, which launched its GRP-bodied GTE (Grand Touring Estate) in 1968, styled by David Ogle. Based on a design commissioned by Triplex in 1966 which utilized the SE4 chassis, the GTE cleverly amalgamated the earlier GT coupé theme with estate-type layout. Like most specialist cars, the GTE used a combination of many mass-car-manufacturers' parts: three-litre V6 engine and gearbox from Ford, suspension units from Triumph, and so on. But this was nothing to be ashamed of. The GTE went well, looked good and consumed yards of people and luggage; it was also in good company when at least one member of the Royal Family took delivery. The time was almost right for Ford UK to introduce their own four-seater sports coupé.

Hard on the heels of the Mk II Cortina Lotus came the Escort Twin Cam, seen here at the Bagshot proving ground. Ford's continued involvement in international motor sport did much to enhance the company's sporting image.

Fascia layout of the Escort Twin Cam. Compare this to the design of the early Cortina GT with its 'add-on' dials. Bucket seats and transmission tunnel consoles had yet to emerge.

The Escort Twin Cam was very much a 'homologation special', developed to accommodate Henry Taylor's wish to campaign a competitive car. The engine had to be offset to the left (nearside) so that it could fit into the Escort's engine bay.

ENTER COLT

The poor sales performance of the Classic Capri of the early 1960s had done little to dampen the enthusiasm of Dagenham for introducing an entirely new coupé, one that was distinctly sporting in design. Using many mechanical components from existing Ford models and offering a wide range of engine options, retail prices of the new car would be kept within reasonable boundaries. As Stan Gillen, Ford UK's Chief Executive had remarked, it would be a car which would put the fun back into motoring. 'We had a Managing Director of Ford called Alan Bark,' Walter Hayes recalled, 'who got hugely ill through eating some resin-infected bread. His illness was so serious he had to be replaced and the man who took over his position was Stanley Gillen, who was one of the nicest of Americans. Immediately he came to Dagenham he became infected by the feeling of youth and vitality.'

Early in 1965 Ford's UK management gave the go-ahead for work to begin on drawing up proposals for Project Colt (a young horse, not unlike the Mustang – right!), the code-name for the next generation of Capri.

As with the Cardinal, design studies for the Colt were undertaken in Britain and Germany to produce full-size models for evaluation and testing. This time, however, Detroit was also involved in the work at the outset, to help the project along and also pass on experience gained from shaping the Mustang. 'The styling facilities at Ford during those days were pretty limited and Detroit sent over some design studies,' Hayes said recently. 'One was a Mustang-type shape produced, I think, by Gordon MacKray. Gillen was enthusiastic and so was I, but we did meet some opposition because there was some feeling that while the Ford range was by no means complete at that stage, if we did the Colt (code-name for the Capri) it could be at the expense of something which could sell in greater volume.'

ROD MANSFIELD

Born in Bristol in 1935, Rod Mansfield is the link between almost all the sporting models Ford has produced over the last twenty years.

After attending Battersea Polytechnic and the Chelsea College of Aero and Automobile Engineering, Rod started his career as a young designer working for AC Cars in Thames Ditton. Then followed National Service in REME, during which time he began racing in, of all things, an Austin A35 van, the only concession to competing being the removal of the hub-caps!

National Service completed, Rod applied to over thirty companies, the most attractive reply being from Ford who offered him a post as Development Engineer. Then followed a period in NVH (noise, vibration, harshness), before taking on the responsibility for front-suspension and steering development. Meanwhile, his interest in motor sport continued; he was 750MC Trials Champion two years running, going on to set up his own racing team with two friends, racing Anglias, Cortinas and Twin Cam Escorts, as well as competing in the Mexico Challenge series.

A youthful Rod Mansfield poses with one of the Escorts he raced in the Escort Challenge Series. His name needs no introduction to Capri fans!

Promotion followed in the exciting AVO, Rod selling performance parts, building replica rally cars and manufacturing cars like the RS1600 and Capri RS2600. (Rod was also involved with the still-born four wheel-drive Capri project.) Next, Rod spent a short time working in Public Affairs.

In February 1980 the idea was hatched to set up an all-new department within Ford: SVE. The proposal was for a special department responsible for developing low-volume, high-performance versions of Ford's mainstream product line. Gerhart Hartwig, Ford Europe's Director of Vehicle Engineering, asked Rod if he would set up such a department. Ironically, the first car to receive the SVE treatment was the Capri which, history records, was a tremendous market success.

Then came the Fiesta XR2, the Escort Cabriolet, Escort RS Turbo, Sierra XR4×4, Sierra RS Cosworth and on to the Granada 4×4. All have vindicated the original idea for SVE and the purpose of a specialist group within Ford's empire.

Mansfield then moved away from SVE to work in another low-volume section under the Ford umbrella – Aston Martin – taking the post of Engineering Director where, no doubt, his talent and enthusiasm was well received.

Two very different sketches of the future Capri. The rear view shows typical American treatment, while the front aspect indicates a more European look, illustrating closely the shape of the final proposal.

At the time, Ford was very enthusiastic about the use of 'customer clinics' as a way of judging public reaction to design proposals, and so members of the public were asked for their comments without being told who was responsible for each of the designs. In the case of the Colt programme, these clinics were held in Geneva, Milan, Hamburg, Brussels, Cologne, Amsterdam and London, two versions being put on display – 'GBX' and 'Flowline' – along with other in-house sketches and some designs produced by outside suppliers. Both of Ford's themes represented a compromise between a GT and a sports coupé.

In terms of styling, the GBX and Flowline shapes mirrored the Mustang's successful lines, encompassing a long bonnet, a cabin large enough to accommodate seating for four adults, and an adequate boot. In line with Ford's established policy of offering a range of power units for its model ranges, Colt would be available with engine options varying from 1,300cc to a 2.0-litre V4. No new engine was to be designed specifically for Colt and no mention was made either of

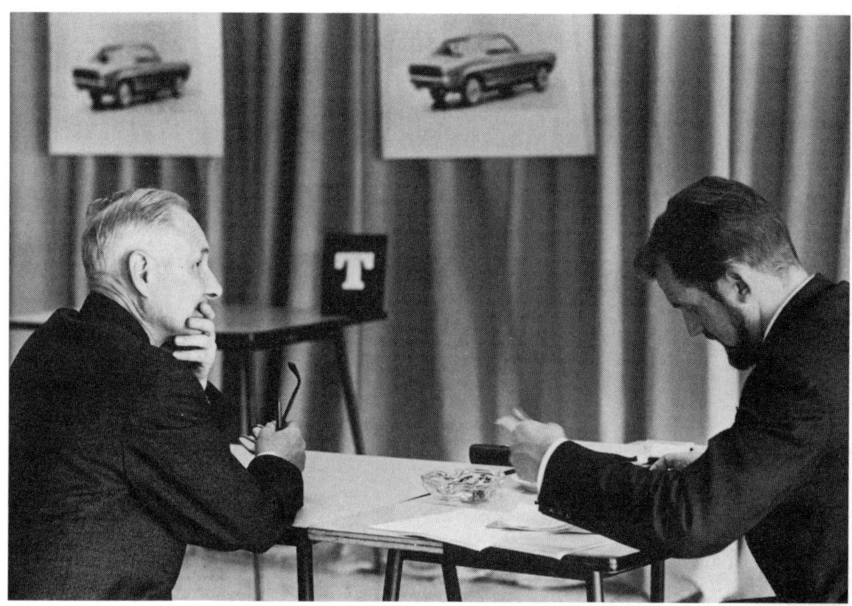

A Project Colt Clinic in 1966 with one 'patient' looking pensively at the display of drawings. Ford put great emphasis on this method of gaining public reaction to their private styling treatments.

installing the V6 Essex 3.0-litre engine, although it was clear that the Colt's voluminous under-bonnet space could accommodate it with room to spare.

Feedback from the various clinics was immensely important to Ford's Product Planning team in gauging public reaction, for the car's appearance had to be attractive enough to carry a premium price-tag with no detrimental effect on sales, despite the fact that it would have proportionally less cabin and luggage space than equivalently priced Ford saloons. Investment, budget control and profit revenue would be even more crucial to the Colt's programme because of the perceived sales volumes. (In the event, sales far outstripped Ford's projected production quantities, as we shall see later.)

'It was a very naïve time, there wasn't a computer anywhere,' recalled Rod Mansfield with candour. 'I remember we had bad vibration problems with the 109E. We took it up to Boreham for tests and thought the cause was a bending moment in the prop shaft. So I asked the fitters to cut longitudinal slots at each end of the shaft to try to establish a different bending moment to counterbalance it. Of course, it didn't work. But, on the way back, driving flat out, the shaft snapped and pole-vaulted down the road, nearly destroying five Ford Development Engineers.'

A significant time in the Colt's evolution was in the summer of 1966, when a final decision had to be made over its future. Stanley Gillen, Ford UK's Chief Executive, was sufficiently encouraged by the feedback he had received on the programme to give it the go-ahead, using GBX as the foundation for the production version. John Hitchman, a Ford development engineer who had been involved with the Consul Capri GT and the wedge-nosed Corsair GT, was given the task of taking care of the Colt project. 'Luckily, Gillen was very bold and we took it to the Product Committee and it was agreed we should go ahead,' mused Walter on reflection. 'Even so, I think it was only a £20 million programme so it was never a major enterprise.'

It was also during this period that Ford

A Project Colt scale model being evaluated in the wind tunnel for aerodynamic efficiency during 1966.

put considerable effort into its NVH (noise, vibration and harshness) programme, championed by Director of Engineering, Harley Copp. The effects of this research were certainly to benefit the overall ride quality in future production models. Suspension development for the Colt was initiated using a Cortina as a development study, this being fitted with revised suspension geometry and spring rates. To put curious people off the scent, the car was fitted with an additional glass panel, held in place by chrome sticky tape! Such was the handling and ride qualities of this car that it became a firm favourite with the development team, far outstripping that of the standard Cortina.

'It was through suspension development work on the Capri that I first met Sir John Whitmore, whom we hired to undertake handling evaluation for us,' recalled Rod Mansfield. 'The actual development was being done on a Cortina using an Alfa Romeo as a comparison. And I remember we were very pleased with our efforts, despite the fact that it was probably just lowering, widening and stiffening more than we'd done before on other cars. Brian Peacock did a lot of work on the front suspension. There's just no substitute for persistent testing, changing and then testing again.'

As the Colt programme continued, more customer clinics were held to gauge public reaction. Significantly, there was strong feeling about the shape of the rear side-window of the GBX which, because of its limited size and upward-slanting trailing edge, gave back-seat passengers a marked feeling of claustrophobia. As a result, Ford's stylists got to work and produced a graceful half-ellipse portal which neatly followed the sloping rear roof-line. In October 1967, the new rear window shape was agreed for production and the following month 'Colt' became 'Capri', the name, like that of the Cortina, having strong links with Europe. Ford's favoured pronunciation for its proposed coupé, by the way, was to emphasize the first syllable.

With the wind-tunnel testing completed, a full-scale model was produced in GRP. In this version the bonnet has been given subtle air scoops and the rear transom panel is recessed with the registration plate mounted below the bumper.

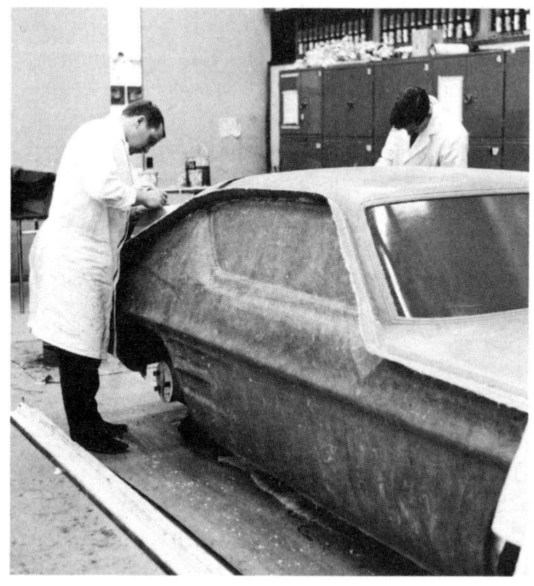

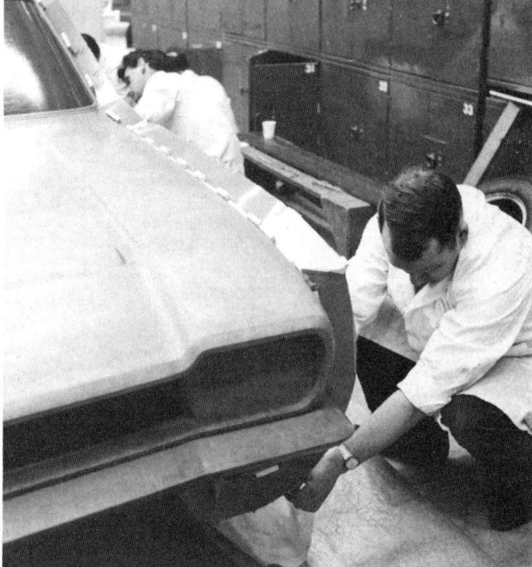

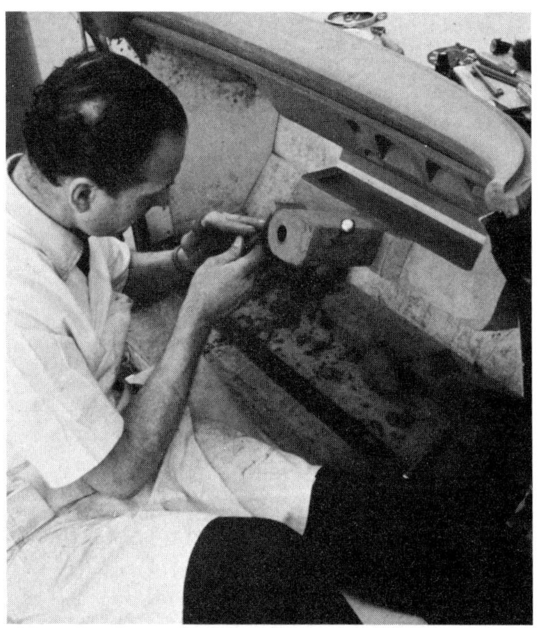

At the same time as the GRP bodyshells were made in 1966, a fascia layout for the Colt was sculptured from timber and clay. In this version the instruments have been recessed into the dash panel.

INTERNATIONAL RELATIONS

Meanwhile, much had happened to affect Ford's European operations. In the years leading up to 1960, plans were drawn up by Detroit to amalgamate Ford's European divisions. This began with Ford America increasing its holding on Ford UK from 54.6 per cent to 100 per cent, thereby ensuring that schemes hatched in the UK would be implemented without a hitch. Fundamental to Detroit's plans were the increased integration of Ford's European facilities and improved co-ordination of its worldwide operations. The notion was to create total flexibility between manufacturing and design centres, and to remove any perceived boundaries – such as national borders and language barriers. Ford Europe would work together, styling, designing, developing, testing, standardizing and manufacturing. It was an elaborate and far-sighted vision which had to be sold to Ford's managers in Europe first.

During a formal visit to Europe in mid-

A full-sized mock-up on display at another of Ford's clinics, set off by some rather nice alloy wheels. Notice the notchback styling. Clearly, the frontal treatment was agreed well in advance of the side and rear window treatments.

June 1967 by Henry Ford II, the plan was officially set up and Ford Europe was put under the control of John Andrews. It was at this same meeting, incidentally, that the Capri was given the blessing of Ford's Board of Directors.

'Henry Ford always got very mad because he felt that Ford's European companies would treat each other like distant cousins,' said Hayes, recalling the feelings of his master. 'In Germany they had the Taunus 12M, which was front-wheel drive, and in Britain we had the Cortina, which was rear-wheel drive. This all meant separate manufacturing assemblies, which Henry thought was bizarre. So he got us all together and said, "I, Henry Ford, have decided to set up Ford Europe. John Andrews will be President. Go away and do it".'

While the first true pan-European passenger vehicle to emerge from Ford's closer working operations would be the Capri (due for launch in early 1969), a large degree of commonality was achieved with the Escort, the Anglia 105E's replacement, which would appear in January 1968. Development work on the Escort had started in 1964 and it became the first production car to be finished at Halewood (in mid-November 1967). Ford engineers referred to the Escort as a new concept in small/medium mass-market saloons. The knowledge gained with the Anglia over model variants led to the Escort being marketed in 1100, 1300, 1300GT and Twin Cam versions, the latter model reflecting Ford's performance image.

The Escort's raked windscreen, and lower yet longer outline, gave the car a sleeker appearance than the 105E model it replaced, while boot accommodation had also increased markedly. As with the Capri, considerable attention was paid to reducing NVH in the Escort by using specially designed exhaust systems, particular types of interior trim materials and a one-piece gearbox/clutch bell-housing casting. This was the first Ford to use rack and pinion steering, and the valuable experience gained in creating it would prove invaluable when this type of steering was developed for the Capri.

Production of the Escort was planned to take place in Halewood, as well as at Ford's Ghent plant, while the company's Saarlouis plant in Germany would supply body pressings to the production lines in the UK and Belgium. It must be said that initially, however, the German product planners treated the scheme with considerable scepticism. They felt that the Escort's conventional engine and transmission layout, plus its simple, straightforward engineering, would not find a responsive market when competing with the new, innovative range of FWD cars. How wrong they were!

In 1972 the Escort took over from Austin's 1100/1300 to become Britain's second best-selling car, the prime spot being taken up by the fast-becoming-legendary Cortina. In Germany, the Escort also proved its worth by helping to increase output from 207,763 cars in the year of its launch (1968) to 300,856 units the following year, thereby boosting Ford Germany's position in the market-place by 2.2 per cent. 'Undoubtedly, there were worries in the company over the effects of amalgamating Ford's European operations,' Mansfield explained, 'But it was the right thing to do and Ford showed the way to other manufacturers.'

PUBLIC IMAGE

Over all, as every Ford enthusiast knows, much went on during the mid-1960s to elevate Ford's performance image world-wide: 1964 saw the GT40 taking on the might of Ferrari at Le Mans for the first time, Carroll Shelby's Cobras won the GT Category in the States, and a Cortina won the Safari Rally; in 1965 Jim Clark won at Indianapolis in a rear-engined Ford Lotus; in 1966 the Mk II

GT40s won at Le Mans to take the World Championship of Makes, a Lotus Cortina won the RAC Rally and Graham Hill won at Indianapolis; in 1967 Ford won again at Le Mans, while the new Ford-Cosworth race engine took four Grands Prix trophies; and 1968 saw Ford Cosworth and Graham Hill take the World Driver's Championship, and the beginning of the Escort's legendary rally career. In the following years Jackie Stewart won the World Championship no less than three times with Ford (1969, 1971 and 1973), and the Capri became the car to beat on the tracks.

By 1968 Carroll Shelby, who had also played a key part in Ford's image-making campaign, had become part of the establishment, having set up four companies to look after his interests: one for bolt-on parts for Ford engines, a second for accessories, a third for special project management and a fourth for racing. It was the latter that was responsible for developing Shelby versions of production Mustangs, marketed as the GT350 and GT500. Globally, Ford's impact on the competition world was enormous, a factor that would dramatically increase the Capri's chances of gaining status in the performance market.

DESIGN DETAILS

There was, however, still much to be done in terms of project development before the Capri was ready for unveiling, for the car presented Ford's suspension-design technologists with a very daunting set of operational parameters. The car's unladen stance was specified as having a pronounced nose-up, tail-down attitude. This meant that the rear suspension travel from full rebound to full compression was limited to just 6.65in (16.89cm), compared to 8.3in (21.1cm) on the more softly sprung Cortina. Moreover, when the car was carrying rear-seat passengers and a full complement of luggage, this movement was even more restricted.

By late 1968 they were almost there! The rear side-window, however, still had to be reworked into the half-ellipse so characteristic of the Mk I Capri. Just look at those skimpy crossply tyres!

Tough testing of a Colt prototype in 1967; an LHD car undergoing suspension evaluation in Belgium. Rear suspension design created demanding tolerances because of the limited travel available.

Rod Mansfield recalls the period: 'In 1967 we moved from Averley to Dunton, Ford's new research centre. We were working on the suspension for the Capri at the time. I, with my team, were involved with the front suspension and John Allfield with his team sat next to me handling the rear suspension. One day we had a telephone call to say our Chief Engineer, George Halford, would be late in because a wheel had come off his Zodiac. John and I looked at each other. Luckily, it was the rear wheel so it was Allfield's problem.'

The solution to Capri was rear radius arms with high-friction rubber bushes that would restrict movement, together with rubber bump-stops and stiffer semi-elliptic leaf springs rated at 100lb/in compared to 90lb/in on the Cortina. At the front, the coil springs were increased from 74lb/in for the Cortina to 90lb/in on the Capri, while suspension travel was reduced from the Cortina's 8in (20.32cm) to 6.25in (15.88cm) in the two-door coupé. This created, improved handling characteristics that outstripped those of Ford's saloon range.

A considerable amount of tough test driving

Cold-weather testing in the Arctic. Much work was carried out to perfect the throughflow ventilation system in order to ensure its performance in European countries; despite the use of production power units, tests were also carried out on engine cooling systems in vastly contrasting climates.

Road testers gathered in Cyprus in January 1969 to test Ford's new coupé. Ford had laid on four cars – a 1600, a 1600GT, a 2000GT and a BDA-engined car (which never made production). The Autocar *team covered some 800 miles (1,290km) of tough testing in the four Capris, driving conditions varying from the fast, well-engineered roads of the lowlands to snow-covered mountain tracks at altitudes of 6,000ft (1,800m) plus.*

was done using some ten prototype Capris at facilities such as the Lommel test track in Belgium, as well as the surrounding public roads. The already proven power trains were tested vigorously in their new environments, with a specific watch being kept on heat dissipation from the engine compartment and the effects of weight distribution on handling, to ensure that the Capri had the kind of road-holding its look suggested. 'The Capri was based on pretty straightforward engineering,' smiled Rod Mansfield at the memory. 'MacPherson struts, solid rear axle. Nothing wrong with that, but no one would have designed it like that any later than 1970.'

PROMOTION PROGRAMME

During 1968 a photographic session was organized using a couple of prototype cars. This gave Ford's marketing people a focus on the best promotional emphasis for the Capri, the intention being to standardize the advertising campaign throughout the car's European markets. 'Capri, the car you always promised yourself' was the promotional catchphrase coined for the international launch.

Six Capris, plus a whole entourage of engineers, fashion models and public relations staff went off for an eight-week stint in Portugal, where around 100,000 photographs were

A novel view of the tohc 1.6-litre Cosworth-developed BDA engine. A prototype Capri was hand-built and sent to Cyprus for evaluation by the press. 'It was nothing more than a Walter Hayes kite-flying exercise to judge reaction,' remarked Rod Mansfield.

taken for what would be a major advertising campaign covering newspapers, magazines and poster hoardings. At the same time, journalists were taken off to Cyprus where a group of special Boreham-built cars – including a hand-built Cosworth BDA-engined Capri, complete with 6in-wide (15cm-wide) Minilite wheels – were waiting to be put through their paces.

In late January 1969, *Autocar* printed a review of the Capris which had been tested in Cyprus. The *Autocar* team of two had four different models to play with: the 1600; the 1600GT; the 2000GT; and the sixteen-valve tohc 1600 BDA-engined car. Cyprus had proved to be a good choice for putting Ford's new sporting model through its paces, and *Autocar*'s two representatives covered almost 800 miles (1,300km) over various road conditions ideally suited to evaluating both high-speed and town conditions. The team concluded that the Capris handled better than any previous production Ford model, with light and precise steering, and a suspension that was almost harsh on smooth roads but which performed better when the car was fully laden. The brakes provided lots of feel, although the testers did experience front-wheel lock-up when braking hard into a corner on uneven surfaces.

Of the engine options reviewed, the 1600GT was considered the most 'sporty', revving freely to 6,000rpm, while the 2000V4 GT produced more power yet was less than happy with anything more than 4,000rpm. As with all Fords, the ventilation system came in for praise, the throughput of air dealing happily with variations in temperature and conditions. There was, however, criticism over rear-seat leg room when the front seats were

The 1600GT, perhaps the most popular of all the Capri models, with Rostyle wheels. It offered good performance at reasonable economy; sadly, there are few left in this condition.

moved back, while reversing manoeuvres required familiarization with the car (not surprising, considering the fall-away shape of the boot-lid). Overall, however, the body shape was found to produce little wind noise; the NVH (noise, vibration and harshness) team had apparently done a very good job in keeping potential problems at bay.

The 1600 BDA-engined car was thought to be an altogether more responsive machine, its 6in-wide (15cm-wide) road wheels (5in, or 13cm, for the GTs and 4.5in, or 11cm, for the 1600s) giving a more compliant ride quality. The Cosworth-developed engine revved freely to 7,000rpm in the gears, reaching 5,750rpm quickly in top gear which gave an indicated speed of 100mph (161km/h).

The Capris were something altogether new from Ford, and were thought by testers to be quite outstanding in many ways – particularly in the areas of stability, quietness and controllability. 'The Capri came about because of the way Ford was at the time,' recalled Walter Hayes, ex-Vice-Chairman of Ford Europe. 'We found there was magic in performance cars, although they didn't have to be 150 mph cars. Certainly, the Cortina GT wasn't, yet it sold strongly.'

An under-bonnet view of the 1600GT showing the crossflow Kent engine and tubular exhaust manifold. Based on the 80.97 × 77.62mm 1,599cc engine, the unit produced a healthy 88bhp.

AVAILABLE OPTIONS

At the time of its launch the Capri was available with five engine options, ranging from the 1,298cc Escort unit which produced 52bhp at 5,000rpm, to the V4 1,996cc Corsair engine, with changes made to its carburettor, camshaft and exhaust manifolding to boost power from 88bhp to 92.5bhp at 5,500rpm. The latest single-rail Corsair 2000E type gearbox was fitted to all models of Capri, but with varying ratios depending on engine

Interior of a 1600 showing the twin-instrument fascia, period Radiomobile car radio and mock-leather three-spoke steering-wheel.

FORD CAPRI MK I – 1600GT (1969)

LAYOUT AND CHASSIS
Two-door coupé/monocoque construction

ENGINE	
Type	Kent
Block material	Cast iron
Head material	Cast iron
Cylinders	4
Cooling	Water
Bore and stroke	80.98 × 77.62mm
Capacity	1,599cc
Valves	ohv
Compression ratio	9.2:1
Carburettor	Weber
Max. power	82bhp @ 5,400rpm
Max. torque	92lb/ft @ 3,600rpm
Fuel capacity	10.5 gallons (47.7 litres)
TRANSMISSION	
Gearbox	4-speed
Ratios (internal)	2.97:1, 2.01:1, 1.40:1, 1.00:1
Final drive	3.55:1
SUSPENSION AND STEERING	
Front	MacPherson strut
Rear	Semi-elliptic springs
Steering	Rack and pinion
Tyres	165 × 13
Wheels	Steel
Rim width	4.5in
BRAKES	
Type	Hydraulic disc/drum
Size	9.625in disc, 9 × 1.75in drum
DIMENSIONS (in/mm)	
Track: front	53/1,346
rear	52/1,321
Wheelbase	100.8/2,560
Overall length	167.8/4,262
Overall width	64.8/1,646
Overall height	50.2/1,275
Unladen weight	2,030lb/921kg
PERFORMANCE	
Top speed	98mph (158km/h)
0–60mph	13.4sec

FORD CAPRI MK I – 2000GT (1969)

LAYOUT AND CHASSIS
Two-door coupé/monocoque construction

ENGINE	
Type	German V-4
Block material	Cast iron
Head material	Cast iron
Cylinders	V-4 60deg
Cooling	Water
Bore and stroke	93.66 × 72.44mm
Capacity	1,996cc
Valves	ohv
Compression ratio	8.9:1
Carburettor	Weber
Max. power	92.5bhp @ 5,500rpm
Max. torque	104lb/ft @ 3,600rpm
Fuel capacity	10.5 gallons (47.7 litres)
TRANSMISSION	
Gearbox	4-speed
Ratios (internal)	2.97:1, 2.01:1, 1.40:1, 1.00:1
Final drive	3.55:1
SUSPENSION AND STEERING	
Front	MacPherson strut
Rear	Semi-elliptic springs
Steering	Rack and pinion
Tyres	165 × 13
Wheels	Steel
Rim width	4.5in
BRAKES	
Type	Hydraulic disc/drum
Size	9.625in disc, 9 × 1.75in drum
DIMENSIONS (in/mm)	
Track: front	53/1,346
rear	52/1,321
Wheelbase	100.8/2,560
Overall length	167.8/4,262
Overall width	64.8/1,646
Overall height	50.2/1,275
Unladen weight	2,115lb/959kg
PERFORMANCE	
Top speed	107mph (172km/h)
0–60mph	10.6sec

size: the 1300, 1300GT and 1600 utilized the Cortina wide ratios; the 1600GT and the 2000GT used the ratios from the Corsair. Final drive ratios were 4.125 for the 1300 and 1300GT, 3.9 for the 1600, 3.78 for the 1600GT, and 3.55 for the 2000GT.

All models except the 1300 were fitted with Corsair 9.625in (24.4cm) diameter front discs and 9 × 1.75in (23 × 4cm) rear drums with servo as standard on the top two models. The 1300 utilized Cortina brakes – 9.5in (24.1cm) diameter front discs and 1.5in (3.8cm) rear drums – without servo assistance. The front suspension followed the same practice favoured on the new Escort range, with MacPherson struts and an anti-roll bar attached to the base of the suspension leg to form a semi-trailing arm. The steering also followed that in the Escort, being precise rack and pinion, mounted ahead of the front-wheel centre-line, and using many Escort components.

The rear axle utilized the usual semi-elliptic springs with telescopic dampers. Much work had been done in producing a tidy axle location arrangement for the Capri which would keep axle tramp under control yet transmit the minimum of road noise and vibration to the car's interior. The result of this research was to fit trailing arms and position the bottom location points of the dampers on the axle, one on either side of the tube.

The wheelbase shared the Corsair's 100in (2,540mm) measurement, yet used the Cortina's 52in (1,321mm) front and rear track dimension. Considerable thought had gone into giving the Capri's monocoque bodyshell above-average stiffness, and despite being larger than the Escort the Capri was some 5 per cent lighter and more rigid. An additional cross-member located by the front footwell helped reduce resonance in the 2,700–3,000rpm rev band. Vibration was also kept to a minimum by stiffening crucial body panels and enlarging and softening rear spring bushes. The rear engine hanger was relocated and a stiffener placed between the sump and clutch housing. Work was also carried out to produce a quieter, longer-lasting exhaust system, and carefully chosen sound-deadening material was fixed to both sides of the bulkhead panel and the transmission tunnel. These modifications all helped to give the Capri its highly praised, smooth, vibration-free ride.

THE FAMILY FASTBACK

The advertising campaign launched at the time of the Capri's introduction hailed the car as 'Ford Capri: the family-size fastback'. The small print talked of the family man's responsibilities, with 'fidgety kids, a wife and maybe a mother-in-law to ferry around'. Ford reckoned they had pulled off the impossible by styling a car which looked like a racy two-seater, yet had room in the back for two adults plus a boot to take all their luggage. With typical Ford value-for-money, there seemed to be a Capri priced to suit most pockets.

Finally, we must remember the Capri custom 'packs' – 'extras' that could be fitted to the car after purchase so the new owner at least felt he or she was buying something individual:

X-Pack (£32 12s 0d)	**L-Pack (£15 0s 4d)**	**R-Pack (£39 3s 4d)**
Reclining seats	Bumper overriders	5in road wheels
Bucket rear seat	Dummy side-vents	15in steering-wheel
Second interior light	Locking petrol cap	Spot/fog lamp
Handbrake warning light	Extra brightwork	Map-reading lamp
Dipping rear-view mirror		Matt-black bonnet, door sills and boot panels
Two-tone horns		
Reversing lights		

Two types of road wheel seen on the Mk I Capri. The first is the standard steel wheel with chrome hub-cap seen on the 1300 and 1600 models; the second is the Rostyle wheel, fitted to sports versions of the Capri and also seen on the Cortina 1600E.

By bulk-buying you could save a few quid: the XL-Pack was just £44 7s 10d, while the XLR-Pack of goodies came to £79 12s 10d. Then, of course, there was £14 0s 9d for the obligatory inertia-reel seat-belts.

'Another crucial aspect of Capri was its timing,' explained Hayes. 'It came at the time we were setting up Ford Europe. The potential sales volume for the UK market alone just would not have made it viable, but considered as a project undertaken in conjunction with Ford Germany – with the European market – it made good economic sense.'

Without doubt, the Capri was an exciting concept in Ford's model line-up, encompassing style and flair in a family fastback. The Mustang had proved highly successful in the States, substantiating the need for this type of car. Even so the Capri was launched into a world of uncertainty, with abundant credit squeezes and industrial unrest. What sort of future would it have?

DISCONTENT

Sadly, even Henry Ford could not have envisaged the government's squeeze on the economy and the 1968–9 labour disputes that were to have such a savage effect on Britain's motor industry. During the first three months of 1969, Ford's output dropped to 71,981 – compared with 113,715 units produced during the same period of 1968. In an *Autocar* interview in July 1969, Henry Ford explained that strikes in the UK had affected parts supplies to Ford Germany. While he would not be drawn on the issue of investments being made in Germany rather than in the UK, it was clear, that he put great store on the value of Saarlouis's contribution to Ford's potential in Central Europe, using the Capri as a specific example of the total co-operation between Ford's European centres. Looking back from the stable labour-relations period of the mid-1990s, it is difficult to picture the prolonged and damaging effect Britain's industrial disputes had on manufacturing and the country's image internationally.

CAPRI MK I CHASSIS/DATE IDENTIFICATION DETAILS

Capri 1300 and 1600					
4-cy ohv 80.98 × 62.99 1,298cc Alt eng 1968–72 4-cy ohv 80.98 × 77.62 1,599cc	Nov 68	ECD ECG	ECH.76519 ECH.03773 ECH.76520 ECH.09751	1300 1600 1300GT 1600GT	Two-door fastback saloon first produced (announced Jan 1969). Servo on 1600GT, auto transmission option on 1600 only. Models available with L, X and R packs (*see* text).
	Sep 70	ECD ECG	ECK.33236 ECK.33313		1300 and 1600 More powerful. 1300GT and 1600GT eng. Servo brakes standard on 1300GT and 1600. X & R packs no longer available separately. Nylon trim option.
	Oct 71	ECG	ECM –		1300GT no longer available.
	Feb 72	ECG	ECM –		1600GT Standard saloon no longer available.
	Jun 72	ECG	ECM		Special 1600GT introduced. Special colours. Bonnet power bulge. Black console, fascia and trim. Opening rear windows. Auto transmission optional.
	Sep 72	ECD ECG	ECM.31536 ECM.31558		1300 and 1600 Bonnet power bulge. 1600GT Larger headlamps and rear lamps. Modified fascia, larger dials, glove box. Two-spoke steering wheel. Revised suspension. 1,599cc ohv engine replaced by 1,593cc ohc. Options limited to 1300L, 1600L, 1600XL, 1600GT. XL has reclining front seats. GT has high bhp engine, black fascia and clock. Auto transmission optional.
	Dec 73	ECG	ECN 50987		Capri Mk I discontinued.
Capri 2000GT					
V-4 ohv 93.66 × 72.44 1,996cc	Mar 69	ECH	EC1 09646		Two-door fastback saloon. As for 1600GT but with 1,996cc engine. Trim as for 1600GT. Auto transmission optional.
	Jan 71		ECL 36279		X and R options no longer available individually. Nylon upholstery optional.
	Oct 71		ECL		Capri Special introduced. XLR trim, special colour, black vinyl roof, black seat trim. Rear window slats and spoiler.
	Feb 72		–		Standard saloon no longer available.
	Jun 72		ECM		Capri Special 2000GT introduced. Trim as for 1600GT. Auto transmission optional.
	Sep 72		ECM 36482		Modified as for 1600GT. Options restricted to 2000GT. Auto transmission optional.
	Dec 73		ECN 36656		Capri Mk I discontinued.

Capri 300				
V-6 ohv 93.66 × 72.44 2,994cc	Sep 69	ECG	ECJ 22021	3000GT two door fastback saloon. Similar to 2000GT but with bulge on bonnet. Twin exhaust tail pipes. Trim options as 2000GT.
	Nov 69		ECJ 42425	3000E (announced Mar 70). Luxury of 3000GT. XLR with opening rear window and 3000E trim.
	Jan 71		ECL 36306	GT and E unchanged. X and R packs no longer available individually. Nylon trim available as an option.
	Oct 71		ECL 07209	Increased bhp.
	Feb 72		–	GT standard saloon no longer available.
	Jun 72		ECM	Capri Special 3000GT introduced. Trim as for 1600GT. Auto transmission optional.
	Jly 72		ECM 52597	Saloon E discontinued. Replaced by GXL.
	Sep 72		ECM	Modified as 2000GT. Options restricted to 3000GT.
			ECM	3000GXL introduced. As for 3000GT but with twin headlamps, sports wheels, waist chrome strip and opening rear window. Grained dash. Auto transmission optional. Sports pack on GT.
	Dec 73		ECN 36355	Capri Mk I discontinued.

CAPRI MK I PERFORMANCE FIGURES

Model	Performance (0 to 60 mph)	Max. speed	Fuel consumption	Standing quarter mile
1600GT	13.4 sec	98mph (158km/h)	24.8mpg (11.4l/100km)	18.8 sec
2000GT	10.6 sec	107mph (172km/h)	22mpg (12.8l/100km)	18.2 sec
3000GT	10.3 sec	113mph (182km/h)	16.7mpg (16.9l/100km)	17.6 sec

FURTHER DEVELOPMENT

The issue of *Autocar* that carried the feature on the group Capri test in Cyprus also featured another article entitled 'Ford's new twin-cam'. It was appropriate that this interesting new unit should be discussed as one of the Cyprus prototype Capris had been fitted with a similar unit. There was also talk of a hundred more Capris being fitted with BDA engines for reliability evaluation before production proper began at the end of 1969. Referred to as the Cosworth BDA (BD standing for belt drive), the unit utilized the 1,600cc Cortina block assembly with an extended crankshaft nose to take the toothed-belt drive pulley. The original camshaft was also retained to drive the petrol and oil pumps and the distributor.

The cylinder head consisted of two LM8 aluminium castings, the lower forming the head itself, with valves set at 40 degrees in

At the top end of the Capri range was the 3000GT. Giving almost unparalleled performance for the price, the car really could be described as 'The car you always promised yourself'.

the pent-roof-design combustion chambers. The upper casting carried the camshaft bearings, the camshafts themselves driven by the toothed belt. The valves and timing gear were manufactured from good but not expensive materials, while the crankshaft and connecting rods were standard 1600 Cortina, thus imposing a rev limit of 7,000rpm and a peak power of 120bhp at 6,200rpm. Significantly, the *Autocar* article mentioned that there were no plans at that stage to terminate production of the Lotus twin-cam unit (by then almost ten years old). The initial production batch of BDAs were destined for racing and assessment by 'selected users', including the *Autocar* team.

In the event, the BDA-powered Capri never reached production. Supplies of these units (built by Harpers of Letchworth) were instead channelled into Escort assembly for the delightful RS1600, rally versions of which were to become so successful on the world's toughest stages. In its place was to come an altogether different 120+bhp motor, which gave the Capri a relaxed cruising speed of 100mph (161km/h) plus.

V6 POWER

The Mk IV Zodiac, launched in 1966, was Ford's less-than-pretty model-range flag-

FORD CAPRI MK I – 3000GT (1969)

LAYOUT AND CHASSIS
Two-door coupé/monocoque construction

ENGINE	
Type	Essex
Block material	Cast iron
Head material	Cast iron
Cylinders	6
Cooling	Water
Bore and stroke	93.66 × 72.4mm
Capacity	2,994cc
Valves	ohv
Compression ratio	8.9:1
Carburettor	Weber
Max. power	128bhp @ 4,750rpm
Max. torque	173lb/ft @ 3,000rpm
Fuel capacity	10.6 gallons (48 litres)
TRANSMISSION	
Gearbox	4-speed
Ratios (internal)	3.16:1, 2.21:1, 1.40:1, 1.00:1
Final drive	3.09:1
SUSPENSION AND STEERING	
Front	MacPherson strut
Rear	Semi-elliptic springs
Steering	Rack and pinion
Tyres	165 × 13
Wheels	Steel
Rim width	5.0in
BRAKES	
Type	Hydraulic disc/drum
Size	9.625in disc, 9 × 1.75in drum
DIMENSIONS (in/mm)	
Track: front	53/1,346
rear	52/1,321
Wheelbase	100.8/2,560
Overall length	167.8/4,262
Overall width	64.8/1,646
Overall height	50.2/1,275
Unladen weight	2,330lb/1,057kg
PERFORMANCE	
Top speed	113mph (182km/h)
0–60mph	10.3sec

ship. It was big, with a huge bonnet (long enough to accommodate the spare wheel in front of the engine, Reliant Scimitar style), a stumpy boot and very American-influenced styling. Powered by the 93.7 × 72.4mm 2,994cc V6 unit, power output was set at 136bhp at 4,750rpm. The manual gearbox had wide ratios to support its non-sporting saloon status, although most customers opted for the automatic version.

In order to fit the Zodiac's 60-degree V6 engine into the Capri, the bonnet had to be given a power bulge that was sufficient to clear the air cleaner on the centrally mounted carburettor. The radiator was uprated to dissipate the heat generated from the largest UK Ford-manufactured engine, a 13.5gal (61.4l) fuel tank was substituted to feed the car's thirstier appetite, and a bigger battery was also specified. The standard wide-ratio Mk IV gearbox was fitted, with a modified remote-control gear linkage, driving a 3.22:1 final drive.

Underneath, the suspension was uprated by the addition of harder anti-roll bar bushes, beefier shock absorbers all round and stiffer springs – 122lb (55kg) on the front and 125lb (57kg) on the rear. Tyres were increased to 185 (70) Goodyear Grand Prix, fitted to 5.5in-wide (14cm-wide) road wheels.

To overcome oil surges caused through the sporty Capri's higher cornering speeds, the 3-litre engine was given uprated crankshaft bearings, a modified oil pick-up and a baffled sump. The body was also stiffened around the suspension-locating points to handle the 263lb (119kg) of the V6 over the 217lb (98kg) weight of the small V4 unit.

In terms of performance, the Capri 3000GT proved to be spirited rather than impressive, with a 0–60mph (0–97km/h) time of 10.3 seconds and a maximum gallop of 114mph (183km/h). Above all else, however, it was the car's lazy power that endeared it to the buying public, for it was a car that produced the goods in a most unfrenzied fashion. 'There is no question in my mind that the Capri was Europe's Mustang,' remarked Mansfield, thoughtfully. 'It just illustrates that Ford is an American-owned and dominated company.'

Fitting neatly under the Capri's voluminous bonnet, the Mk 1V V6 Zephyr Zodiac power unit gave the car a relaxed performance that was more than a match for its competitors: a top speed of 115mph (185km/h) and a 0–60mph (0–97km/h) time of 9.2 seconds.

NEW MODELS

At the 1970 Geneva Motor Show Ford launched two new versions of the Capri. One was the 3000E ('E' for executive, of course), which was fitted with all the top-of-the-range extras; in addition to the XLR-Pack options, these included a Ford push-button radio, opening rear windows, heated rear screen, a vinyl roof and cloth panels for the seats. The overall result was a comprehensively equipped value-for-money fast sports coupé, more than capable of competing head on with its rivals. The other new Capri had been developed by Ford Cologne. It had a special fuel-injected competition version of the 2.6-litre in-line six-cylinder engine which had shown its colours at the 84-hour endurance race at the Nürburgring, at the Tour de Corse and at the Tour de France. Available in silver-grey only (the colours of the German Ford motorsport team), this version of the Capri had GRP doors, bonnet and boot-lid, and 6in road wheels.

April of that year also saw the Capri being introduced on to the American market with a launch at the New York Motor Show. The car could be bought in 1.6- and 2.0-litre forms only which used the newly introduced ohc Pinto engine, the unit that had suffered so many problems in the early days through high camshaft wear. The car was an immediate success and orders for over £3 million were put on the books. Parts for the US Capris were initially supplied from Britain – until industrial disputes sharply affected output and supplies were moved to Cologne.

Meanwhile, Ford UK had been improving

the output of its four-cylinder Kent engines, and changes to carburettor and valve timing had resulted in 4–8bhp of extra power. Brakes and lights were also improved, and a degree of rationalization was made to the L-, XL- and XLR-Pack options.

FAVO

In 1970, also, FAVO (Ford Advanced Vehicle Operations) was established, an Anglo-German arrangement for low-volume specialist versions of Ford's mainstream products. The first cars to come off the South Ockendon-based factory production line were the RS1600 and less-powerful RS Mexico Escorts, the mouth-watering RS2600 Capri being manufactured in Cologne. FAVO quickly blossomed into a thriving mini-industry in the UK, with around 200 staff working under the expert guidance of Ray Horrocks in the 85,000sq. ft (7,900sq. m) ex-parts department. The very lucrative Rallye Sport programme was also launched and, in addition to selling the cars themselves, promoted after-market spares and accessories – a very lucrative side of the business.

'Setting up FAVO was very much the culmination of all the excitement which had been generated during the 1960s,' said Rod Mansfield as he explained the background recently. 'But, mainstream engineering said "You want a sporting version of the Escort? Fine, but we can't make a start for three years and it'll take two years to develop." Walter Hayes said "That's ridiculous, we want it now". So it was the inertia of mainstream engineering which caused FAVO to be located remotely. Although, I was told that if I joined FAVO, I would never be able to go back to mainstream engineering.'

There was also a down side to 1970, for it was revealed in the press that the British motor industry had lost an unbelievable 8.8 million days that year through industrial

WILLIAM 'BILL' HAYDEN CBE

William 'Bill' Hayden was born in West Ham, East London, in January 1929 and was educated at Romford Technical College. He then went on to gain considerable experience in the commercial and finance world through working in stockbroking and insurance during the late 1940s, a background which was to serve him well when he joined Ford.

Hayden joined Ford in 1950, becoming a member of the Cost Accounting Department of Briggs Motor Bodies Limited of Dagenham. His experience in the City assured rapid promotion, Bill broadened his knowledge in the finance and cost-controlling fields before moving on to senior management in manufacture in 1966.

Starting as Assistant Manager, Transmission and Chassis Division, Hayden then moved on yet again to become General Operations Manager and, later still, Director of Manufacturing, Ford of Britain. It was during his time in this job that he was able to bring about the arrangements necessary for establishing FAVO at South Ockenden, responding to Walter Hayes' suggestion for a 'factory within a factory'. 'Bill winked at me and it just seemed to happen like magic,' recalled Hayes. Hayden was later promoted to Vice-President, Power Train Operations, Ford of Europe.

In 1971 Hayden was appointed Vice-President, Truck Manufacturing Operations, Ford of Europe, becoming a member of the Board of Ford Motor Company the year after. In 1974, he was promoted yet again to become Ford of Europe's Vice-President Manufacturing, being awarded the CBE for his services to export two years later. In 1989 Hayden was appointed to the newly created post of Vice-President, Manufacturing Group, Ford of Europe.

A close-up of the rear light cluster fitted to early Mk I Capris. Compare this to the larger lenses on the face-lift Capris of 1973.

action (the highest since 1926), a proportion of which had been centred around the docks, thereby affecting exports. A surprise defeat of Harold Wilson's government in June put Edward Heath in the hot seat, who immediately began a campaign to pass legislation that would curb wild-cat strikes; it was to be an uphill battle which would affect the motor industry directly.

In 1971 the Capri Special (based on the 2000GT) was introduced, finished in bright Vista Orange. Among the standard fittings were a heated rear screen, cloth-covered seats, push-button radio and vinyl roof. Its most obvious additions, however, clearly influenced by the Boss Mustang in the States, were a rear boot spoiler and rather tasteless GRP window slats fitted over the outside of the rear screen.

At the London Motor Show later that year Ford introduced a revised 3000E and 3000GT. According to Ford's PR men, these were 'the fastest production line cars ever to be marketed by Ford of Britain,' with engines producing 8 per cent more power yet with no corresponding increase in fuel consumption. The bulk of the changes were focused on the combustion chambers, where alterations to inlet valve size, ports and manifolding improved gas flow. Modifications to the air cleaner, carburettor jets and a revised exhaust system also played their part, reputedly reducing the level of hydrocarbons in the exhaust gases.

The transmission was given a higher 3.09:1 final drive (which produced 22mph, or 35km/h, at 1,000rpm), and the dreadfully low Zodiac second-gear ratio was changed so it was now possible to reach 63mph (101km/h) in the second cog before changing up. There was an increase in servo size (from 7in up to 8in), revised, softer rear springs and slightly different road wheels, and slightly modified lenses on the auxilliary driving lights. The changes were all pretty basic, but they were sufficient to give Ford's PR people something to go on. 'Just think,' ran a typical Capri advertisement of the time, 'for the same kind of money you could have an ordinary family saloon.'

In 1972 Ford's design studios produced a set of add-on body panels for the Mk I car which included front air dam, bonnet air scoop, front and rear wheelarch extensions, and boot spoiler. It was, however, only an exercise and the panels never became available for sale.

In the middle of 1972 a series of special Capris were introduced, with 1,600cc, 2.0- and 3.0-litre engines, and coachwork finished in emerald-green or ebony-black with red and gold side-body stripes. Power bulges in the bonnets, matt-black dashboards and centre consoles were among the features. This was simply Ford's way of keeping the market interested. At Brands Hatch that year a group of 3.0-litre Capris took part in the second celebrity challenge, the result being a pile of very bruised cars!

For the 1973 model year, Ford introduced the face-lift Capri range. The big give-away from the front was the much larger oblong-shaped headlamps (which finally overcame criticism of the Capri's poor lighting performance) with sealed-beam inserts, and twin circular lights with halogen lamps on the top-of-the-range 3000GXL model. Also, all Capris had by then gained bonnet bulges and restyled grilles, while at the rear there were enlarged light clusters. The rather nice black and silver 5in steel road wheels were standardized, and the rear axle trailing arms were withdrawn and replaced by an anti-roll bar. Spring rates were softened, though this did have the effect of increasing roll and pitch.

Inside, there were restyled dashboards, two-spoke steering-wheels and better shaped seats with woven material inserts. Concave knee recessions in the rear panels also gave back-seat passengers more space.

The Capri range at this stage included the 1300 (the 1300GT was dropped) two 1600 Pinto-engined cars in standard and GT form, the 2.0-litre V4 GT, and the top-of-the-range

The face-lift Capri introduced on to the UK market in 1973, seen here in 1600GT form with sports steel wheels and vinyl roof. The engine is the ohc Pinto unit first seen in the Mk III Cortina.

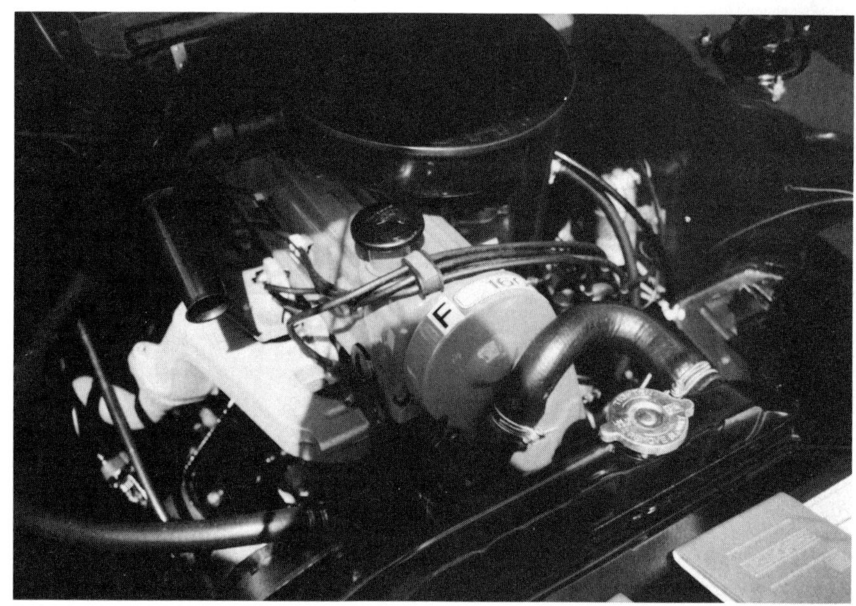

An under-bonnet view of a 1600L model, showing the ohc 80.97 × 72.57mm engine. Early engines proved troublesome, with poor camshaft lobe lubrication; modified feed pipes and regular oil changes cured the problem.

Interior of the GXL model, with wool seat fillets and improved fascia. Considerable thought had gone into improving the breed – better instrumentation and headlamps, improved seating – and few could fault it.

3.0-litre GXL and GT models, which, incidentally, had been given the German 2.6-litre Hummer gearbox. The Hummer was a marked improvement over the earlier Zodiac box, the 'top loader' remote-control mechanics being less likely to baulk at quick changes the way its predecessor did. Moreover, the Ford people rationalized the option packs so that only the L, XL, GT and GXL were available. Even so, with these packs plus the various choices in engine size and trim options, there were still nineteen versions of the UK Capri over which the enthusiast could drool.

The Cologne team meanwhile had gone ever further in its rationalization programme, with the result that all German Capris, save for the V6 units, were ohc Pinto units – including the 1300. A quick look at the sales figures for the Capri in 1969, 1970 and 1971 reveals that Ford Germany were consistently selling roughly twice as many cars as Ford UK. It is not surprising, then, that when the millionth Capri came off the production line – an RS2600, produced on 29 August 1973 – it was German-built.

As Ford prepared to launch the Capri II, the company's range of cars for the Euro-

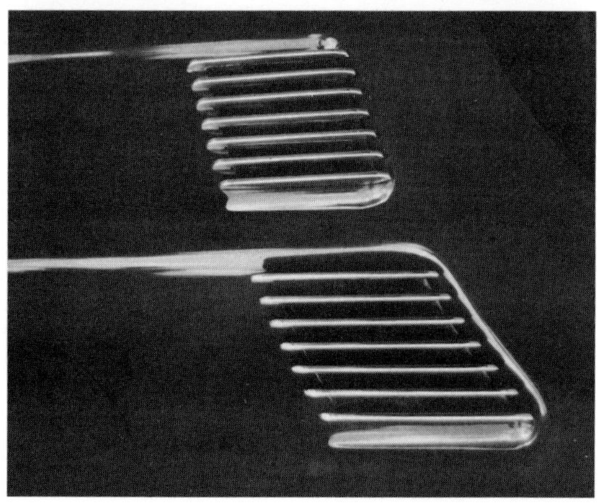

Details of the face-lift Capri: sports-style steel road wheels replaced the Rostyle-type; side-grille flashes were reduced in length; and larger rear light clusters were added.

pean market looked comprehensive – from the base Escort 1100 to the evergreen Cortina (by then in Mk III form) and the flagship Granadas, of which there was even a coupé version. Yet on the horizon loomed the spectre of petrol rationing as the Energy Crisis began to gather momentum. Some 16 million petrol ration books were printed and by the end of 1973 roughly 200 petrol stations had closed. The future for both the motor industry and the individual motorist looked bleak indeed. How would it affect Ford and the impending new Capri?

3 Major Changes

As Ford moved cautiously into the 1970s, the vice-like grip of the Energy Crisis was beginning to take effect world-wide; several well-known and established specialist manufacturers – such as Jensen – would succumb in the next few years. Meanwhile, in line with true motor-industry ideology (which decrees that a new model must be introduced while its predecessor is still selling strongly, rather than wait for its popularity to wane), the Capri Mk II was launched on to an unsuspecting market in February 1974. A total of 1,172,900 Mk Is had been built in exactly five years, and no subsequent version of the Capri would sell anywhere near this quantity. The new model, however, was an altogether more versatile machine than its earlier sibling. Load-carrier, shopping car, family transport or fast continental GT; the Capri II could be all these things.

PROBLEM-SOLVING

If the Capri was nicknamed the poor-man's Aston Martin – and there was no shame in the title – then the irony had to be that Ford would one day own AML Ltd. The next generation of Capris would then ape the ageless, classic lines of the late William Towns' shaped DBS model introduced in 1966, adding a lifting tailgate for practicality and emulating Jaguar's legendary E-Type. But there were other reasons for the changes. Early Capris (the 1969–73 models) had been criticized for poor rear three-quarter vision and limited

The addition of a third hatchback door gave the Capri II (launched in February 1974) a broader market potential. However, in mid-1977, during its production run, sales of the Capri to the USA were stopped while the Energy Crisis did its share to dampen the market.

boot space. Ford's designers had listened, yet therein hung a dichotomy: on the one hand the stylists aimed to make the Capri sleeker, more elegant and more like the cars that caught the hearts of the enthusiasts, while on the other the advertising men wanted to promote the Capri as a four-seater family car, thereby making it attractive to those drivers who needed more room. And, after all, the MGB GT, the Triumph GT6 and even the Jaguar E-type were really only two-seaters with vestigial accommodation in the rear for children enduring short journeys.

The answer, then, was clear: restyle the rear of the Capri, giving it a sloping roof/window-line and make the window itself open on gas-assisted struts, thus increasing the boot volume at a single stroke. If you added to this the facility to lower and raise the rear seats, the load-carrying capacity was boosted considerably. The spin-off from this clever redesign treatment was that the rear side-window could also be made larger, thereby overcoming the second complaint of the early Capris. There were influences from outside, too, like Reliant's very successful GRP-bodied GTE. Interestingly, an article in the July 1965 edition of *Autocar* illustrated a collection of drawings showing possible Ford cars of the future. One artist's impression depicted a two-door coupé design not that dissimilar to the shape which finally became the Capri II, with a fastback rear and folding back seats. In marketing terms, the new Capri was certainly better designed than its predecessor to align itself with the sort of product that Ford's management perceived should be made by a volume carmaker.

'With the considerable sales success of the first generation of Capri, the dealers were able to say that if the model was made more versatile with an opening rear tailgate and fold-flat rear seats it would have wider appeal,' Hayes recalled. 'But I feel that the Capri was talking more closely to its true market in its original form than it did in Mk II and Mk III forms.'

WORK BEGINS

In 1970, work began on 'Diana' (Ford chose girls' names as project titles – the restyled Escort was known as Brenda, after a secretary of one of Ford's top executives), the code-name given to the next generation of Capri. The 100.8in (2,560mm) wheelbase and the 53.5in (1,359mm) front track of the earlier Capri were retained. However, to create extra boot space, the rear track was increased from 52.3in (1,328mm) to 54.5in (1,384mm). The bodyshell itself was widened by 2.1in (53mm), and roughly 1in (25mm) was added to the height and the overall length.

Most of the changes to be integrated into the underside of the Capri II had, in fact, already been introduced on to the current model. Ford talked grandly of some 151 modifications in total. This may sound a little hard to believe, until you realize that it took into account the complete modification shopping list – including specification changes to items such as bolt sizes and suspension component alterations that the majority of buyers would hardly notice!

In terms of styling, Capri II gained considerably from an increase in glass area: some 14 per cent in the side-windows – due partly to the downward sweep of the door window ledges and increased size of rear side-windows – and a huge 30 per cent in the rear tailgate. This in turn was responsible, at least in part, for the corresponding increase in overall weight – a gain of 145lb (66kg) in the case of the luxury 3.0-litre top-of-the-range Ghia model. The balance of this extra weight came from the additional metal that was used to strengthen the boot area (effectively weakened by the gaping hole created by the tailgate aperture) and the increase in torsional rigidity necessary for

The launch of the Mk II Capri saw the introduction of the ohc Pinto engine family (this is the [illegible] version) in 1.6-litre (72bhp and 88bhp) and 2.0-litre (98bhp) forms.

the body tub. There was a bonus in having this extra body metal, however, in that it strengthened the roof area to give the Capri II an effective roll-over cage.

Inside, the improved dashboard layout of the latest Mk I Capri was rolled over into Capri II, and included an easy-to-read speedo and rev counter on the more expensive versions. As discussed previously, the rear seats could be folded flat to give a large deck space, this facility being further improved by making the seats individually hinged on the range-leading Ghia and GT models.

Under the bonnet, the Capri II range came powered by a variety of engines, from the 57bhp crossflow 1.3-litre Kent unit to the 1.6-litre engines in the 72bhp and 88bhp forms, both being later-generation ohc Pinto units. Also in ohc form, making its début in the Capri II, was the 2.0-litre version available in 98bhp form only. This came straight out of the Mk III 'coke bottle' Cortina that was launched in 1971. Finally, there was the 3.0-litre engine, the same as before but with twin exhaust tail pipes which marked it down as the V6 version of the team. For German buyers, there was a 55bhp version of the 1.3-litre engine. Then came the 1.6-litre units available in similar 72bhp and 88bhp tune. However, rather than opt for the 2.0-litre engine, Cologne chose the 2.3-litre V6, which produced 108bhp, while the British V6 3.0-litre Essex engine was listed as an option for the 2300 GT and Ghia cars.

In Britain there were differences in gearbox ratios, too. The 1.3-, 1.6- and 2.0-litre cars used a 'close ratio' box which only found its way on to the 1.3 model in the German range. The Germans themselves used their own ratios in these cars, although the 3.0-litre gearbox was the same on both sides of the Channel; it was, in fact, the box from the 1972 Granada.

Final drives also varied, depending on engine size and tune. The English Cortina-

FORD CAPRI MK II – 1600S (1975)

LAYOUT AND CHASSIS	
Two-door coupé/monocoque construction	
ENGINE	
Type	Pinto
Block material	Cast iron
Head material	Cast iron
Cylinders	4
Cooling	Water
Bore and stroke	87.7 × 66.0mm
Capacity	1,593cc
Valves	ohv
Compression ratio	9.2:1
Carburettor	Weber
Max. power	88bhp @ 5,700rpm
Max. torque	92lb/ft @ 5,700rpm
Fuel capacity	13 gallons (59 litres)
TRANSMISSION	
Gearbox	4-speed
Ratios (internal)	3.58:1, 2.01:1, 1.40:1, 1.00:1
Final drive	3.75:1
SUSPENSION AND STEERING	
Front	MacPherson strut
Rear	Semi-elliptic springs
Steering	Rack and pinion
Tyres	165 × 13
Wheels	Alloy
Rim width	5.0in
BRAKES	
Type	Hydraulic disc/drum
Size	9.625in disc, 9 × 1.75in drum
DIMENSIONS (in/mm)	
Track: front	53/1,346
rear	54.5/1,384
Wheelbase	101/2,565
Overall length	167.8/4,262
Overall width	67/1,702
Overall height	51/1,295
Unladen weight	2,293lb/1,040kg
PERFORMANCE	
Top speed	106mph (171km/h)
0–60mph	11.4sec

FORD CAPRI MK II – 2000S (1975)

LAYOUT AND CHASSIS	
Two-door coupé/monocoque construction	
ENGINE	
Type	Pinto
Block material	Cast iron
Head material	Cast iron
Cylinders	4
Cooling	Water
Bore and stroke	90.3 × 77.0mm
Capacity	1,993cc
Valves	ohc
Compression ratio	9.2:1
Carburettor	Weber
Max. power	98bhp @ 5,200rpm
Max. torque	111lb/ft @ 3,500rpm
Fuel capacity	13 gallons (59 litres)
TRANSMISSION	
Gearbox	4-speed
Ratios (internal)	3.65:1, 1.97:1, 1.37:1, 1.00:1
Final drive	3.44:1
SUSPENSION AND STEERING	
Front	MacPherson strut
Rear	Semi-elliptic springs
Steering	Rack and pinion
Tyres	175 × 13
Wheels	Alloy
Rim width	5.5in
BRAKES	
Type	Hydraulic disc/drum
Size	9.8in disc, 8 × 1.75in drum
DIMENSIONS (in/mm)	
Track: front	53/1,346
rear	54.5/1,384
Wheelbase	101/2,565
Overall length	167.8/4,262
Overall width	67/1,702
Overall height	51/1,295
Unladen weight	2,273lb/1,031kg
PERFORMANCE	
Top speed	110mph (177km/h)
0–60mph	10.4sec

type was used on small, less-powerful Capris, while the tough German-made Atlas axle was fitted to the 2,000cc and 3,000cc cars. Automatic transmission was available as an option on 1600, 2000 and 3000 models, and was made standard wear for the sumptuous V6 Ghia, the boxes being made in Ford's Bordeaux plant. The box itself was common to all models, although settings and torque converter sizes varied with engine capacity. Customers for GT versions, however, did not have the manual/automatic transmission dilemma to worry about as these cars were available as manual only.

FORD CAPRI MK II – 3000S (1975)

LAYOUT AND CHASSIS
Two-door coupé/monocoque construction

ENGINE

Type	Essex
Block material	Cast iron
Head material	Cast iron
Cylinders	6
Cooling	Water
Bore and stroke	93.7 × 72.4mm
Capacity	2,994cc
Valves	ohv
Compression ratio	9.0:1
Carburettor	Weber
Max. power	138bhp @ 5,000rpm
Max. torque	174lb/ft @ 3,500rpm
Fuel capacity	13 gallons (59 litres)

TRANSMISSION

Gearbox	4-speed
Ratios (internal)	3.35:1, 1.94:1, 1.41:1, 1.00:1
Final drive	3.09:1

SUSPENSION AND STEERING

Front	MacPherson strut
Rear	Semi-elliptic springs
Steering	Rack and pinion
Tyres	185 × 13
Wheels	Alloy
Rim width	5.5in

BRAKES

Type	Hydraulic disc/drum
Size	9.75in disc, 9 × 1.75in drum

DIMENSIONS (in/mm)

Track: front	53/1,346
rear	54.5/1,384
Wheelbase	101/2,565
Overall length	167.8/4,262
Overall width	67/1,702
Overall height	51/1,295
Unladen weight	2,574lb/1,168kg

PERFORMANCE

Top speed	117mph (188km/h)
0–60mph	9.0sec

Underneath, the spring rates had been changed yet again, and given softer settings to align the ride quality more with the broader 'family' attraction of the new Capri range. To handle the additional weight of the 3.0-litre cars, the front disc brakes were increased to 9.75in (24.8cm) diameter and the rear drums were enlarged to 2.29 × 9in (5.8 × 22.9cm).

Meanwhile, the NVH (noise, vibration and harshness) people had been busy with the bodywork, and the Capri II used a considerable amount of polyurethane foam to fill in blind-body panel sections. The aim was to combat resonance and help reduce body rot through water ingress, a problem already becoming obvious on earlier 'notchback' Capris.

The new Capri II offered four levels of interior trim, ranging from the base L through the XL and GT variants to the luxurious Ghia in ascending order of price, luxury and complexity. And, although this would appear to indicate an almost infinite number of variations, not all were available on every model. The base L pack, for example, was only found on the 1300 and 1600 cars, while only the 1600 Capri II could be ordered with the intermediate XL package. Finally, the top-of-the-range 2.0-litre and 3.0-litre cars were only available in either Ghia or GT form. Desirable features on the latter included an efficient, sliding-steel sun roof and 5.5in alloy road wheels. The Ghia also came with a vinyl roof which, although only a cosmetic frill, did set the car off rather well. Incidentally, all Ghia versions were built in Germany from the start, and de-

As Capri production progressed, more attention was paid to rust protection. In this photograph (taken in 1975 before manufacture had been moved to Germany), bodies are being sprayed prior to assembly. Ghias, of course, were available with metallic paint finish.

A 2.0-litre Ghia with alloy wheels and vinyl roof. The beauty of the Mk II Capri for the family owner was the versatility of the carrying space: the car could be a four-seater with conventional boot; a three-seater with one of the rear seats laid flat; or a two-seater with extended load deck.

veloped in conjunction with the Ford-owned coachbuilding firm of Ghia in Turin. Other additions in the Ghia package were a rear wash/wipe facility for the tailgate, rubber side-body mouldings, radio, halogen headlamps and tinted glass – a pretty comprehensive list all in all.

COMPETITION

As they lined up against their competitors, the new Capris continued to offer value for money, good performance and cheap running costs, all in a stylish presentation. The table below shows how the Capri shaped up to the more popular alternatives.
It was clear that competition in this sector of the sporting market was increasing, and while it was true that the Mk I Capri had sold well, other contenders had arrived on the scene, including the Japanese. Often criticized during this period for producing cars with poor road-holding, the inscrutable engineers from the East were learning fast. The tough terrain of international rallies, where road-holding – and reliability – were primary considerations, provided first-class experience. No one, not even Ford, could afford to be complacent.

By the time the updated Capri was launched in February 1974, Ford's product line looked comprehensive. It started with

Capri Mk badging on an S-registration 3.0-litre Ghia. Notice the size of the light cluster when compared to the large lenses fitted to the face-lift Mk I cars. Runners let into the carpet covering the load deck helped prevent damage when carrying heavy objects.

Model	Max speed (mph/km/h)	Acceleration 0–60 mph/ 0–97 km/h (sec)	Fuel consumption (mpg/km/l)	Cost (£)
Capri 3000S	117/188	9.0	23.1/8.17	2,927
Alfa Romeo Alfetta GTV	118/190	8.9	23.3/8.25	4,799
Datsun 260Z 2 + 2	120/193	9.9	23.9/8.46	5,247
Lotus Elite 503	124/200	7.8	20.9/7.40	9,782
MGB GT	102/164	13.0	23.7/8.39	3,060
Triumph Stag	116/187	9.3	20.7/7.33	5,419

the Escorts, from the base Popular to the rally-proven RS1600 and more practical Mexico versions. Then came the Mk III Cortina in all its forms (though this Ford evergreen would never be offered with the tohc engine), including the 2000E with its 98bhp 2.0-litre Pinto engine and luxurious interior, which had taken over from the popular 1600E. Then came the Capri, followed by the top-of-the-range Granadas, cars that won acclaim from the press for their space, comfort, good rideability, performance and value for money.

In contrast, a quick glimpse at what Detroit had up its sleeve for the 1974 Mustang reveals an altogether smaller, almost 'Europeanized' car available in notchback and fastback forms. Lee Iaccoca, back at the Ford helm, had instigated the small fixed-hardtop approach for this version, known as Mustang II. What emerged was an amalgamation of European engineering trends (rack and pinion steering, and German 2.3-litre and 2.8-litre V6 engines that had been much reduced in power by the addition of detoxification equipment) and Japanese-like styling. Taste, sadly, was not Mustang II's forte.

In May 1974 the Ghia versions of the 2-litre and 3-litre Capris began arriving in the UK from Germany in order to satisfy orders. This would be the way forward for Capri production, with all manufacturing moving to Cologne in 1976. But that was still some way off.

By 1972 Ford Europe had completed its complex and adventurous scheme to integrate its European activities, with particular emphasis being placed on the British and German operations and the headquarters based at the ex-Army barracks at Warley, near Brentwood in Essex. At a time when other British motor manufacturers were experiencing real problems, Ford alone was running at a profit, the only exception being 1971 when the books showed a £30.7 million deficit. This loss was due to a crippling ten-week strike, the longest in Ford's history, which focused on securing parity for all Ford workers when the highest paid staff were based in the Midlands. In monetary terms this would have meant an increase of up to 50 per cent on basic rates. A deal was finally struck which involved an initial payment of 16.2 per cent, followed by instalments stretching over the next two years which pushed pay rates up by 33 per cent. The offer was accepted and in 1972 Ford saw a profitable trading year once more. In an interview some years later, Sir Terrence Beckett remarked that the basis for Ford's industrial relations was established just after World War II and centred on a national system of pay bargaining, held at the same time each year, with a simple system of staff grading common to all Ford plants. In short, Beckett's recipe for Ford's success was to 'manage' their way from day to day, thereby ensuring the company did not get into controversial situations.

MARKETING SUCCESSES

Initial interest in the Capri II was reflected in strong sales volumes: a total of 183,000 cars were sold in the first year of manufacture. However, this figure dropped back markedly in 1975 (100,000 units) and in 1976 (101,000). This was the year that the Capri lost the American market, although the effect (as the figures illustrate) was not as dramatic as it might otherwise have been had Ford not launched a major marketing campaign (called Realignment Program in Fordspeak) which clearly boosted sales in other areas.

In June 1975 Ford launched the all-black John Player Capri II S Special, a version based on the 2.0-litre GT and the 3.0-litre GT cars. First shown at the Geneva Motor Show in March of that year, the striking S cars were finished entirely in black with

A German LHD version of the all-black JPS Capri series launched at the Geneva Motor Show in March 1975 (notice the headlamp wipers). Available in 1.6-, 2.0-and 3.0-litre forms, the only hint of colour other than black came from the gold coachlines, wheel spokes and seat panels.

A detail shot showing the gold coachlines on a JPS Midnight Capri. (Such stripework can be a real problem for the accident repair team.) The coachwork echoed the colour scheme of the JPS colours used on the Lotus GP cars, and did much to continue Ford's sporty international image.

gold coachlines: the body, interior, bumpers (finished in an epoxy powder coating), and even trim fittings such as wipers, badges and so on, were all black. The cars even boasted black-tinted glass. Only the seats were allowed a degree of colour, with gold panels let into the black squabs and backrests! Even the headlining was black. Outside, there were gold-finished alloy wheels, a rear wash/wipe facility and halogen headlamps for midnight drivers.

In October the same year Ford introduced its value-for-money scheme, a key point in the Capri II's career as the many optional extras became standard fittings, thereby boosting sales interest. To begin with, a bargain basement 1300 model was introduced, powered by a detuned 49.5bhp engine (wow!) and a dechromed body offered at a low showroom-attracting price. Also on offer was the GL model, which replaced the earlier XL model, available in either 1,600cc or 2.0-litre forms, which boasted sports wheels, a centre dash console, halogen headlamps,

Gold-sprayed FAVO-type alloy wheels on a JPS S Capri. In all, three types of alloy wheel were fitted to S cars. The S Capri was also fitted with uprated springs, dampers and anti-roll bars to firm up the ride, in parallel with the more sporty look.

Top-of-the-range 3.0-litre Ghia with vinyl roof, sliding sun hatch, eight-spoke alloy wheels and tinted glass. Ford bought Ghia of Turin in 1972, the name adding a cachet to its top-line models. The Italian company worked in harmony with Ford's Cologne team to ensure the Capri Ghia could boast luxury fittings.

The streamlined door handle on the Mk II Capri featured this trigger mechanism, which was carried through to the Mk III cars. This move away from the thumb-press button used on the SB60 and Mk I Capris was all part of a trend to improve aerodynamic efficiency.

The remote-control door mirror fitted to the 3.0-litre Ghia Capri – notice that it was not colour-coded, a feature that was to come later on Mk III cars. The mirror angle was controlled by a small lever on the inside face of the door panel.

With the introduction of the lifting rear third door, Capri IIs were fitted with a wash/wipe facility, although this was initially included only on the top-of-the-range model specification. Notice also the opening rear window which gave improved ventilation.

rear wash/wipe and sporty bucket seats.

Such was the success of the S models that GT versions for the 1976 model year were dropped in September 1975. For the 1600 range, many 'extras' – such as reclining front seats, sports wheels, brake servo and divided folding rear seats – were made standard fittings. The ever-popular 2000S was similarly uprated, while the 3000 was given new alloy wheels and power steering as standard.

All S cars were given a bolt-on front chin spoiler, while the spring rates were increased (Ford's development engineers could

The interior of a 3.0-litre Ghia. This is a late model car with three-stalk steering column light controls and automatic transmission as standard, although a manual gearbox could be ordered.

Designed to take in-line four-cylinder engines, the under-bonnet space was more than enough to accommodate the stubby V6 engine – in this case the 3.0-litre Essex unit, once described by Keith Duckworth as 'nothing more than a boat anchor'.

not resist the temptation to keep changing the Capri's springs throughout its life), and a stiffer anti-roll bar and Bilstein gas dampers added. The model was made available in a full range of body colours, though the rather boy-racerish Midnight Capri body decals were retained. Finally, in February 1976 the 'sonic idle' range of carburettors was launched, fitted to the 1.3- and 1.6-litre engines. These used sonic shock waves to transpose fuel droplets into vapour, thereby making the carburettors more efficient. (Clearly this system must have worked, because Ford won a Design Council Award for the idea.)

Ford's Total Performance image on the world stage continued to flourish as full-page advertisements depicted the rich and famous driving the company's products. Emerson Fittipaldi narrowly won the F1 World Championship in 1974, and a Ford Cosworth-engined Gulf Mirage triumphed at Le Mans in the same year. Two years on, James Hunt won the F1 Championship after the famous wet-weather scrap at Mount Fuji in Japan. Escorts also continued their successes unabated, although Stuart Turner, the head of Ford's Competitions Department at Boreham, was criticized for signing up Scandinavian drivers for the works team in preference to British drivers. In reply, Turner was characteristically unrepentant, saying 'the only way a British driver would get into the team would be by beating Roger (Clark) regularly'. The launch of the even faster Escort RS1800 opened another chapter in the team's history.

For the sports-car enthusiast, however, things looked bleak, and by the mid-1970s many of the best British sports-car manufacturers – such as Healey and Sunbeam – had gone for good. However, in 1973 MG bravely launched the MGB GT V8 powered by the Buick-derived Rover engine, a smooth and powerful unit that transformed the rugged, much-loved 'B'. And in the following year the controversial Abingdon black-bumpered cars were introduced, the result of increasingly stringent American regulations. Very soon the MGB would be replaced by the contentiously styled wedge-shaped TR7. MG-lovers felt cheated.

PRODUCTION MOVE

The year 1976 would be a significant one in the Capri's history, for between August and October production of all models moved from Halewood to Cologne. Production of the RS1800 Escort had been located at Saarlouis (much to the disgust of many true RS enthusiasts), Ford's argument being that, since there was space on the German production line for these low-volume cars, they should be built there. Moving the Capri's production line to Germany also made production sense to Ford Europe's management.

This period also saw changes being made to the Capri's specification, not least of which was that automatic transmission was dropped from the S models. Three-stalk steering-column controls for lights, indicators and wipers were also introduced in June. There were some additions to Capri's engine options, too, although these were not available on the British market: a 1,999cc V6 engine was introduced which produced 90bhp at 5,000rpm. This was linked to the UK-specification 2.0-litre gearbox and final drive. Also introduced was a low-compression version of the 1300 and 1600 ohc engines, which produced 54bhp and 68bhp respectively.

It was during this period that the Capri began to feel the effects of one of its closest rivals, the Opel Manta, marketed in the UK as the Vauxhall Cavalier Coupé. The international Energy Crisis also did much to reduce interest in sporting cars like the Capri: in January 1975 the collapse of Burmah Oil, Britain's second-largest oil company, wiped over £1,000 million off share values, while

CAPRI MK II CHASSIS/DATE IDENTIFICATION DETAILS

Capri 1300 and 1600

Engine	Date	Plant	Chassis no.	Model	Details
4-cy ohv	Feb 74	ECL	BAECPL15439	1300	Capri Mk II three-door saloon with opening rear tailgate. XL has servo brakes, heated rear windows and carpet. GT has higher bhp engine. Rear seats fold down separately. Four extra dash dials. Options include sports wheels, auto transmission on 1600. Sports pack on GT.
80.98 × 62.99			BAECPL15481	1600L	
1,298cc				1600XL	
Alt eng 1974–78		ECG	BAECPL18308	1600GT	
4-cy ohv					
87.65 × 66					
1,593cc					
	Jan 75		BAECPR		Folding rear, divided seats optional on XL
	Jun 75	ECL			1600GT 'S' Midnight introduced Based on GT with black interior and exterior. Gold alloy wheels, cloth trim, sports steering wheel and head-rests.
	Sep 75		BAECRJ51412		1300XL and 1600XL discontinued. Replaced by GL.
		ECG	BAECRJ06106		1300GT and 1600GT discontinued. Replaced by 'S'.
	Oct 75	ECL	BAECRJ44752		1300L and 1600L. Sports wheels, reclining front seats, brake servo on 1600.
			BAECRJ10359		1300 introduced. As L version but with black bumpers and window surrounds. Fixed front seats. Fixed rear seat, steel wheels.
		ECG	BAECRJ12472		1600GL replaces XL with sports wheels, waist rubber protection strip, cloth seats, centre console with clock. Divided rear seats. Auto transmission optional.
		ECL	BAECRJ10361		1600S replaces GT with black bumpers, alloy wheels and three-spoke steering wheel. Head-rests.
	Feb 76		S		1300 fitted with economy engine.
	Apl 76				Auto transmission optional on 1600S.
	Aug–Oct 76	ECL & ECG			Production transferred to Germany.
	Aug 76		GAECSE02506	1600S	First German cars to UK
	Sep 76		GAECSL18558	1600GL	
	Oct 76		GAECSY49000	1300; 1300L; 1600L	
	Sep 76		BAECSK22921	1600S	Final German cars to UK
	Oct 76		BAECSY30668	1300	
	76		BAECSY37319	1300L & 1600L	
	76	ECG	BAECSL51574	1600GL	
	Jan 77		GVECT		New prefix.
	Feb 78				Mk II range discontinued.

Model	Date	Code	Chassis No.	Changes
Capri 2000GT				
4-cy ohv 90.82 × 76.95 1,996cc	Feb 74	ECG	BAECPL18317	Capri Mk II sdr saloon. Similar to 1600GT but with 2,000cc eng as for 1600GT.
	May 74	ECT	GAECR	2000 Ghia introduced. Vinyl roof, alloy wheels, sun roof, special internal trim and head-rests. Auto transmission optional. Built in Germany.
	Jun 75	ECL		2000S Midnight. Similar spec to 1600 version.
	Sep 75	ECG	BAECRJ06106	2000GT replaced by S.
	Oct 75	ECL	BAECRJ10361	2000S with black bumpers, alloy wheels, three-spoke steering wheel. Head rests
		ECG	BAECRJ12472	2000GL. Special as 1600XL.
		ECT	GAECRM08515	2000 Ghia. Remote door mirror.
	Apr 76	ECL		Auto transmission no longer available on 2000S.
	Aug–Oct 76	ECL & ECG		Production transferred to Germany.
	Aug 76		GAECSE02506	2000S } First German
	Sep 76		GAECSL18558	2000GL } cars to UK
	Sep 76	ECL	BAECSK22921	2000S } Last UK-built
	Oct 76	ECG	BAECSL51574	2000GL } cars
	Jan 77		GVECT	2000S; GL and Ghia: new prefix.
	Feb 78			Mk II range discontinued.
Capri 3000				
V-6 ohv 93.66 × 72.44 2,994cc	Feb 74	ECG	BAECPL15474	Capri Mk II introduced. Similar to 2000 but with 2,994cc engine. Optional extras as for 2000.
	May 74	ECT	GAECR	Capri II Ghia introduced. Similar to 2000 Ghia. Power steering. Produced in Germany.
	Jun 75			3000GT S Midnight introduced
	Sep 75	ECG	BAECRJ06106	3000GT discontinued.
	Oct 75	ECL	BAECRJ10361	3000S introduced. As GT but for black bumpers, alloy wheels, three-spoke steering wheel, power steering and head-rests.
	Oct 75	ECT	GAECRM08515	3000 Ghia has power steering and remote door mirror as standard.
	Apr 76	ECL		Auto transmission no longer available on S type.
		ECT		Auto transmission standard on Ghia. Manual transmission available.
	Aug–Sep 76	ECL		Production moved to Germany.
	Aug 76		GAECSE02506	3000S. First German car to UK.
	Sep 76		BAECSK22921	3000S. Last UK-built car.
	Jan 77		GVECT	New prefix code.
	Feb 78	ECL		Capri Mk II discontinued.

CAPRI MK II PERFORMANCE FIGURES

Model	Performance (0–60 mph)	Max. speed	Fuel consumption	Standing quarter mile
1600S	11.4 sec	106mph (171km/h)	27.4mpg (10.3l/100km)	18.2 sec
2000S	10.4 sec	110mph (177km/h)	24mpg (11.8l/100km)	17.9 sec
3000S	9.7 sec	119mph (191km/h)	23.1mpg (12.3l/100km)	17.0 sec

Figures by kind permission of *Autocar*

the following year OPEC agreed a huge 15 per cent increase in the price of crude oil.

The Mk II Capri had but a limited four-year production life, during which time 403,612 cars were built. During 1976 the German market bought some 18,000 Capris, while the British were responsible for buying 36,000. When these figures are compared to the 105,000 UK sales of the Cavalier in the same year, it is easy to see why Ford badly needed to rejuvenate the Capri's image. That said, when Capri II was launched, sales of Opel's Manta nose-dived from 80,000 units in 1972 to just 30,000 in 1974. The Capri had, however, far exceeded its planners' best hopes, continuously grasping 2.5–3 per cent of the British market and 3.5 per cent of the German market, an impressive achievement when viewed alongside the volume sales of the fleet market saloons. Meanwhile, Ford's model range had been extended still further by the introduction of the front-wheel-drive Fiesta in 1975, and the all-conquering Escorts (available in RS1800 and RS2000 form for the enthusiast). Meanwhile, Cortinas were continuing to feature high up in the company's list of top-selling models.

In establishing Ford Europe – a project which, incidentally, was well in advance of the similar General Motors Vauxhall/Opel rearrangement that took place some years later – Ford had taken a considerable financial risk. In the event, by the mid-1970s the wisdom of Ford's forward-thinking was starting to pay off, the Capri and Escort pro-

A 1976 3.0-litre S model with 'bolt-on' GRP front air spoiler. Initially available to special order only, the 'S' suffix replaced the questionable 'GT' title. Retaining some of the body coachlines and matt-black embellishments of the JPS cars, the S Capris were available in various body colours other than black.

A detail view of the front lamp/grille aperture on the Mk II 3.0-litre S Capri; note the extensive use of self-tapping screws for mounting the grille panel and headlamp unit. In reaction to criticisms of poor lighting performance on early Mk I Capris, later cars and subsequent Mk II and Mk IIIs benefited from halogen lamps.

grammes taking full advantage of the close working relations of Ford's European headquarters. Further huge investments would be made in Spain to manufacture Ford's first FWD 'baby-car' gamble, the Fiesta.

In the States, the smaller, Europeanized Mustang was still managing to retain a portion of the coupé sports-car market. Indeed, Bob Lutz, Ford of Europe's Chairman, admitted during an interview in *Autocar* that while there would never be a large market for US cars in Europe, there was never-

The eight-spoke alloy wheel fitted to the S and Ghia Capris. Development in suspension technology – and Ford's programme to reduce vibration and harshness – involved concerted and harmonious work by damper, tyre and brake manufacturers, much of which was the direct result of experience gained through competition.

Interior of a Mk II S, with its late 1976 three-stalk lighting controls and three-spoke steering-wheel.

theless the opportunity to sell luxury V8 Mustangs in small quantities, rather than Ford Europe developing a Mustang equivalent of its own. He went on to reveal that competition from GM and Japan was having a grave effect on Ford's US business. Moreover, the situation was to be aggravated by the retirement of Henry Ford II, who not only had put a very personal stamp on the company and its products world-wide, but who also had the ability to talk with government leaders worldwide.

Restrained yet sporting treatment for S Capri: the view many motorists got of the 3.0-litre version. With its 117mph (188km/h) top speed and 0–60mph (0–97km/h) time of 9 seconds, the car offered unbeatable performance for its price of £3,081.

4 Best in Class

The early 1970s were seen by those in the motor industry as the threshold of a period which promised increased production allied to improved technical design and greater performance. Sadly, this overall feeling of optimism was soon dashed as the repercussions of the Arab-Israeli War of October 1973 created the Energy Crisis, OPEC's subsequent decision to double the price of crude oil in December of that year, and hence the creation in the UK of the three-day working week. At the same time strikes continued to paralyse British industry, the areas most affected being coal and transport, as well as the automobile business. British Leyland, for example, lost a monstrous £31.9 million on their car and light-commercial operations in 1977, while Vauxhall suffered an after-tax loss of £1.9 million in 1976 and £2.2 million the following year. In an effort to be more cost-effective, European car manufacturers were forced to consider Pan-European co-operation agreements, the best example being that set up between Volvo, Renault and Peugeot. This particular agreement resulted in a new design of V6 petrol engine, one which none of these three manufacturers could have justified financially had they attempted it alone.

In the mid-1970s the 'big twelve' European car companies in Britain, France, Germany and Italy were responsible for producing some 28 per cent of the world's 38 million unit output. However, this situation was about to change markedly with the enormous growth in car manufacturing. The world's top manufacturers in 1978 were: General Motors (16.5 per cent of world production); Ford (7.8 per cent); Toyota (6.5 per cent). The biggest motor manufacturer in Europe was Renault, which lay sixth in the world table behind Nissan and Chrysler (US), while British Leyland's troubles during 1976 lost them their slot in the top-ten league.

CHANGING FASHIONS

This period also saw competition hotting up in the two-door coupé market, with manufacturers such as Opel, Lancia, Toyota, Datsun and even VW (with the Scirocco) all offering essentially similar packages, albeit with different mechanical configurations. In all cases the attraction lay in the coupés' stylish presentation – although critics and cynics wrote them off, saying mass manufacturers were simply charging more for less-roomy versions of their bread-and-butter saloons. In 1977 the Capri was rated seventh in the UK's list of top-ten bestsellers, outstripping the smaller, yet more versatile volume-market Fiesta saloon. This was just a year after the Fiesta's introduction, so style and chic clearly did count for a great deal!

The 1970s also saw the emergence of an altogether different market – the front-wheel-drive sports hatch – led in 1976 by Volkswagen with the introduction of its GTi, a hot little number indeed with four seats *and* road-holding/performance which would happily see off most traditional sports cars. While Vauxhall had followed with the Chevette 2300HS (admittedly not FWD but a 'hot hatch' none the less), Ford fans would have to wait until 1980 for the launch of the FWD 'Erika' Escort range and the XR3 before anything comparable was offered.

A view of Capris Mks I, II and III. This shows how, with subtle changes to grille shape and front-apron design, the car became more sportily aggressive in appearance.

Against this shifting market, Ford's management decided that while it was indeed true that the Capri needed a face-lift (always replace or uplift when sales are at their strongest!), the extent to which this programme would be allowed to change the car's specification and styling would have to be kept under a tight rein. In fact, it was for this reason that the Capri III (launched in 1978) was both the best model so far yet the least exciting, and also why it did so little in capturing the attention of the world's press, receiving less – though not unenthusiastic – coverage.

IMPROVED AERODYNAMICS

The majority of changes incorporated into the Capri Mk III involved aerodynamic modifications, a result primarily of developments made in the competition arena.

By the 1970s much of the hard work that had been done on race-car aerodynamics by men such as Len Bailey a decade earlier (whose handiwork on the legendary GT40 and GT70 is now the stuff of textbooks) was beginning to reflect on high-street showroom models. Indeed, if the trend for big-bore silencers and wider wheels started in the 1960s, then the bolt-on body-parts boom really began ten years later.

Ford's stylists began looking at the Escort and the Capri to see how they could benefit from aerodynamics technology, at the same time adding trend-setting image wear such as body panels, spoilers and special wheels to improve their appearance. The threshold coefficient of drag (Cd) figure of the day was 0.4, and anything better was considered good. While Vauxhall's team, led by the clever and colourful Wayne Cherry, came up with the 'droop shoot' Firenza in 1974, Ford's designers added a nose cone with integral chin and boot spoiler to the evergreen Escort, producing the Mk II RS2000 in 1976. The cone itself added some 8.6in (21.8cm) to the car's overall length, the crucial Cd figure dropping from 0.45 for the standard Escort saloon to 0.383 for the Rallye Sport car. Ford also reckoned that the new design had reduced front-end lift by 25 per cent and rear-end lift by a remarkable 30 per cent, as well as pushing the maximum speed up 6–7 per cent over a similar 2.0-litre car without the 'sporty' bits. Such aerodynamic add-ons were first seen on race Capris. Jochen Neerpasch began successfully campaigning Capris with highly tuned V6 motors, which in turn spurned the RS2800 and RS3100 road cars that boasted front apron and rear boot spoilers for effect as well as show.

In 1976 the young Ford stylists showed the world what they had in mind for the future Capri when they introduced the 'Modular Aerodynamic' development Capri at the Geneva Motor Show, just twelve months after the public preview of the Escort RS2000 which had caused so much interest in March 1975. The Capri's frontal treatment clearly resembled the angled, louvred grille and recessed twin headlamps of the RS2000 Escort. As with the S-type Capri, the interior trim was finished in black, with black wrap-around bumpers back and front, and indicators set into the front-bumper moulding. The wheel embellishers, flat discs extending to the rim edges, were another interesting feature. It would be nice to know the drag factor for this particular Capri!

CORPORATE CAPRI

Sadly, the car Ford so proudly launched to the world on 2 March 1978 was not as radical and dramatic in its appearance as Modular Aerodynamic. It was, however, an improvement over the Capri Mk II, despite the assessment of the cynics, who just wrote it off as nothing better than a 'face-lift'. In fact, the Capri Mk III was better integrated within Ford's model framework than its predecessors, sharing many visual trademarks with other cars in the range. Also, the Capri Mk III had a bolder, stronger character, its selling points being style, value for money and, thanks to the car's success in motor sport, a sporty, performance-orientated image.

Starting at the front, the Capri Mk III shared the same twin 5.3in (13.46cm) headlamp treatment with Modular Aerodynamic, the prototype Capri seen at Geneva. Market research had shown that twin headlamps created a more upmarket image and provided improved lighting power, necessary on the faster Capri versions. They also allowed a lower bonnet line, the bonnet itself reaching further forward. Sadly, however, the sloping grille of Modular Aerodynamic had given way to the in-house design style first seen on Ford's Fiesta and Granada. The grille slats were aerofoil in section and, according to Ford's experts, some 15 per cent more efficient, reducing air resistance by 1.5 per cent over the previous design.

Returning to aerodynamics, the add-on spoiler from the previous S-type cars was incorporated into a new front-apron pressing, which reduced lift and drag by 7 per cent and 6 per cent respectively. A rear RS2000-type boot-lid spoiler was added to S models to aid high-speed stability and improve windflow. Overall, Ford reported that the Capri Mk III had a Cd factor of 0.403, while the bespoilered S cars did rather better at 0.374. As was the case with Modular Aerodynamic, the Capri Mk III also had wrap-around front and rear bumpers which (on all but the S models, which featured S graphic decals along the body flanks), married

Ford's code-name for the Mk III Capri was 'Carla'. Changing a Mk II into a Mk III can be done, but it is expensive: new wings, valance, bonnet, tail lights, grille, bumpers and headlamps. Work on aerodynamics created a Cd figure of 0.403. (Incidentally, this is a 3.0-litre S model.)

up with heavy-duty side-body rubbing mouldings. At the rear were larger light clusters with 'ribbed; stay-clean lenses.

For Britain the Mk III engines included the base 1300 which was given a power increase to 57bhp. The 1600Ls and GLs had a sohc 72bhp unit, while the 1600 S model had a heartier Weber carburettor engine with better 'plumbing', this producing 88bhp. The 2.0-litre Pinto engine gave 98bhp, and the lusty V6 unit produced 138bhp. A tuned 1300 GT model, with 73bhp on tap, was available for the French and Italian markets, while a detuned 63bhp 1600 Capri was produced for the Swedish market. For the German market, in addition to the 1300 and 1600 engines, the Capri was available with four and six cylinder 2.0-litre units and a 2.3-litre V6, as well as the familiar 3.0-litre V6 engine. No changes were made to the drivetrains. The C3-type automatic gearbox was still available on all but the 1300 model, and standard wear on the 3.0-litre Ghia.

Underneath the car, the roll bars were increased in diameter to improve handling, while all but the basic versions were given gas-filled Bilstein rear dampers (clearly a German influence, since they were reckoned to give improved ride quality and were almost totally fade-free). Ford did make reference to the possibility of gas-filled inserts for the front struts and the option of S-type dampers for non-sporting variants, although this proved to be a hollow promise. Brakes remained as before.

As a result of criticism concerning the shape and materials used on the seats in the Mk II, Ford had clearly worked hard at improving this important aspect, the Mk III having a herringbone-pattern upholstery of good-wearing quality. Trim colours included dark red, brown, black and tan. S models had the added option of Recaro competition-type seats finished in tartan check and black, which gave good hip-hugging support even though they did little to cushion the harsher ride given by the S-type suspension. The head-restraint panels of these seats

The fascia layout of a Mk III S, showing the similarity to that fitted to the Mk II Capris. The dash surround is finished in a light grey, thereby reducing the plastic feel.

were given transparent mesh inserts, so rear-view vision was not impaired as it was on cars fitted with standard seats.

A smaller 14in (36cm) steering-wheel was fitted to all but the Ghia models, which retained the larger two-spoke wheel. The dashboard remained little changed except for a move to a satin-type finish for the dash panel itself, with added padding above. Instruments were much as before, but with individual bezels and yellow pointers. Behind, the load-carrying area was given a parcel shelf which could be removed if necessary, a thoughtful addition to counter comments that luggage was always on display in previous models.

For the owner/driver, however, perhaps the most significant mechanical improvement over previous Capris was the move to longer

Ford fitted Recaro seats as an option to the Mk III S cars; rearward vision was enhanced by the 'tennis racquet' inserts. The seats in this car have been covered in non-standard material, replacing the tartan trim.

service intervals. Although electronic engine-management systems had yet to be introduced, Ford was confident that it could market the Capri range with services required every 12,000 miles (20,000km), with only oil changes, contact-breaker adjustment and a brake inspection required at half that distance. Inspection holes located in the rear-brake backplates allowed service engineers to check for lining thickness, while compensation for wear was catered for by the installation of a self-adjusting mechan-

FORD CAPRI MK III – 1600S (1978)

LAYOUT AND CHASSIS	
Two-door coupé/monocoque construction	
ENGINE	
Type	Pinto
Block material	Cast iron
Head material	Cast iron
Cylinders	4
Cooling	Water
Bore and stroke	87.7 × 66mm
Capacity	1,593cc
Valves	ohc
Compression ratio	9.2:1
Carburettor	Weber
Max. power	88bhp @ 5,700rpm
Max. torque	92lb/ft @ 4,000rpm
Fuel capacity	13 gallons (59 litres)
TRANSMISSION	
Gearbox	4-speed
Ratios (internal)	3.58:1, 2.01:1, 1.40:1, 1.00:1
Final drive	3.75:1
SUSPENSION AND STEERING	
Front	MacPherson strut
Rear	Semi-elliptic springs
Steering	Rack and pinion
Tyres	165 × 13
Wheels	Alloy
Rim width	5.0in
BRAKES	
Type	Hydraulic disc/drum
Size	9.60in disc, 9 × 1.75in drum
DIMENSIONS (in/mm)	
Track: front	53/1,346
rear	54.5/1,384
Wheelbase	101/2,565
Overall length	167.8/4,262
Overall width	67/1,702
Overall height	51/1,295
Unladen weight	2,293lb/1,040kg
PERFORMANCE	
Top speed	99mph (159km/h)
0–60mph	12.7sec

FORD CAPRI MK III – 2000S (1978)

LAYOUT AND CHASSIS	
Two-door coupé/monocoque construction	
ENGINE	
Type	Pinto
Block material	Cast iron
Head material	Cast iron
Cylinders	4
Cooling	Water
Bore and stroke	90.3 × 77mm
Capacity	1,993cc
Valves	ohc
Compression ratio	9.2:1
Carburettor	Weber
Max. power	98bhp @ 5,200rpm
Max. torque	111lb/ft @ 3,500rpm
Fuel capacity	13 gallons (59 litres)
TRANSMISSION	
Gearbox	4-speed
Ratios (internal)	3.65:1, 1.97:1, 1.37:1, 1.00:1
Final drive	3.44:1
SUSPENSION AND STEERING	
Front	MacPherson strut
Rear	Semi-elliptic springs
Steering	Rack and pinion
Tyres	175 × 13
Wheels	Alloy
Rim width	5.5in
BRAKES	
Type	Hydraulic disc/drum
Size	9.8in disc, 8 × 1.75in drum
DIMENSIONS (in/mm)	
Track: front	53/1,346
rear	54.5/1,384
Wheelbase	101/2,565
Overall length	167.8/4,262
Overall width	67/1,702
Overall height	51/1,295
Unladen weight	2,273lb/1,031kg
PERFORMANCE	
Top speed	107mph (172km/h)
0–60mph	10.8sec

ism. Tappet adjustment intervals, on all but the 3.0-litre V6 Essex engine (which stayed at 6,000 miles, or 10,000km), had also been doubled.

Fundamental to this increase in servicing intervals was the use of sealed-for-life suspension and steering joints, as well as gearboxes and back axles that had lifelong lubrication. It was calculated that drivers would save some 44 per cent in servicing costs over 20,000 miles (32,000km). The point that still had to be borne in mind, however, was that Capri owners who had always let the Ford dealer take the servicing strain would still have to book their cars in for a service of sorts (including spark-plug electrode and contact-breaker adjustment, and fluid reservoir checks), the result being that these cars would still be off the road. Even so, the Capri ranged continued to offer a variety of packages to suit most pockets, the 3.0-litre models without doubt being unbeatable value for money.

'I think Ford has always been very lucky in having the supreme dealer network,' asserted Walter Hayes. 'There was an important hard-core of dealers who were very supportive of motor sport. They'd already gained experience in selling the Lotus and GT Cortinas, so the Capri was nothing new.'

FORD CAPRI MK III – 3000S (1978)

LAYOUT AND CHASSIS	
Two-door coupé/monocoque construction	
ENGINE	
Type	Essex
Block material	Cast iron
Head material	Cast iron
Cylinders	V6 60deg
Cooling	Water
Bore and stroke	93.66 × 72.4mm
Capacity	2,994cc
Valves	ohv
Compression ratio	9.0:1
Carburettor	Weber
Max. power	138bhp @ 5,000rpm
Max. torque	174lb/ft @ 3,000rpm
Fuel capacity	13 gallons (59 litres)
TRANSMISSION	
Gearbox	4-speed
Ratios (internal)	3.16:1, 1.94:1, 1.41:1, 1.00:1
Final drive	3.09:1
SUSPENSION AND STEERING	
Front	MacPherson strut
Rear	Semi-elliptic springs
Steering	Rack and pinion
Tyres	185 × 13
Wheels	Alloy
Rim width	5.5in
BRAKES	
Type	Hydraulic disc/drum
Size	9.75in disc, 9 × 1.75in drum
DIMENSIONS (in/mm)	
Track: front	53/1,346
rear	54.5/1,384
Wheelbase	101/2,565
Overall length	167.8/4,262
Overall width	67/1,702
Overall height	51/1,295
Unladen weight	2,688lb/1,219kg
PERFORMANCE	
Top speed	119mph (191km/h)
0–60mph	9.78sec

FURTHER IMPROVEMENTS

In 1980 the whole Capri range benefited from a few subtle changes. The Ghia was given an improved radio/cassette-player, a sports steering-wheel, headlamp washers which squirted from jets mounted precariously on the bumpers, and a passenger-door mirror. The S was given integral rear spotlamps, improved sound-deadening and a remote-controlled driver's-door mirror, while GL additions included manual door mirrors and head restraints, and the L was given a medium-and long-wave radio. A change to viscous fans added a further 3bhp to all engine specifications for UK cars, while the German 2.3 V6 unit was uprated to 114bhp by increasing the compression ratio from 8.75:1 to 9:1 and adding larger valves with improved breathing tracts.

This S-type has been fitted with optional twin water jets to the front bumpers, for cleaning the headlamp lenses. There is always friendly rivalry between Capri club members over the relative merits of the 3.0-litre Essex engine and the 2.8 Cologne unit. The owner of this S has 'gone German'.

An under-bonnet view of the same car. The turret-linking tube (first seen on rally Escorts) increases the torsional rigidity of the body tub by reducing flexing at the suspension mounting points.

The same year also saw the introduction of Ford's new front-wheel-drive Escort range, which included the sparkling XR3. This car gave quite extraordinary performance from just 1,600cc, its 96bhp engine returning a 0–60mph (0–97km/h) time of 9.2 seconds and a top speed of 113 mph (182km/h); the only adverse criticism concerned its handling. In most aspects the car quite outshone even the 3.0-litre Capri, while its fuel consumption was markedly better at 27mpg (10.5l/100km).

By the late 1970s and early 1980s performance and running costs were vital considerations when choosing a car. Vicious inflation had bumped up the price of the 1300 Capri from £890 in 1969 to a staggering £3,983 in March 1980 – a rise of 345 per cent! Fuel costs had also rocketed – in 1970 a gallon (4.5 litres) of petrol cost 32p; by 1979 the price was up to £1.20. At the same time, there was a strong US-influenced lobby that found gas-guzzling, fuel-junky 'tanks' from Detroit socially unacceptable. A 1978 UK-run advert for the Mustang – the Capri's older American cousin – stated that 'a Mustang travels like nothing else on British roads'. Sadly, it looked like nothing else too. By 1979 Mustangs sold in the States were available with a 2.3-litre four-cylinder engine as *standard*, although turbo-charged 2.3- and 2.8-litre V6 versions were available, along with a 5.0-litre V8 for extra performance. The huge 7-litre engines were gone for good.

Sadly, the Capri was beginning to lose ground to more innovative modern cars because of its ageing mechanics. While British Capri sales looked good in 1978 and 1979 – 31,642 units and 49,147 units respectively, accounting for 2 per cent and 2.9 per cent overall – total Capri sales were down to 41,753 in 1980, and dropping. Something new was needed to give the Capri a market boost.

Despite the doom and gloom that surrounded market planners in big motor manufacturers throughout the western world during the mid-1970s, thankfully it did not altogether stop the introduction of exciting new models. Jensen brought out the 2.0-litre Lotus-engined Jensen-Healey sports, with its contentious styling and Porsche launched the delightful Audi-engined 924; the revolutionary Mazda RX7 came along with its rotary engine, and Triumph took the plunge with the TR7 wedge. The sceptics of course questioned the wisdom of making such cars in view of the weak economic and energy-conscious climate, but in truth, the market for sporting cars showed critical resilience to such adverse influence. The new breed of sports car was finding ready buyers.

IMPROVING THE BEAST

It was amid this optimism that Ford decided to resurrect the legendary yet short-lived FAVO-type facility of the early 1970s, this time calling it Special Vehicle Engineering. The SVE team was set up in February 1980 and located within Ford's Research and Development centre at Laindon ('Dunton') under the watchful eye of Engineering Chief, Ron Mellor. At the suggestion of Gerhart Hartwig, Ford Europe's Director of Vehicle Engineering, and with support from Public Affairs Chief, Walter Hayes, and Chairman of Ford Europe, Bob Lutz, Rod Mansfield was invited to take up the job of establishing the department and preparing it to take on the task of transforming the ageing 3.0-litre S Capri into the 2.8 injection. Appropriately, a number of the SVE team were ex-AVO engineers.

'It was because of the shortfalls of FAVO being remote from mainstream engineering that when I was asked to set up SVE I made sure it was part of the main fabric of Ford's production,' remarked Rod recently. 'But

A detail view of a late model 2.8 Injection showing the depth of the chin spoiler and the design of the aerofoils on the grille slats. Ford claimed that even this attention to aerodynamic detail reduced drag.

what you could do in the 1980s, you couldn't do in the 1970s. When we built the first six or so Cosworth Sierra 4 × 4 prototypes, they were assembled on the line at production-line speeds and driven off. No favours asked. We claimed that as a first.'

In fact, the idea to 'injectionize' the Capri was not a new one, for a prototype Capri Mk III fitted with a 2.8 engine had been made available for selected press staff early in 1978. This early project was, however, never rolled out since this would have meant re-certification in those countries where Essex-engined Capris were still being sold. Ford took the view that sales volumes did not square with the projected development costs. So what changed? Simply, the 3.0-litre V6 Essex engine fell short of Europe's emission standards, and by 1980 was being built in standard tune only for use in the Capri and the rugged Transit van. However, demand for the Capri – in the UK in particular – suggested that there was perhaps life left in the model after all. To keep the car in production it would need to be updated with an engine of improved design, and Ford's market analysts argued that the necessary development costs could be offset if the Capri's image was elevated and its retail price increased accordingly.

The 2.8-litre Cologne V6 was first seen in the UK in late 1977 fitted in the top-of-the-range Granada. Sharing an identical bore size of 93mm with the British-built V6, the German engine had a smaller 68.5mm stroke, compared to 72.4mm for the bigger Essex unit. However, with the benefit of fuel injection the smaller V6 developed a reliable 160bhp at 5,700rpm, while the 3.0-litre managed only 138bhp at 5,000rpm when fitted with the down-draught twin-choke Weber carburettor. In contrast, torque was rated at 174lb/ft (129Nm) at 3,000rpm for the 3.0-litre engine and only 162lb/ft (120Nm) at 5,700rpm for the 2.8-litre version. Overall, however, it was the clean exhaust-gas profile of the German engine that assured it a place in the Capri's future.

Fundamental to the development work done by Mansfield and his team at Dunton in preparing the 2.8-litre engine for installation in the latest Capri was making the unit

The 2.8 injection Cologne unit fitted to the Capri. Much work was done by Ford's engineers to improve the engine's reliability when fitted in the Capri, where the unit would be subjected to high revs and sustained fast driving.

more resilient to hard use. Consideration was given to the possibility of the engine being revved higher and for longer periods than when fitted in the Granada saloon. Attention was given to the crankshaft in an effort to increase reliability under severe high-speed cornering. An oil/water inter-cooler was fitted which used the faster-heating engine coolant to warm the oil on cold start-up, yet also controlled the oil temperature in the same way as an oil cooler when it exceeded 212°F (100°C). The radiator efficiency was improved by increasing the fin density, and the electronic ignition was set to cut out at 6,100rpm in order to prevent over-revving.

The drivetrain was left as standard 3.0-litre Capri specification, with a four-speed gearbox and 3.09:1 final drive which gave only 21.08mph (33.92km/h) at 1,000rpm in top gear, suggesting that higher gearing might be in order at a later stage. The single-plate clutch was left unchanged, too.

Around the suspension the front and rear anti-roll bars were increased in diameter by 0.08in (2mm) all round: 1in (24mm) on the front and 0.5in (14mm) on the rear, the rear staggered axle/damper location being carried through to the latest Capri, aided by rubber bump-stops. Front and rear spring rates were also increased: up to 122lb/in coils on the front and 140lb/in single leaves on the rear. Bilstein gas-filled telescopic dampers were fitted all round. The alloy wheels were changed to Woolfrace Sonic 7 × 13s, shod with 205/60VR NCT low-profile tyres, which set the car off rather well. Incidentally, the ride height was dropped by 1in (25mm) all round to reduce the roll angle.

Perhaps the greatest improvement for the press-on motorist, however, was the adoption of 9.76in (24.8cm) ventilated disc brakes at the front. In part this was to acknowledge the new EEC regulations which affected front-to-rear wheel-braking bias. A front/rear G-force pressure-sensing limitor valve was also added to make the front brakes take the greater pressure.

The new 2.8i was based on the Capri shell and finished to Ghia specification with the

CAPRI MK III CHASSIS/DATE IDENTIFICATION DETAILS

Capri 1300 and 1600

Engine	Date			Model	Details
4-cy ohv 80.98 × 62.99 1,298cc Alt eng 4-cy ohc 87.65 × 66 1,593cc	Feb 78	ECL	GEV	1300 1300L 1600L 1600GL 1600S	Capri Mk III three-door saloon. Similar to Mk II but with wrap-around black bumpers and side rubbing mouldings. Twin round headlamps. Large oblong rear light cluster. Revised fascia with twin circular dials. S model has side body decals 1600.
	Apr 79				Viscous fan fitted. All models have brake fluid warning light.
	Sep 79				L models have rear fog lamps. GL spec. Improved trim. GL and S have remote door mirror.
	Mar 80				Special Edition based on L with 1,593cc engine, fabric seat trim, extra instruments and sports road wheels.
	Jan 81				All models have trim update including removable rear shelf. S has boot spoiler and Recaro seats.
	Jly 81	ECL			Cameo introduced based on L with 1,298cc or 1,599cc engine. No centre console, clock or radio. Calypso introduced based on 1.6LS. Two-tone paint, tailgate wash wipe, tinted glass and head-rest.
	May 82	ECL			Cabaret introduced based on 1.6L 1,993cc engine optional. Equipment includes a sun roof, LS trim, rear spoiler, sports wheels.
	Jan 83	ECL			Cabaret II introduced based on L with 1,593cc or 1,998cc engine and improved spec.
	Mar 83				Model range reduced to 1.6LS model only with improved trim tailgate wash wipe, remote mirror, and uprated suspension.
	Sep 83				1.6L model has better stereo.
	Jun 84				Laser introduced based on LS with 1,593cc or 1,998cc engine and five-speed gearbox. Improved trim. Colour-coded grille and mirrors. Tinted glass.
	Dec 86				Model discontinued.

Capri 2000GT

Engine	Date			Model	Details
4-cy ohc 90.82 × 76.95 1,996cc	Feb 78	ECG	GEV	2000GL 2000S 2000 Ghia	Capri Mk II Similar to Mk II but with black wrap-around bumpers. Twin circular headlamps and large rear lamp cluster. Revised fascia.
	Apr 79				Viscous fan fitted. All models have brake fluid warning light. 185/70HR tyres fitted to S version.

	Sep 79			L model has rear fog light. GL spec improved with remote door mirror fitted to GL and S. Ghia has passenger mirror, headlamp washers and three-spoke steering-wheel.
	Mar 83			L, GL and Ghia models discontinued. S has opening rear windows, improved trim Escort XR3i seats, sun roof and five-speed gearbox.
	Sep 83	ECL		S fitted with radio/cassette.
	Dec 86			2.0S model discontinued.
Capri 3000 V-6 ohv 93.66 × 72.44 2,994cc 93 × 68.5 2,792cc 1981 on	Feb 78	ECG	GEV	3000S } Capri Mk II 3000 Ghia } introduced. Similar to Mk II but with black wrap-around bumpers. Ghia has side rubbing strip. S has side body decals. Twin circular headlamps and large rear light cluster. Revised fascia.
	Jly 81	ECG		3.0 litre models replaced by 2.8 injection with Bosch K-Jetronic fuel injection. Four-speed gearbox. Servo brakes with ventilated front discs, power steering. 7 × 13 alloy wheels. Uprated suspension. Recaro seats and radio/cassette. Manual version only.
	Oct 82	ECG		Five-speed gearbox fitted.
	Sep 84			Model renamed 2.8 Special fitted with limited slip differential as standard.
	May 86	ECT		Introduction of Capri 280 with 7 × 15 alloy wheels, 195/VR Pirelli tyres, leather covered Recaro seats, steering-wheel gear lever and handbrake gaiters. Available in dark green only.
	Dec 86			Model discontinued.

standard fittings of a tilt/slide sun roof, Recaro seats trimmed with crushed velour side-panels, and a radio/cassette-player. The only real choice left for the 2.8i customer was whether to have metallic paint, in which case the price-tag was £8,095, compared to £7,995 without.

When asked recently to give his opinion over the best car SVE produced, Mansfield was unhesitating in saying that he had a very soft spot for the Capri injection, partly, of course, because it was the first car his department produced. The injection took just fifteen months to develop, which just goes to show what a small, dedicated team can achieve.

Without doubt, the launch of the Capri 2.8i in late June 1981 was a pleasant surprise for Britain's foremost motor-noters, and the press extolled the virtues of its ability to give sheer, uncomplicated enjoyment. The car's simple engineering allied to simple and inexpensive maintenance, together with its dynamic performance and good handling and road-holding, were a tribute to the efforts of Rod Mansfield and his team. Indeed, it says much for the Capri's original design formula that, some seven years after

CAPRI MK III PERFORMANCE FIGURES

Model	Performance (0–60 mph)	Max. speed	Fuel consumption	Standing quarter mile
1600S	12.7 sec	101mph (163km/h)	27.6mpg (10.3l/100km)	19.0 sec
2000S	10.8 sec	107mph (172km/h)	25.6mpg (11.1l/100km)	17.7 sec
3000S	8.6 sec	118mph (190km/h)	19.5mpg (14.5l/100km)	16.6 sec

Figures by kind permission of *Autocar*

the introduction of Capri Mk II, the 2.8i was considered by those who tested it to be more than a match for the opposition.

'The two cars we looked at when we set up SVE were the Capri and the Fiesta,' Mansfield recalls, explaining the background over which car was chosen to be 'Job No 1'. 'We decided the Capri would need less work and could be completed quicker. In view of its reception it proved to be the right decision.'

NEW TIMES, NEW MODELS

The 1980s were to prove almost as exciting as the 1960s for Ford enthusiasts. In September 1981 a prototype of the Escort RS1600i 'homologation special' was exhibited at the Frankfurt Motor Show. Ford had initially planned on making just 500 of these very impressive-looking front-wheel-drive Escorts, but by the time production ceased 8,569 cars had been built. Waiting in the wings were the mean little Fiesta XR2, with its 1.6-litre engine, and the fuel-injected XR3i, which was launched in October 1982. Both cars were the work of Rod Mansfield and his team.

Although there was an ever-increasing number of sporting Fords from which the enthusiast could choose, it was clear to observers which direction things would take. It was quite simply easier (and cheaper) to upgrade showroom saloons than develop a limited-market coupé. In May 1983 the XR4i, powered by the 2.8i engine driving through a five-speed gearbox, was introduced, the car being capable of a top speed of 130mph (209km/h) and a 0–60mph (0–97km/h) time of 7.9 seconds. The Escort RS Turbo was Mansfield's next offering a year later, with a 127mph (204km/h) top speed and a 0–60mph (0–97km/h) time of just 8.6 seconds – not bad for 1,600cc saloon! Ford fans were spoilt for choice, and there was more to come.

As for the Capris, in June 1981, coincidental to the launch of 2.8i, Ford introduced two smaller-engined versions: the Cameo (based on the L model), offered with either the 1,300cc or 1,600cc engine; and the Calypso, which used the LS trim pack as a basis available with the 1.6-litre engine only. The 2000S, however, remained available for those who wanted that much more performance but who did not think they needed the tyre-burning qualities of the 2.8i – nor, for that matter, the insurance costs. This was obviously a sales ploy to keep interest alive in the Capri range, but it was a successful one if the numbers of Capris still around in the mid-1990s is anything to go by. A year later, in May 1982, came the Cabaret – another limited-edition version sold on the UK market only. This was based on the L trim specification and powered by either the trusty 1.6-litre engine or, to special order, by the 2.0-litre unit.

FORD CAPRI 2.8 injection (1981)
(FORD CAPRI BROOKLANDS 280 (1986))

LAYOUT AND CHASSIS	
Two-door coupé/monocoque construction	
ENGINE	
Type	Cologne
Block material	Cast iron
Head material	Cast iron
Cylinders	V6 60deg
Cooling	Water
Bore and stroke	93 × 68.5mm
Capacity	2,792cc
Valves	ohv
Compression ratio	9.2:1
Carburettor	Bosch K Jetronic
Max. power	160bhp @ 5,700rpm (152bhp at 5,700rpm)
Max. torque	162lb/ft @ 4,200rpm
Fuel capacity	13 gallons (59 litres)
TRANSMISSION	
Gearbox	4-speed (5-speed)
Ratios	3.16:1, 1.95:1, 1.41:1, 1.00:1 (5th gear 0.82:1)
Final drive	3.09:1
SUSPENSION AND STEERING	
Front	MacPherson strut
Rear	Semi-elliptic springs
Steering	Rack and pinion
Tyres	205/60 VR × 13 (195/50 VR × 15)
Wheels	Alloy
Rim width	7in × 13 (7in × 15)
BRAKES	
Type	Hydraulic disc/drum
Size	9.8in ventilated disc, 9 × 2.25in drum
DIMENSIONS (in/mm)	
Track: front	53/1,346
rear	54.5/1,384
Wheelbase	101/2,565
Overall length	167.8/4,262
Overall width	67/1,702
Overall height	51/1,295
Unladen weight	2,620lb/1,188kg
PERFORMANCE	
Top speed	130mph (209km/h) (130mph (209km/h))
0–60mph	7.9sec (8.3sec)

It was only natural that the Capri would eventually pick up the XR4i's five-speed gearbox which, incidentally, was also fitted in the Granada during the winter of 1982 and launched in January 1983. The big benefit here, of course, was the increase in overall gearing, the 3.09:1 differential and 205/60 tyres producing a relaxed 25.7mph (41.4km/h) at 1,000 revs in top gear. The change made no marked difference to performance, the Capri still recording a 0–60mph (0–97km/h) time of 7.9 seconds and scoring a flat-out speed of 127mph (204km/h). However, fuel consumption did improve as a result for the five-speed car's longer legs. The constant 56mph (90km/h) and 75mph (121km/h) figures were 34.9mpg (8.1l/100km) and 27.4mpg (10.3l/100km) for the four-speed car and 38.2mpg (7.4l/100km) and 30.1mpg (9.4l/100km) for the five-speed version. The interior of the car was given a spruce-up too. The check-trimmed seats were replaced with mid-grey velour, similar to the material used in the RS1600i Escort, and the rear quarter lights were hinged for added ventilation. The radio/cassette-player used in both the Ghia and the 2.8i was the SRT32P unit.

The Cabaret Mk II was introduced at the same time as Ford launched the five-speed 2.8 injection, and again used the L level of trim pack, the power coming from either the 1.6- or 2.0-litre engine. Two months later, in March 1983, the Capri range was rationalized to include just the 1600 LS, the 2000S and the 2.8 injection. The LS was updated with a specification sheet that listed rear wash/wipe, uprated suspension, restyled seats and trim, and a sun roof, the LS and S models being given radio/cassette-players as standard in September of that year. The 2.8 injection was not forgotten either, its radio/cassette equipment being uprated.

Although the Capri managed sixteenth place in the UK's top twenty car sales in 1983, it was clear nonetheless that its position was slipping. By 1984 motor-market observers were seriously questioning how long the Capri could keep going in view of its ageing design and the increasingly tough competition from other manufacturers such as Toyota, Vauxhall and Nissan. Saleswise, the Capri's biggest market still remained in the UK where, because of the ever-growing world of collectors' cars, the Capri (certainly in 2.8-injection form) was being suggested as a future classic.

In June 1984 the Laser special edition was launched, signalling the gradual demise of the Capri on continental markets. Standard specification included 185/70 tyres on four-spoke alloy road wheels, a trim package special to the Laser model, a top-of-the-range dashboard layout and a quad-speaker stereo system. Outside, the Laser could be identified by its unique badging and colour-coded door mirrors, headlamp surrounds and grille. Again, power-unit choice was limited to the 1.6- or 2.0-litre engines, although there was the option of a five-speed gearbox on the larger engine, and automatic transmission for the more relaxed motorist.

To coincide with the October 1984 London Motor Show, the Capri 2.8 injection's specification list was further enhanced by the addition of 13 × 7 multi-spoke RS alloy wheels shod with 205/60 tyres, and a Salisbury multi-plate limited-slip differential as standard, hitherto only available as options. Inside, leather was used to trim the edges of the Recaro seats, as well as the door inserts, steering-wheel and even the gear-lever knob! The car was called the 2.8 injection Special by way of celebration, with badges and decals to match.

Yet it was clear the end was in sight, for by 1985 the Capri was being built in RHD only. Even so, 4,000 2.8 injections and 12,900 of the 1.6-litre and 2.0-litre versions were sold during 1984 (an interesting balance of sales) although the following year this number had diminished to a less inspiring 11,000 units in total. Ford's marketing experts surely realized that there was only so much dressing up they could do before customers drifted away.

For the fast-Ford fan, the company's line-up that year (1984) included the technically advanced 2.8i-powered XR 4 × 4 Sierra, which brought the bonus of four-wheel drive to an already established quick Ford saloon.

'When I came back from Detroit in 1984, it was to see Ford saloons being beaten on the race tracks,' remarked Walter Hayes with distinct unease at the recollection. 'That was when we put the Sierra Cosworth programme in hand. And there is no point in a company entering into product cannibalism. Once the Cosworth was on the way it spelt death for the Capri. By the late 1980s it was an altogether more sophisticated market.'

THE END OF THE ROAD

Most people agree that Ford must be congratulated for not just letting the Capri drop quietly from sight. Rumours spread of two turbo-charged models, Ford's last fling with their errant coupé; a 200bhp model and an even more brutal twin-turbo-charged 245bhp model, both to be fitted with the long-awaited rear disc brakes. A production run of 500 was planned for the more powerful version, with a '500' badge suitably displayed. But, sadly, it was not to be (reason prevailing over rashness, if there was any foundation to the rumours) and in late 1986 a final run of 1,038 Capris was made, badged as 'Capri 280' and finished in Brooklands dark green, with white and red coachlines. The 15 × 7 alloy wheels were fitted with low-profile 195/50VR Pirellis to maintain the same overall gearing, which, if anything, improved the Capri's already well-respected road-holding. Inside, Ford had excelled themselves with leather trim throughout. Few of these cars were left languishing in

One of the most popular of the Mk I Capris, the 1600GT. Its 82bhp engine gave a 0–60mph (0–97km/h) time of 12.5 seconds and 100mph (160km/h) top speed, with an overall fuel consumption of 25mpg (11.3l/100km). Like all Fords, and Capris in particular, it offered good value for money while spares and tuning parts were easily available, which is still the case today.

In 1972 Ford were preparing to introduce the face-lift Mk I later that year. In-house notices talked of 151 changes to European Capris and 194 for the US cars! Notice the chromed hub caps and vinyl roof on this early 1972 1600L model. Within just a few short months this version would feature the power bulge bonnet of the 3-litre and improved headlamps.

Several British tuning companies, such as Allard of Richmond (south-west London) offered Capris fitted with V8 engines. In Johannesburg, tuning expert Basil Green developed the Perana, which was powered by a slightly tuned version of the 5-litre Mustang engine.

In the Mk I Capri Ford fitted a mock wood veneer dashboard, which tried to emulate the real wood trim of the 1600E Cortina. This is the six-dial GT version, which included gauges for oil pressure, water temperature, battery condition and gallons in the tank, along with the usual speedo and rev counter. The Mk II facia was a great improvement.

Part of the Perana's attraction was its 'Q-car' like appearance, many unsuspecting motorists being shocked by the car's outstanding performance. Only the addition of the V8 badge gives any hint of what lies under the bonnet.

Under the bonnet Basil Green was able to shoehorn a full 4,942cc Mustang engine tuned with a four-barrel 460cfm Holley carburettor, solid lifter valve gear and sports camshaft. Surprisingly, the weight of the American V8 was little more than the British V6, the car tipping the scales at just 14lb (6kg) more than the Capri 3000GT.

During the Capri's design phase Ford relied heavily on feedback from customer 'clinics' held throughout Europe to ensure the car had true international appeal. The frontal treatment was finalized in 1966, a full three years before the car was launched; the overall effect – shallow grille with slim bumper beneath – would remain a Capri feature throughout its life.

The 1960s and 1970s were the halycon days of after-market 'goodies' with tuning shops selling everything from stick-on chequered tape to cylinder head conversions for the DIY enthusiast. A popular 'modification' was the chromed racing wing mirror, which, along with the matt black paint panels, gives this Capri a more sporty look.

When the Capri Mk I was launched road test staff found many commendable aspects, including the comfortable seats and adequate space in the rear for adult passengers, while Ford's ventilation system also came in for favourable remarks. On the down side, however, the minor controls were said to be 'confusing' while the overall effect mirrored Ford's image of the period.

In late 1972 Ford introduced the face-lift Mk I Capri which featured the bonnet bulge of the 3-litre car on all versions and improved headlamps. On this rare RS3100 the single bumper has given way to twin quarter matt black blades with inset indicators. Below is the obvious apron spoiler, which helped reduce lift and aided stability on the race versions.

A major design feature on the face-lift Mk I Capri were the enlarged rear light clusters. In fact, this is an RS3100, which utilized the very last of the Mk I bodyshells before the Mk II model was introduced in February 1974, and full homologation was granted. Indeed, Production Management at Halewood were less than pleased since valuable time was spent in assembling RS3100s, which should rather have been spent in establishing Mk II production!

The RS3100 was Ford's homologation special and since only around 200 were built, they are nowadays perhaps the most sought-after Capri for the enthusiast. Officially, Ford needed to build 1,000 of these cars to be compliant with Group 2 regulations, though it is likely that only 200 were put together before the Energy Crisis took its effect. (Inset:) With the aid of the obvious black plastic rear tail spoiler Ford designers were able to record the best Cd figure of any Mk I Capri – an impressive 0.375. On race cars the aerofoil did work, reducing rear end lift and aiding high speed stability, a feature which was lacking on the earlier RS2600, making it something of a handful at speeds around 150mph (240km/h).

A strong styling characteristic of the Mk I Capri was the heavy swage line which ran from the snout to the rear wheelarch, dropping away behind, giving the car a nose-up/tail-down appearance. On the Mk II Capri the line was softened and extended to the rear improving its side profile.

The overbored 3.1-litre RS3100 engine developed 148bhp at 5,000rpm, some 10 per cent greater than the standard 3.0-litre unit, though the car cost a whopping 37 per cent more to buy. Among the promotional activities to launch the car in November 1973 Ford arranged for three-times F1 World Champion Jackie Stewart to pose with a press car. The launch coincided with the distribution of Energy Crisis petrol rationing books (though they were never used).

The Capri Mk II was intended to attract the family buyer by including a lift-up hatchback, greater glass area and wider rear section. At the top of the range were 2.0-litre and 3.0-litre Ghia models, a reflection of Ford's purchase of the Turin-based firm of coach-builders; these boasted alloy wheels and a sunroof as standard.

In 1978 Ford launched the Mk III Capri with its reshaped front, which included twin headlamps on all versions and a chin spoiler. It was the least publicized of all Capri models (the press taking the view that it was little more than a face-lift). This top-of-the-range 3.0-litre 138bhp Ghia headed up a range of ten models, starting with the 57bhp 1300.

The introduction of the Laser Capris in 1.6- and 2.0-litre versions marked the run-down of the smaller-engined models in Europe. By mid 1984 – the year the Laser was launched – the Capri was suffering harsh competition from Vauxhall/Opel and Japanese cars. In addition to colour co-ordinated headlamp surrounds and door mirrors, Lasers got some snazzy body graphics, alloy wheels and special interior trim.

The last of the line, the Brooklands 280. Tastefully trimmed in leather and fitted with 7J × 15in alloy wheels it is a credit to Ford that they gave their sports coupé a dignified end. Just 1,038 280s were built, making them an instant classic.

Jochen Mass leading at the start of the Zandvoort 4-hours. He was to go on for some thirty laps, wrestling with the unwieldy Capri, until a half shaft broke, which put him out of the event. The second Capri, driven by Fitzpatrick and Larrousse, managed third place, with their car badly misfiring by the time it crossed the line behind the BMW Coupé of James Hunt and Brian Muir.

Gordon Spice at the wheel of the CC-developed Mk III Capri in 1980. Based in Kerbymooreside, Yorkshire, the company became the acknowledged experts in Capri race preparation in the UK with a full house conversion costing around £16,000 – and that was in 1980! The main competition came from Rover with their newly launched SD1.

A Ford publicity shot of the last of the line, the Capri 280. Rod Mansfield suggested to a Ford executive that the Capri be fitted with the Sierra Cosworth engine to extend its life, but he was only joking!

The luxurious interior of the Capri 280, with its leather-trimmed seats. Despite a very full specification there were details missing: electric windows; and air-conditioning. Sadly, the competition went one better.

The interior of a late model Capri 280, showing an after-market accessory burr-walnut fascia panel. The addition of wood fillets to door cappings and dashboards is a throwback to the once-thriving British coachbuilding industry, which few other countries can boast.

Ford dealership windows, despite the £11,999 price-tag. 'I think we should have gone for larger diameter wheels at a much earlier stage,' admitted Rod candidly. 'But it is always easy to say what we should have done after the event.'

And so the Capri finally came to a respectable end, after 324,045 Mk IIIs had been built during eight years of production. Time has proved the collector right after all, for the Capri – especially in the Mk III and RS forms – has indeed become a classic, with

An under-bonnet view of the same Capri showing the very neat Turbo Technics installation, with extensive use of armoured hosing to protect against the huge under-bonnet temperatures. Such a conversion produced 200bhp at 5,500rpm, resulting in a 0–60mph (0–97km/h) time of 6.5 seconds and a 143mph (230km/h) top speed.

On 19 December 1986 the media witnessed the very last Capri 280 coming down the Cologne production line, after a total of 1,886,647 Capris had been made. Well-respected motor-noter Mike McCarthy was lucky enough to borrow the car before it was 'mothballed'.

happy, proud owners turning out to club days to share in their mutual enjoyment.

'I remember taking one of Ford's directors around the test track in a Capri, saying that SVE could modify it to take the Cosworth engine,' laughed Rod. 'But it was not meant seriously. So much of the remainder of the car would have needed updating, too, that it wouldn't have been a viable proposition.'

Waiting in the wings to take over the mantle of 'the car you always promised yourself' was the Sierra RS Cosworth, introduced in July 1986. This car, truly impressive by any standards, was capable of 153mph (246km/h) and a neck-snapping 0–60mph (0–97km/h) time of 6.2 seconds. It lacked the coupé's style and individuality, but it was a sporting Ford nonetheless. Developed by the redoubtable Rod Mansfield, the Sierra was a car to keep the Ford flag flying. As Walter Hayes said recently, 'The Capri was just a rung on the ladder of excitement which so typified everything Ford did in the 1960s.'

ENTER PROBE

And that, as they say, was that . . . well, not quite.

An excuse to show Glen Bullen's immaculate 280 Brooklands. This car is fitted with automatic transmission, making it a rarity among just 1,053 cars built.

Links between Ford and Mazda were first established in the early 1980s when Ford was busy developing the front-wheel-drive Escort programme. It was to prove a fruitful alliance with wind-tunnel, chassis-engineering and body-styling collaboration resulting in the remarkable similarities between the Escort and the Mazda 323. Then, during the 1980s, Ford undertook a number of design studies which went under the title of Probe. The first three were concept cars conceived in Europe to improve aerodynamics through body-shape efficiency, while Probe IV and V were proposals developed by Ford US that involved advanced powertrain technology concepts.

In 1988 a production version of the Probe was launched. The new sports car, a 2 + 2 coupé, was powered by a four-cylinder twelve-valve 2.2-litre engine, available in both carburettor and turbo-charged form, driving a front-mounted transaxle. Probe production was located at a newly built factory established by Mazda Motor Manufacturing (USA) Corporation (MMUC), a wholly owned subsidiary of Mazda Motor Corporation. The factory, built between 1985 and 1987, made use of the most modern automotive manufacturing techniques and was located on a 395-acre (160-hectare) site at Flat Rock, Michigan, some 25 miles (40km) south of Detroit. Almost 500,000 Probes were sold throughout the North American market.

Significantly, while demand for the Capri had dwindled during the mid-1980s (with the exception of the UK market, sales of the Capri had dropped to almost nil across the remainder of Europe), sales of sports and high-performances saloons doubled in Europe between 1989 and 1991 as new European and Japanese cars were launched, stimulating demand still further for this type of car. Rather than go to the expense of developing a new car from scratch, Ford began looking closely at the possibilities of introducing a 'Capri replacement' on to the European market by importing the Probe from North America.

At the end of 1991 a group of senior Ford

executives and engineers put a Probe through its paces. They carried out extensive tests on all types of road condition, including a German *autobahn*, the Zolder racing circuit and Ford's Proving Ground at Lommel in Belgium, making comparisons with similar coupés. The outcome of this exhaustive programme was a decision to redevelop the Probe into a car more suitable for the discerning European enthusiast and the driving conditions encountered on this side of the Atlantic.

In reality, the updating programme was really nothing short of a complete redesign, with a new floorpan, totally revised body styling developed by Mimi Vanderm Oelen, with a drag coefficient of 0.34, uprated suspension and different engine options. Probe was born.

DESIGN ALTERATIONS

The Probe's front suspension utilized Ford's favoured MacPherson struts, heavily angled in an effort to give good road-holding. Short, large-diameter coil springs were offset to one side in relation to the strut/damper to minimize side-loads and reduce strut friction. A 1.1in (27.2mm) tubular anti-anti-roll bar, locating with each suspension leg using drop links, was added to reduce body roll and increase steering response.

At the rear, a fully independent Quadralink set-up was used which included two laterally located horizontal links connecting above and below each wheel hub, a trailing arm running rearwards from the body, with the coil spring/damper strut forming the fourth link, and a 12mm anti-roll bar. The arrangement, which was similar to that used on the Mondeo saloon, gave a form of passive rear-wheel steering, creating excellent poise and wheel control when cornering. Under straight-line running or quick steering manoeuvres the rear wheels maintained a 0-degree toe-in. As lateral forces built up during cornering, small relative movements in the link system created a toe-in effect, reducing tyre-slip angles and stabilizing cornering behaviour.

The steering was fitted with speed-sensitive power assistance, which was designed to give greater assistance at low speeds when tyre friction was greatest. As speed increased, the power assistance reduced to compensate for the correspondingly lighter steering loads. The lock-to-lock steering ratio was set at a sporting 2.9 turns.

Two engine choices were available: 2.0 litres and 2.5 litres. The 1,991cc 83.0 × 92.0mm four-cylinder sixteen-valve unit utilized an alloy cylinder head with two chain-driven overhead camshafts mounted on a cast-iron block. To help reduce vibration at high crankshaft speeds, the crankshaft itself was given five main bearings and eight counterweights. Controlled by electronic engine management with multi-point fuel injection, the engine developed 165bhp at 5,500rpm to give this version of the Probe a 0–62mph (0–100km/h) time of 10.6 seconds and a maximum speed of 127mph (204km/h).

The 2,497cc 84.5 × 74.2mm six-cylinder 60° V6 engine utilized twin alloy cylinder heads, each with twin overhead camshafts and mounted on an alloy cylinder block. As was the case with the smaller unit, the 2.5-litre engine was fitted with electronic engine management and multi-point fuel injection, though with the added benefit that the induction tracts were given a variable length section which changed with engine speed and load, thereby improving fuel economy and reducing exhaust emissions. This relatively short stroke allowed the engine to rev freely, the unit producing 165bhp at 5,500rpm which resulted in a 0–62mph (0–100km/h) time of 8.5 seconds and a maximum speed of 136mph (219km/h). Both the 2.0-litre and the 24V versions of the Probe were fitted

FORD PROBE 24V (1994)

LAYOUT AND CHASSIS
Two-door coupé/monocoque construction

ENGINE

Type	Mazda
Block material	Aluminium
Head material	Aluminium
Cylinders	V6
Cooling	n/a
Bore and stroke	85.0 × 74.0mm
Capacity	2,497cc
Valves	4 per cylinder, doch
Compression ratio	9.2:1
Carburettor	Multiple-point injection and fully mapped electronic ignition
Max. power	164bhp @ 5,600rpm
Max. torque	160lb/ft @ 4,800rpm
Fuel capacity	12.8 gallons (58 litres)

TRANSMISSION

Gearbox	5-speed
Ratios	3.3:1, 1.83:1, 1.31:1, 1.03:1, 0.79:1
Final drive	4.39:1

SUSPENSION AND STEERING

Front	Struts, coil springs, anti-roll bar
Rear	Multi-link, coil springs, anti-roll bar
Steering	Power-assisted rack and pinion
Tyres	225/50 VR × 16
Wheels	Alloy
Rim width	7in × 16

BRAKES

Type	Hydraulic disc anti-lock
Size	259mm ventilated disc, 262mm plain disc

DIMENSIONS (in/mm)

Track: front	59.8/1,520
rear	59.8/1,520
Wheelbase	102.9/2,615
Overall length	178.9/4,545
Overall width	69/1,773
Overall height	51.5/1,310
Unladen weight	2,809lb/1,274kg

PERFORMANCE

Top speed	134mph (215km/h)
0–60mph	7.9sec

with closed-loop three-way catalytic converters.

Drive on both cars was taken via a hydraulically operated single-plate clutch to five-speed transaxles, the ratios of the first three gears in the gearbox fitted to the 2.0-litre version being slightly lower to compensate for the smaller engine. Final drive ratios were 4.1:1 for the 16V and 4.39:1 for the 24V.

Rigorous testing of the Probe during 1991 led to a number of suspension changes, including alterations to damper-valve pressure settings in order to reduce ride harshness. More tests were then carried out over various road surfaces to ensure the best ride performance – from sports-car-style driving techniques at speeds around 75mph (121km/h) on minor B road, to flat runs at speeds of up to 85mph (137km/h) on concrete-paved *autobahns*.

Considerable thought was given to the inclusion of safety features, the Probe incorporating ABS braking, twin air bags and integral side-intrusion bars in the body design. The computer-designed body was given high-energy-absorbing sections to protect against heavy front or rear damage, creating a rigid cockpit area for both driver and passengers.

The Probe was fitted with a commendably high level of standard equipment, including alloy road wheels (three-spoke 6J × 15 on the 16V; five-spoke 7J × 16 on the 24V), Ford anti-theft system, heated/power door mirrors, rear wash/wipe for the tailgate, driving lights, central locking, electric windows, tinted glass and power radio aerial. The list on the 24v was even more comprehensive, with an electrically operated sun roof, footwell illumination, and leather-covered steering-wheel and gearstick knob. CFC-free air-conditioning and metal paint were options on both cars, with leather trim possible in the 24V.

FUTURE THOUGHTS

In June 1992 Ford acquired a 50 per cent equity in MMUC, the company changing its name to Auto Alliance International Inc. Total production output capacity of the Flat Rock plant is some 280,000 vehicles, with a staff level of 3,500 working a two-shift system. A total of 400 up-to-date robots are used in manufacturing processes, including welding, body-panel pressing, body assembly and plastics moulding for interior parts. The latter uses fifty robots and ten automatic machines capable of handling twenty-five body colours in batches to reduce the waste caused by nozzle-pipe cleaning. There are seven clear-coat metallic finishes for European markets, with white and red available as non-metalic colours. Each Probe covers 12 miles (19km) before reaching the final trim and assembly process area. Here both automatic and manual methods are used – powertrain and glass panels are installed automatically, while underbody components are fitted by hand. Both sixteen-valve and twenty-four-valve engines are imported from Japan, although around 180 US-based companies supply parts direct to the Flat Rock factory, this qualifying Probe as a domestic product under US Government guide-lines.

The Probe made its British début at the London Motor Show in October 1993, the star of Ford's special-theme stand which included a futuristic marquee with exhibits promoting vehicle styling and safety. However, Ford's exciting new coupé was to have some tough competition from the likes of Rover, Honda, Vauxhall and Volkswagen, and while Ford UK are content to promote Probe as the replacement for the well-loved and much-missed Capri, Britain was the only market where Capri was mentioned as the Probe's predecessor. The Germans, for example, weren't interested.

And so the Probe finally came to the UK in March 1994. Despite the thorough testing which Ford had implemented for the Euro-

A replacement for the Capri? The Probe was launched on to the British market in early 1994 in 2.0-litre four-cylinder and 2.5-litre V6 forms. Although competition is fierce, it is thought that the Ford will win by a short head because of its sleek – albeit distinctively Japanese – appearance.

pean market, the company was still unhappy about certain aspects of the Probe's ride for British buyers. As a result of these concerns, the dampers and steering were more subtly tuned, encouraging the authoritative boys at *The Autocar* to state that Ford had turned a 'seriously flawed also-ran into a genuinely good car'.

Despite this, under test the Probe was found wanting in both performance and fuel economy when set against the other coupés in its class, its 0–60mph (0–97km/h) sprint of 7.9 seconds and 23.4mpg (12.1l/100km) not faring at all well. The decidedly low final-drive gearing – equating to 20.6mph (32.2km/h) at 1,000rpm – made for a noisy car at speed. All was not bad news, however, for ride, road-holding and brakes all came in for compliments, although the tweaks made to the suspension had served only to improve the ride and handling qualities rather than make them top of the class.

The *Autocar* team also felt the Probe to be second best to its biggest market rival, the Vauxhall Calibra, in terms of interior design, build quality, materials, performance, comfort and even driver satisfaction. And yet for all that the Probe won the day – just – through being the better-looking of the two, the difference, it was felt, being sufficient to win hearts, and buyers. This was, after all, the same reason the late-lamented Capri had continued to be so popular and why, ultimately, the Opel Manta lost out. Let's hope the Probe is just as successful – only time will tell.

DIETER HAHNE

Dieter Hahne was born in Germany in 1942 and was educated at Braunschweig University where he graduated with an MSc in Mechanical Engineering.

In 1970 Dieter joined Ford Europe as a graduate trainee and two years later was appointed to the post of vehicle Systems Engineer in Ford's Product Development area where, apart from a short period in Parts Operations, he has spent the major part of his career with the company.

Dieter has held a number of key positions, including Manager, Driveline Engineering. Later, he was appointed Manager for Medium Car Programmes, where he was responsible for vehicle testing and development.

With the appointment of Rod Mansfield as Director of Engineering at Aston Martin, Dieter Hahne was made Manager, Special Vehicle Engineering and Vehicle Component Engineering, at Ford's Research Centre at Dunton, Essex.

Dieter Hahne is married with three sons. His interests include sport and unusual cars.

5 Capri Rallye Sports

While the average Ford fan could be forgiven for thinking that Ford competitive motor sport began with the Mk I Zephyr and Zodiac of the 1950s, the company's ties with the sport actually date back almost to the turn of the century.

EARLY SUCCESSES

It was in 1901, even before the founding of the present Ford Motor Company, that Henry Ford built his first racing car with the specific intention of creating publicity, which in turn would finance the establishment of his company. The car Ford built was powered by a twin-cylinder 8,848cc engine, and despite never having driven in a race before he won the Groose Point event in fine style. Ford's success also won him the financial backing he sought, and in November 1901 he set up the Henry Ford Company. His ties with the company were to be short-lived, however, for after a huge row with his fellow directors, the following year, he left, the company going on to become Cadillac!

It was back to the drawing-board and the race-track. Ford built two race cars, 999 (named after a steam locomotive which ran on the New York Central Railroad and achieved a record of 112.5mph, or 181km/h) and Arrow, both cars being powered by 27.9-litre engines. Drive was taken via huge fly-wheels through wooden clutches direct to massive crown-wheel and pinion final drives. There were no gearboxes or universal joints, while the crown wheel and pinion gears had no casings and were open to the elements. Nor was there any rear suspension, the axle being located directly on to the wooden chassis side-members. Basic technology indeed.

Yet for all their crude simplicity, these cars proved highly successful in the hands of the brave Bernie Oldfield and others during the 1902 and 1903 seasons. Indeed, they were so successful that Ford was able to achieve his dream, setting up the Ford Motor Company in June 1903. To reap even more publicity, Ford made a successful attack on the World Land Speed Record in freezing conditions on Lake St Clair, Michigan, in January 1904. Driving what is usually agreed to have been Arrow, Ford achieved 91.37mph (147.04km/h) in a remarkable show of determination and bravery, the car being in an almost continuous state of slide for most of the run. It was a remarkable display of nerve and demonstrated a little of the style Ford would exude later when running the firm that bore his name.

Between the wars, Model T Fords, powered by twin overhead cam engines that were developed by the Chevrolet brothers, could be seen at Indianapolis and other race-tracks around the States. However, they were not always successful. For example, there was the sad saga of the front-wheel-drive V8-powered cars. In 1935 Ford officially entered ten of these Harry Miller-built racers at Indianapolis, only to have them all eliminated. Heat from the cars' exhausts had melted the steering-box grease, the boxes being mounted too close to the exhaust pipes, causing the steering mechanism to seize.

In stark contrast to these failures, works rallying in post-war Britain got off to a more leisurely start with the impossibly upright Anglias winning international rally events during the late 1940s. With the advent of the legendary Mk I Zephyrs, Ford's rally team at last had a competitive car, these ruggedly reliable machines being more than a match for the opposition. Driven by the likes of Maurice Gastonsides, the Mk I Zephyrs started Ford on a remarkable career of rally successes across the world. For example, Ann Hall's 1956 Zephyr had triple Zenith carburettors, special suspension, bucket seats, extra instrumentation and alloy body panels – a true 100mph (160km/h) car with handling to match.

The 1950s also saw a dramatic upsurge in club racing on both sides of the Atlantic, the 100E side-valve Ford engine providing the power for many a clubman's special (including, of course, the illustrious Colin Chapman). In the States, Americans loved the European sports cars for their speed, agility and handling. To gain a measure of the public's reaction to European-styled sports cars, Ford Detroit set up its Advanced Concepts Division with the Yorkshireman Roy Lunn in control.

LE MANS

The work of the Ford Advanced Concepts Division (FACD) became public in 1962 with the launch of Mustang I, a mid-engined sports car designed by the division's Styling Chief, Eugene Bordinat, and Engineer, Herb Misch. The car made a dramatic début at Watkins Glen, driven by the world-famous racing driver, Dan Gurney. *Car and Driver* magazine said it reminded them of the first two-seater Coventry Climax-engined Cooper, and certainly its low sweeping bonnet-line, vestigial windscreen and thick pillared roll-over bar presented a very impressive visual impact. Called the '100-day project', for this was how long it took to build the car, Mustang I was the archetypal Ford parts-bin special: front disc brakes from the Cortina and 1.7-litre V4 engine from the German Taunus. With just 65bhp available from its rear-mounted engine, performance was remarkably sparkling with a 0–60mph (0–97km/h) time of 10.5 seconds and a top speed of 112mph (180km/h).

There were, however, some serious shortcomings with the car's design, not the least of which was its shape. Lee Iacocca felt the design was too radical and the car therefore was not a volume product, instructing the stylists to go back to the drawing-board. What emerged, of course, was the legendary Mustang four-seater coupé, FACD at least proving that Mustang I was a concept that should not be pursued.

Meanwhile, it seemed that Henry Ford II had inherited his father's passion for motor racing. The Le Mans GT40 programme and Ford's Total Performance promotion of the 1960s made powerful international marketing tools which spearheaded the company's drive to create a sporting image. Ford's decision to set up the GT40 project was made after news got out that the German Consul in Milan had mentioned to Ford's German General Manager that Ferrari might be interested in selling as Enzo Ferrari himself was only interested in his racing team, not the road cars, and the company was losing money. The deal, so the informant suggested, was for Ford to buy the whole operation, contracting Ferrari to manage the F1 racing team. With a possible £6 million on the table and negotiations almost at the point of signature, the astute Italian pulled out over fundamental differences in cultural backgrounds and business operations. Whatever, it did make Henry very determined indeed that he would signal the go-ahead for an in-house project for designing and building a Ferrari-beater, the whole thing being undertaken with an almost blank-cheque approach to cost.

As every Ford fan knows, the foundation

JOHN WYER

John Wyer

The name of John Wyer and the GT40 are synonymous in most enthusiasts' minds. When Wyer died in April 1989 at his home in Scottsdale, Arizona, motor racing lost one of its most remarkable and capable personalities.

An engineer by profession, it was Wyer's analytical approach to team management throughout the years which gained him such success. Wyer also had a knack of surrounding himself with talented people who were only too happy to work under his leadership.

Wyer began his career in 1948 at Monaco Motors, a London-based garage which specialized in the preparation of racing cars for the wealthy, Wyer running Dudley Folland's Aston Martin in the prestigious 24-hour race at Spa. It was while he was there that he was spotted by entrepreneur David Brown, who later invited Wyer to take charge of his Aston Martin DBR2s for the 1950 season. The appointment was contracted to last for twelve months, but Wyer remained for thirteen years, during which time he was promoted to Technical Director and later Managing Director of one of the world's best known sports car manufacturers. During that time he had the satisfaction of seeing the team win both Le Mans and the Sports Car World Championship for 1959.

In 1963 Wyer was lured away to join Ford, taking charge of the GT40 – Ford's new weapon with which to beat Ferrari at Le Mans. Based at Slough, Buckinghamshire, the operation was called Ford Advanced Vehicles where, with input from such masters as Len Bailey and Eric Broadley, the team designed and built what is arguably the most attractive and legendary of all sports racing cars. The proof of the GT40's performance was victory in both the 1966 and 1967 Le Mans events.

By this time Ford felt it had made its point and Wyer took over operations with his friend John Willment, calling the team JW Automotive Engineering. Despite running what some criticized as out-dated cars, the GT40s won again, this time in their orange and blue livery.

Such was his performance that Porsche asked Wyer to take charge of its exciting 917 programme. Again, sponsorship was to come from Gulf Oil, and while the cars failed to win at Le Mans they did win eleven out of the seventeen events they entered during the 1970 and 1971 season – an impressive achievement.

At 62 John retired. He had had enough of company politics although, as President of Gulf Oil, he was persuaded to take charge of the GT40-based Mirage team cars (again designed by Len Bailey), their Le Mans victory making it five wins in a row for Wyer.

for the GT40 (so-called because it was 40in high) began with the Lola GT which raced at Le Mans in 1963. The car showed potential but no more, although its performance encouraged Lola's boss, Eric Broadley, to sign a twelve-month 'co-operation' deal with Ford. The Ford Advanced Vehicles (FAV) team, including the Englishman Roy Lunn as well as Len Bailey (who had been sent over from Detroit), moved into a tiny workshop in South London. Unfortunately, personality clashes fuelled by restricted accommodation soon saw the team moving to a trading estate in Slough. At the time, Ford Advanced Vehicles was under the watchful and determined eye of ex-Aston Martin manager, John Wyer. The move proved to be the impetus the team needed. By March 1964 two cars had been completed and were undergoing tests at MIRA, the second car (much against Wyer's wishes) going on to be displayed at the New York Motor Show.

The GT40's first race was in 1964 at the Nürburgring, where the car's potential was there for all to see until suspension and transmission troubles intervened. Then came more testing and racing before Le Mans itself, where, despite showing true promise, unreliability destroyed the car's chances again. In July, Eric Broadley's contract with Ford expired and he went back to running Lola Cars, hence quashing the rumour that the Ford Motor Company had bought out his little race-car business. By the end of the same year, Roy Lunn had also gratefully backed away from the Slough operations. Taking a handful of FAV staff with him, Lunn accepted Ford America's offer to set up Kar Kraft, the US equivalent to FAV, based some few miles from Dearborn where there were assembly facilities and office accommodation.

For the 1965 season, Ford Advanced Vehicles took on Carroll Shelby, the Cobra king, who brought with him the talented Phil Remmington (who had spent much time at AC Cars' Thames Ditton factory helping to turn the AC Ace into the Cobra). The GT40's 4.2-litre alloy Indy engines were discarded in favour of cast-iron-blocked 4.7-litre units, these cars becoming known as Mk Is. The Mk II GT40 was developed by Roy Lunn at Kar Kraft and powered by the monstrous 6,997cc Ford V8 engine, while Mk IIIs were simply road-going versions of the Mk I. Finally, there was a Mk IV version, which utilized a honeycomb chassis and was powered by a tuned version of the 427 engine.

As every Ford fan knows, 1966 turned out to be *the* year of the GT40, with Mk IIs crossing the line at Le Mans in first, second and third positions, actually taking the flag three abreast! In 1967 Mk IVs finished the same event in the first and fourth positions. Ford had achieved what it had set out to do, the programme costing the corporation a reputed $9 million – yet who can compute what value was generated in publicity and added sales? Suffice it to say the GT40 entered the stable of memorable cars, shared only by the truly great marques. However, the story doesn't stop there. Ford withdrew its interest in FAV and as 1966 drew to a close the enterprising John Wyer set up JW Automotive in the same premises with the same staff. The GT40 went on to win at Le Mans again in 1968 and 1969 – an impressive achievement.

FAVO

Ford Advanced Vehicle Operations (FAVO) was an altogether different set-up to FAV. In truth, it was always likely that FAV would have a short career, being a subsidiary of Ford's main empire but with a budget and authority geared specifically to win Le Mans. In this, it achieved its goal. FAVO, however, was established as a low-volume specialist manufacturing unit within Ford, supported with all the financial backing of a multi-million-pound international company, yet with all the benefits of an almost hand-built assembly line.

FAVO was championed by the colourful and energetic Walter Hayes. Flying in the face of the large-scale production, the unit was located in an ex-engineering/spare-parts warehouse in South Ockenden (sometimes referred to as Averley) covering some 85,000sq. ft (7,900sq. m), with a photographic studio alongside. Dunton took over the engineering research element, while the spares section was moved to Thurrock. As Hayes was to relate recently, it was pure opportunism that FAVO was based at South Ockenden, the spares warehouse being large enough to convert into a small assembly line (complete with overhead track capable of handling in excess of 120 units a week), and a photographic studio where publicity shots could be taken for use by the FAVO promotion department. Another key component of FAVO's facility was a planning and design section where future RS models could be developed.

Asked why he had such an impact on influencing Ford to enter competitive motor sport, Hayes replied candidly, 'Ford had a Public Relations Manager, Col Maurice Buckmanster, who was well known for his World War II exploits with SOE [Special Operations Executive]. But Sir Patrick Hennessey, Ford's Chairman, wanted someone different. Coming from the world of journalism, when I joined Ford in 1961 I found I had experience in areas where they knew little. They knew the car-manufacturing business but little about world affairs. Then I was lucky enough to meet Henry Ford so quickly. With the Total Performance programme running there were no limitations to launching new ideas.'

Hayes turned to Ford's production supremo, Bill Hayden, to help bring his fledgling factory to reality, and put the able Ray Horrocks in charge. Horrocks was to tell Ford expert, Jeremy Walton, much later that working in FAVO was the most exciting period of his life. One of the first engineers to join the team during November 1969 was Rod Mansfield. At the time FAVO was being set up, Mansfield was working in the company's truck planning department. As a motor-racing enthusiast himself, Rod wasted no time in getting in touch with Horrocks, becoming the fifth member of the élite FAVO 'club'. In fact, no sooner had Mansfield been hired to join the engineering

Walter Hayes, who left Fleet Street journalism to head up Ford's Public Affairs Department and was the major force in putting Ford on to the international motor-sport map.

team than he found himself interviewing prospective staff. Later, Mansfield would be promoted to run FAVO's High Performance Programme.

As Rod was to recall recently, such was the attraction of Averley that it soon had some very talented people on its books: Alan Wilkinson (who later went to Toyota Team Europe); Mike Bennet (who went on to Reliant); and Mike Moreton (whose name became synonymous with the RS200 and RS500 projects, before he left to run Jaguar's XJ220 project). Horrocks himself, an unknown before being put in charge of FAVO by Hayes, would end up in charge of BL Cars Ltd. That was the calibre of people at FAVO.

FAVO opened its doors to the world on 14 January 1970 and was announced to the press at the prestigious Brussels Motor Show. Some sixty-five outlets had been selected from Ford's main dealer chain to act as 'Rallye Sport' specialists. The plan was that they would deal in RS cars as well as a new range of after-market products, such as bolt-on performance parts (Escort turret kits, alloy road wheels and the like) as well as clothing, this all aimed at enhancing Ford's sporting image.

From the outset there was never any doubt that Averley (FAVO) would be little more than an assembly plant, where the myriad bits from major Ford manufacturing plants were screwed together (by hand-picked and enthusiastic staff, mind you): bodies fully dressed and trimmed from Halewood; engines from Dagenham; rear axles from Swansea. Other factories and suppliers provided the rest. Parts peculiar to RS cars, such as the seats and trim decals, were bought in and added during assembly. And while most people usually associate Averley with the Escort (which is hardly surprising in view of the numbers made there), the unit also played a major role in the early development of sporting Capris.

WORK STARTS

No sooner had the engineering team been formed in late 1969, than it got down to building a prototype RS2600 Capri. Jochen Neerpasch, a former Porsche works driver who had set up German Ford Motorsport on 7 January 1968, argued astutely that, in addition to homologation rules (which demanded quantities of showroom cars to be built), a road-going version of the Capri he would be campaigning in German motor sport would add promotional weight to his race programme. This was fed back to the embryo Averley team, and in November, just one month after FAVO had begun operations, authority was given for the RS Capri development programme to start.

RS 2600

In late 1969 the FAVO team got down to building two prototype RS2600 Capris, which were completed in January the following year. Both cars were in left-hand-drive trim and were used to analyse the RS2600 build process. Next came a directive to put together a third car for display at the Geneva Motor Show in March, a tight time schedule indeed. In fact, to ensure the Show car was ready on time, the engine featured only a mock-up of the Kugelfischer fuel-injection system that would be fitted to the production version. Moreover, such was the cliff-hanger completion date that the Liaison Manager, Richard Martin-Hurst, had to break company rules by ordering an aeroplane to fly the car to Geneva in order to make the press day since bad weather looked sure to delay the car's transit by road. It was a bold move, but it saved Ford from a potential promotions disaster!

To comply with Group II regulations, the team's next headache was to ensure that fifty Capris with long-throw crankshaft en-

Mean, moody, dramatic: the RS2600 was Ford's first fuel-injected production car. The first cars lacked bumpers and spoilers. Nearly 4,000 were built between 1970 and 1973.

The interior of an early RS2600 showing the first generation dashboard, though RS Capri customers got better rally-style reclining seats and a strongly dished steering-wheel.

Of 2,637cc the RS2600 engine produced a true 150bhp at 5,600rpm with a higher compression ratio of 10.5:1, and used the Capri 2300GT camshaft together with siamesed ported cast iron cylinder heads.

gines, yet missing fuel-injection systems, were built on the line at Ford's Cologne plant by mid-April. The four-bearing 2,673cc engines were reckoned to be safe to 6,500rpm and, fitted with the uprated 2300 camshaft, developed 150bhp at 5,700rpm. Those involved with the programme – Rod Mansfield, Harry Worral and Mike Smith – have fond memories of these Capris, the cars being as marginal as possible without being barred by the German authorities as unsuitable for use on German roads. Lack of carpets and glass side-windows was one thing, but as no heaters were fitted either demisting could be a real problem; electric rear windows were subsequently installed. Worse, the GRP bonnet, boot and doors (made by BBS – now a well-known alloy-wheel manufacturer) did not fit properly, and the Perspex side-windows had a habit of vibrating in their sliding channels. Even Ford's own Quality Control Department often refused to allow cars through for sale! To show the measure of attention the team paid to bodyweight, the number of paint coats was reduced to three 'thin' layers, back and front bumpers were left off, and the rear registration plate was illuminated by a pair of Halford's trailer-board lamp units! To complete the inventory, cars were fitted with bucket seats and Minilite magnesium-type road wheels.

With assembly of the first fifty lightweight Capris complete and inspected by a representative of the Paris-based commission for international motor sport, Capris were granted a racing weight in Group 2 specification of 1,984lb (900kg). This category called for some 1,000 units to be built annually, and, as we shall see, nearly 4,000 were built between 1970 and 1974, by which time the rules allowed such freedom that Ford dropped the 2600 in favour of the RS3100 model powered by the V6 Essex 3.0-litre engine.

To comply with the homologation rules, production of the road car had to be put in hand quickly; many years later, those involved with the RS2600 programme look back on the speed with which the car reached series production with pride. Sign-off for the restyled RS2600 front end, which included an air-damm spoiler and twin headlamp arrangement modified to take Cibié inserts, was given approval in mid-July 1970. The engineering green light for the RS2600 was given a month later, the first car rolling off the line a month after that – a fast time schedule by any standards. However, no sooner had production started than immediate panic set in. The smart 6in-wide alloy wheels, lowered ride height and re-drilled front cross-member (which gave some useful negative camber) caused the wheels to touch the front wing arches. Luckily, Cologne's pilot plant at Niehl speedily produced a press tool which gave slight flares to the front wing panels, thereby solving the situation. Had it been a mainstream model the rectification process would have taken months!

'In FAVO you had to be fast on your feet and people who worked there did tend to miss out on what was happening in mainstream engineering,' Rod said with feeling. 'Also, mainstream engineering had a complex release/sign-off procedure for model development. Had we in FAVO adopted the same procedure, the amount of clerical support would have killed the department, so we created our own processes.'

The most obvious deviations of the RS2600's engine from the standard Taunus V6 was the installation of the Kugelfischer fuel-injection system. Its ribbed cast-alloy plenum chamber was located midships of the cylinder V, and the injection pump mounted high up above the alternator and driven by its own toothed belt. Much of the engine development was undertaken by the Rye-based firm of Weslake Engineering Ltd. The engines utilized the longer 69mm-stroke crankshaft with high-compression 10:1 pistons and a 'hotter' camshaft borrowed from the 2300GT Capri. (Alloy cylinder heads were used on the Group 2 race Capris only.) The sump was also taken from the 2300 car and modified to accommodate the different crankshaft. Finally, the exhaust was unique to the RS2600; there was no balance pipe, each tube running from the cylinder head, through a heater box and an expansion box to a squared-off rear pipe.

The RS2600's suspension consisted of uprated competition front springs and a single leaf on the rear, again stiffened up with Bilstein dampers all round. The wheels were Richard Grant alloys with Pirelli CN36 185HRX13s. Brakes were standard 2600GT, with Ferodo competition pads and linings. The gearbox was the standard unit fitted to the V6 Taunus, driving through to a 3.22:1 axle to give a lowly 20mph (32km/h) at 1,000rpm – hardly ideal for prolonged *autobahn* driving. (Only the race cars boasted a five-speed ZF gearbox, while a limited-slip differential was available as an optional extra.) Other changes included interfacing the cable-operated clutch system to a hydraulic slave cylinder using a pivoting arm mounted on the gearbox casing. To give the interior of the RS2600 a sporty feel, racing austerity had given way to Grand Touring luxury with comfy looking, reclining cord-covered rally seats and a deeply dished leather-trimmed steering-wheel, although there was no centre transmission console over the handbrake.

FORD CAPRI RS2600 (1971)

LAYOUT AND CHASSIS
Two-door coupé/monocoque construction

ENGINE	
Type	Cologne
Block material	Cast iron
Head material	Cast iron
Cylinders	V6
Cooling	n/a
Bore and stroke	90.0 × 69.0mm
Capacity	2,637cc
Valves	ohv
Compression ratio	10.0:1
Carburettor	Kugelfischer mechanical
Max. power	150bhp @ 5,800rpm
Max. torque	165lb/ft @ 3,500rpm
Fuel capacity	12.8 gallons (58 litres)
TRANSMISSION	
Gearbox	4-speed
Ratios	3.65:1, 1.97:1, 1.37:1, 1.00:1
Final drive	3.22:1
SUSPENSION AND STEERING	
Front	MacPherson strut
Rear	Semi-elliptic springs
Steering	Rack and pinion
Tyres	185/70 HR × 13
Wheels	Alloy
Rim width	6in
BRAKES	
Type	Hydraulic disc/drum
Size	9.6in disc, 9 × 2.3in drum
DIMENSIONS (in/mm)	
Track: front	54.2/1,377
rear	53.2/1,351
Wheelbase	100.8/2,560
Overall length	168.5/4,280
Overall width	64.8/1,646
Overall height	50.7/1,288
Unladen weight	2,519lb/1,143kg
PERFORMANCE	
Top speed	126mph (203km/h)
0–60mph	7.3sec

Today, people who were involved with the project are happy to report that, as is often the case with homologation specials, the RS2600 was modified as production went along, and early assembly was very much dependent on what parts and units were available at the time. Alterations to improve the fuel-injection system included the addition of a cold-start mechanism, changes to the fuel-injection timing and a move from a two-dimension to a three-dimension injection camshaft. The latter read throttle opening, engine speed and intake manifold vacuum, thereby making the engine smoother and more economical.

MORE MODIFICATIONS

In October 1971 the grey-coloured Richard Grand road wheels of the RS2600 gave way to the four-spoke FAVO type. The opportunity was taken to add chromed bumpers – quarter-type at the front as on the fast Escorts (but with inset flasher units), and a full-width bar at the rear. The disc brakes were also updated to the type being developed for the latest Granada, with the M16J calliper assembly, but with a ventilated disc and hub unique to the Capri. At the same time, the team took a long, hard look at the suspension, raising the ride height using production front coil springs and revised damper settings. This reduced the harshness of the ride, bringing the specification more in line with the standard road cars and making it less of a parts-bin special. Finally, the gearbox was changed to the Granada-type box, similar to that used in the British 3.0-litre Capri.

June 1972 saw the last alterations made to the RS2600. Inside, the bucket-seat material was changed to a more refined ribbed pattern and the head-rests were im-

When RS2600s were fitted with bumpers – quarter type at the front and a full width bar at the rear – they were chromed, just like those found on Ford's family saloons. Note, too, the 5.5in FAVO-styled alloy road wheels.

proved. The steering-wheel was changed to the standard RS flat-spoke type, while the transmission tunnel was given an arm rest/ oddments locker. The fascia was changed to a matt-black finish and the rear quarter lights were adapted to open for improved ventilation. In addition, more aggressive body decals gave the car a strongly sporting appearance. In terms of performance, the 2600 could sprint from 0 to 60mph (97km/h) in a shade over 8 seconds and hit 124mph (200km/h) at full stretch; the lightweight cars could do the 0–60mph (0–97km/h) timed run about a second faster. All were built in left-hand drive form for sale on the Continent, with the exception of a handful of

In 1972 the RS2600 was given the later type of twin headlamp cluster and matt black bumpers, while Mike Cadby's development had resulted in a change to the Granada gearbox, a 3.09:1 final drive and 9.75in ventilated front disc brakes.

Ford first used quarter bumpers on the Lotus Cortina and later on the Escort Twin Cam and RS1600 saloons. These allowed the flashing indicators to be moved from the front apron on the first RS2600 to the bumper itself with small driving lights below.

specially converted cars which reached people like Walter Hayes and Stuart Turner in Britain. British enthusiasts meanwhile would have to wait for the RS3100, waiting in the wings, and the exciting race version.

Without doubt, Weslake made a fundamental contribution to the development of the RS2600 engine, their expertise in gas-flow science (masterminded by Harry Weslake himself, who did much research into gas-flow technology and metallurgy) resulting in an on-going improvement programme on what was, after all, just a cooking production engine, manufactured by the thousand. However, the decision was made to leave Weslake with the 2600 unit and turn instead to Cosworth, whose name had been linked with Ford from the early days of the 105E Anglia, the power unit of which the brilliant Keith Duckworth had turned into the SCA engine, tuned to produce a formidable 115bhp at 8,750rpm. Cosworth had established an enviable reputation for producing batches of top-quality race engines almost without parallel in the industry.

Ford went up to Northampton to talk with Mike Hall and the Cosworth team about utilizing the 3.0-litre Essex unit as the basis for an engine to take over from the German 2.6-litre V6. In fact, Ford's brief to Hall was quite general, simply indicating a desired power output of 400bhp using the Essex V6 cast-iron cylinder block. On to this block

The view many drivers got of the Capri RS2600. The word 'Injection' is balanced by the notation 'Capri RS' on the opposite side of the boot lid decal.

KEITH DUCKWORTH

Keith Duckworth was born in Blackburn, Lancashire, in 1933. His mother taught domestic science at the local school while his father worked on the Manchester Cotton Exchange before setting up his own mill. Duckworth describes him as a bright, intelligent man who, while not an engineer, became something of a car enthusiast, making many mechanical modifications to improve reliability and performance, his favourite car being a pre-war Riley.

Keith was educated at Giggleswick boarding school, taking his 'A' levels before going on to serve his National Service in the RAF. A keen model maker, his interest in things practical matured to motor bikes and assembling a Scott Squirrel from a box of bits.

Next came a degree course in engineering at Imperial College where he became smitten by the motor racing bug (a fellow enthusiast at the time was Roger Brockbank, son of cartoonist Russel Brockbank). Keith managed to persuade his mother to let him spend some of the money he had inherited from his father on a Lotus VI kit, which he built during the summer holidays. The same period the following year saw the young Duckworth working full time for Chapman. It was then that he met his future business partner, Mike Costin.

While still at College, Keith had applied to Napier and Rolls-Royce for a place on their graduate apprenticeship courses. The likelihood of filing metal blocks for many months did not appeal, so, despite having decided to take the Napier job, he contacted Chapman, who offered him the job of Gearbox Development Engineer working on a five-speed gearbox.

However, Keith was far from happy about its design. He had already talked over the idea of setting up an engineering company with Mike Costin, so, after just ten months with Lotus, in 1958 Duckworth left to set up Cosworth (the amalgamation, of course, COStin and DuckWORTH). Costin joined him in their North London workshops in 1962.

Initially, Cosworth was to offer a composite engineering service chassis incorporating suspension and design and power-unit tuning. Very shortly this was dropped in favour of concentrating on engine development alone, with the introduction of the legendary 997cc 105E Anglia engine in 1959. Keith soon had this producing very respectable horsepower figures, initiating what has proved to be a long-standing liaison with Ford which has included the 105E ohc SCA; the FVA; the DFV; the BDA; the GAA; and, more recently, the tohc turbo unit for the Sierra Cosworth.

In 1980 Cosworth became part of the Unit Engineering Industries Group. Keith has now retired, allowing him more time for his hobbies, such as piloting his own helicopter and water skiing – as well as keeping in regular touch with his friend, Mike Costin.

Hall designed identical cylinder heads with four valves per cylinder, actuated by belt-driven twin overhead camshafts. The combustion chambers used the well-known Pentroof V-shape with triple (really!) spark plugs. From talks with Cosworth it was agreed that the engine would utilize a stroke of 72.42mm with a bore size of 95.19mm for road trim (giving a 60 thou overbore size of 3,091cc), but increased to 100mm for race use, thereby resulting in a capacity of 3,412cc. In fact, the decision to start development work on the Essex engine at that time proved to be fortuitous.

It was inevitable that the arrival of BMW's stylish 3.0-litre coupés on to the racing arena in 1973 would mark the beginning of the end for Ford's RS2600 Capri warhorse. Initially, the racing Capris seemed unaffected by the German CSLs' good performances at Monza, Nürburgring and Mantorp Park in Sweden. But by mid-season, the BMWs had taken on the bat-like rear wind-spoiler contraptions (designed, incidentally, by former Ford em-

MIKE COSTIN

Mike Costin, brother of Frank Costin – who is nine years older and whose name is linked with many of the early, sleek Lotus sports racing cars – was born in Harrow, Middlesex, where he was educated at a local private school. Mike happily recalls his childhood days, saying that because he was lazy and his parents did not push him he did not excel at exams. In the days before World War I, his father had undertaken a considerable amount of exploration in Africa before settling in the UK, where he quickly became established as a marble engraver of some repute. He was, however, something of an inventor and while not an engineer, he did make things like radios.

Mike Costin's interest in engineering emerged gradually as he became fascinated by bikes and motor bikes. Meanwhile, Frank was already working in the aircraft industry, so it was hardly surprising that Mike should join De Havilland as an apprentice in 1946. Then came National Service. Back at De Havilland he developed test equipment, working on the first air-conditioning system.

An introduction to Colin Chapman in 1952 (who at the time was a Project Engineer with British Aluminium) resulted in Mike becoming involved with Lotus at a very early stage. The prototype Mk VI had just been completed, Costin's role being to help with the car's development. Gradually, his contribution to Lotus increased and in 1955 he finally left De Havilland to work full time for Chapman.

Soon after, Keith Duckworth joined the team and the idea was hatched to set up Cosworth, Costin joining the company full time in 1962. From there the company grew in stature, becoming the internationally famous firm it is today. However, Mike is quick to point out the immense amount of hard work he put in, both at Lotus and with Cosworth. Like Duckworth, Costin has now retired from the company and is able to enjoy his many pastimes, these including skiing and gliding.

ployee Martin Braungart), with the result that the German cars seemed uncatchable. Ford knew they had to have an answer.

RS3100

In September 1973 the approval was given at a product-planning strategy meeting for a right-hand-drive version of the RS3100 Capri, to be built at Halewood during November and December (which itself gives an idea of how hurried the programme would have to be to comply with the proposed time-scales). The specification sheet for suspension, brakes and wheels was similar to that for later RS2600s, but with the 3.0-litre British V6 engine over-bored to 3.1 litres. The car would be referred to in sales catalogues as the RS3100 (though not badged as such), available through the very successful Rallye Sport outlets. Production target was set at 500 units, to comply with homologation rules.

Capri RS3100 assembly at Halewood began in early November 1973, with a launched schedule to take place at the Kelvin Hall in Glasgow by World Champion racing driver Jackie Stewart on 19 November. A Ford press release talked of the car being based on the face-lift Capri 3000GT, with suitable photos illustrating a very young-looking, long-haired Jackie alongside one of the press publicity cars.

Under the bonnet, the 3.1-litre engine had gas-flowed cylinder heads with polished ports and inlet tracts, although the carburation relied on the dinky single EGAS Weber unit, identical to that fitted to the standard 3.0-litre Capri. The compression ratio, exhaust manifolding and camshaft profile were also identical to those found on the 3.0-litre Capri. There were, however, blue-coloured rocker covers on the cylinder heads to indicate at least something was a little different. Anyway, Ford felt sufficiently encouraged by the modifications to quote a power output of 148bhp at 5,200rpm, some 10 per cent above the standard 3.0-litre specification.

As with the RS2600, the RS3100 front suspension utilized a re-drilled cross-member to give negative camber, with a 1in (2.5cm) reduction in ride height. Spring rates – 142lb/in at the front and 112lb/in at the rear – were again similar in specification to the latter-day 2600 Capri; that is to say, stiffer than standard although not as tough as those used on the first RS Capris. In fact, this half-way house approach to the car's suspension must have been a deliberate move by Ford's engineers, for the Bilstein gas dampers were marked as 'directors', thus indicating a more compliant set-up. At the rear, the 3100 shared the same single-leaf spring with the 2600, though the anti-tramp radius arms of the earlier RS car had given way to the less harsh anti-roll bar/axle location links as fitted to 3.0-litre production Capris. The brakes were also borrowed from the last of the RS2600s, with ventilated 9.75in discs on the front. At the rear, the 9.0 × 2.25in brake drums were taken from the standard 3.0-litre car, as was the 3.09:1 final drive, while the servo was the 8in unit fitted to the British Capris.

High-speed stability and an impressive wind-tunnel Cd figure (quoted at 0.375) on the 3100 were gained from the earlier RS car's front-apron spoiler and boot-lid fin, mandatory for the 180mph (290km/h) speeds of the race cars, although they were probably less effectual during around-town cruising. The RS3100 was also given the usual body decals, together with sporty quarter bumpers at the front and a full-width bar at the rear – in matt-black finish, of course, although the window trim was left in its natural colour.

Little effort was spent on giving the interior of this version of the RS Capri Grand

FORD CAPRI RS3100 (1974)

LAYOUT AND CHASSIS	
Two-door coupé/monocoque construction	
ENGINE	
Type	Essex
Block material	Cast iron
Head material	Cast iron
Cylinders	V6
Cooling	n/a
Bore and stroke	95.19 × 72.4mm
Capacity	3,091cc
Valves	ohv
Compression ratio	9.0:1
Carburettor	Weber
Max. power	148bhp @ 5,000rpm
Max. torque	187lb/ft @ 3,000rpm
Fuel capacity	12.8 gallons (58 litres)
TRANSMISSION	
Gearbox	4-speed
Ratios	3.163:1, 1.95:1, 1.412:1, 1.00:1
Final drive	3.09:1
SUSPENSION AND STEERING	
Front	MacPherson struts
Rear	Semi-elliptic springs
Steering	Rack and pinion
Tyres	185/70 HR × 13
Wheels	Alloy
Rim width	6in
BRAKES	
Type	Hydraulic disc/drum
Size	9.6in disc, 9.0 × 2.3in drum
DIMENSIONS (in/mm)	
Track: front	54.2/1,377
rear	53.2/1,351
Wheelbase	100.8/2,560
Overall length	168.5/4,280
Overall width	64.8/1,646
Overall height	50.7/1,288
Unladen weight	2,519lb/1,143kg
PERFORMANCE	
Top speed	123mph (198km/h)
0–60mph	7.2sec

The RS3100 was developed through the desire to win back the European Touring Car Championship supremacy from BMW. The programme resulted in a contract with Cosworth for a dohc V6 unit based on the Essex V6, which produced well over 400bhp.

Touring trim, save for the addition of a 14in (36cm) three-spoke RS-type flat steering-wheel. The seats and dashboard remained unchanged from the showroom 3000GT. It was not so much a homologation special as a homologation compromise!

Today, almost exactly twenty years after the RS3100 reached production, rumours are rife over its brief career. It seems that some 500 RS3100 kits (wheels, suspension parts and so on) were dispatched to Halewood and the production line. Remarkably, only 200 arrived on site ready for assembly! First, the rather nice FAVO alloy wheels mysteriously disappeared, followed soon after by the ventilated front discs. Equally difficult to comprehend is the suggestion that two RS3100s went from dealer to dealer in advance of the FIA officer's official tour of Ford agents.

Equally interesting are tales told of the FAVO staff's antics, such as the time when Ray Horrocks' 3.1-litre Zodiac was damaged when someone reversed it off the service hoist. The lads apparently spent hours racing around the local Ford dealerships in an attempt to trace aubergine-coloured body panels before the boss got back! Or the time when someone 'borrowed' an RS1600 Escort which had been built with all the usual RS goodies, only to report it stolen after his weekend's enjoyment. The police later recovered the accessories on the borrower's premises, at which point his career with Ford came to an abrupt end.

Sadly, the timing of the RS3100 coincided

The RS3100 was really a 1973 RS2600 chassis and brakes powered by an overbored version of the 3-litre Essex V6, giving 95.19 × 72.44mm resulting in 3,091cc and producing 148bhp at 5,000rpm.

with the dramatic Energy Crisis which did so much to harm the British motor industry, resulting in the car being less than a success in sales terms. Moreover, by the time the car reached production the team at Halewood was concentrating on launching the Mk II Capri. In fact, in January 1975 the new Capri and the last of the RS cars were built alongside each other, much to the annoyance of the Halewood Product Planning staff who, as was probably true of the promotions staff in the Public Affairs Department, looked on

In sharp contrast to the RS2600 the RS3100 relied on standard specification 3-litre seats, steering-wheel and dash panel, making this version of Ford's sporting Capri the least exciting visually from the interior.

The RS3100 was fitted with the 6in FAVO-type alloy wheels used on the earlier RS Capri along with the bump stops. 'Director' setting gas dampers gave a less harsh ride although spring rates were a hard 142lb/in in the front and 112lb/in in the rear.

the RS3100 as yesterday's model.

In 1972 Ray Horrocks was replaced by Stuart Turner, though even his considerable management skills could not prevent the inevitable. In 1974 plans began to emerge that FAVO would be closed down, the majority of its 200 staff going their different ways. In fact, the department's closure did not take place until 1975, the Motorsport parts section lasting longer still.

In 1975, Mike Moreton, one of Ford's Product Planners, drew up a scheme for a

High-speed stability was provided by the pronounced RS3100 spoiler, which reduced tail end lift at speeds of 160mph (258km/h) and over. Note that on this RS3100 the rear decal reads 'Capri GT' and not 'Capri RS', as on the 2600.

CAPRI RS2600 AND 3100 DATE PROFILE	
March 1969	First appearance of Capri 2300GT on Lyons–Charbonnières Rally as prototype. Engine producing 170bhp (DIN) at 6,500rpm.
October 1969	Approval at FAVO for RS Capri programme.
December 1969	Work begins on first LHD Capri RS2600 prototypes at FAVO.
March 1970	Capri RS2600 on show at the Geneva Motor Show.
May 1970	First fifty pre-production Capri RS2600s built at Cologne.
August 1970	FAVO gets approval for Capri RS2600 technical specification which includes fuel injection and modified suspension.
September 1970	First production Capri RS2600s built at Cologne. Powered by 2,637cc V6 engine with Kugelfischer mechanical fuel injection developing 150bhp at 5,800rpm. MacPherson front suspension with re-drilled Capri cross-member, leaf springs and radius arms on the rear. Bilstein dampers. Richard Grant 6J × 13in alloy road wheels. Interior as German Capri 2300GT but with dished steering-wheel and reclining cord-covered front seats. Car not for general release in UK.
October 1971	Changes to production specification including an increase in ride height, alloy road wheels changed for FAVO four-spoke type, chrome bumpers fitted, later changed to matt-black type. Cortina 3-litre ventilated-type front disc brakes.
June 1972	Fascia changed to matt-black finish. Also, changes to interior trim material including softer cord for seats and modified head restraints. Three-spoke flat steering and opening rear quarter lights.
September 1973	Approval given for Capri RS3100 in RHD form to be built at Halewood from November 1973.
October 1973	First six pre-production Capri RS3100s built at Boreham.
November 1973	Introduction of Capri RS3100 available through Rallye Sport dealers only. Based on Capri 3000GT with 3,091cc Essex-based engine with single Weber carburettor and polished ports and inlet tracts producing 148bhp (DIN) at 5,000rpm. Front brakes as Capri RS2600. Rear brakes, servo and final drive, as Capri 3-litre. Lowered ride height with modified front spring rates and cross-member. Rear suspension utilized anti-roll bar from Capri 3-litre Bilstein dampers. Interior trim as Capri 3000GT but with three-spoke RS-type steering-wheel. Matt-black bumpers (quarter type at front) and boot mounted flick-up rear spoiler.
December 1973	Capri RS2600 model discontinued.
February 1974	Capri RS3100 model discontinued. Introduction of Capri Mk II model range announced (with three-door coachwork).

Capri RS2.8i. Unfortunately, however, so much time was spent in productionizing the Mk II Escort RS2000 in Germany (a decision which even now rankles some Ford fans) that, despite being given management approval, this Capri never reached fruition. Later still, RS2800 prototypes were built in Mk III form, but again did not reach the production stage. With the decision made to set up the Special Vehicle Engineering team, the Capri 2.8i was productionized but without any competition involvement.

In Germany, Zakspeed and Ford co-operated over the development of the Capri 2.8 Turbo, which was marketed through German Rallye Sport dealerships during

1981 and 1982. Fitted with a KKK turbocharger linked to a standard V6 carburettor, the boost was set at a modest 5.51psi (0.38bar). Later, the KKK turbo unit was replaced by the more popular Garrett Ai-Research unit which, boosted to 7.25psi (0.5bar), produced 188bhp at 5,500rpm. These exciting Capris, built in LHD form, certainly looked the part, with outrageous rear aerofoil spoilers and X-pack body kits providing huge wheelarches to house the wide 6.5in – and sometimes even 7.5in – alloy wheels, and huge front spoilers. The interior trim was finished in grey dralon, the seats being similar to those found in the Escort RS1600i. These Zakspeed cars were a fitting finale to the Capri's RS career. Despite a predicted production run of 300–400 cars, only 200 of the fast road Capris were ever built.

6 Competition Years: 1969–77

As news of the Capri's launch, scheduled for 1969, began to filter through Ford's various departments, there were those – such as Henry Taylor, Ford's Competitions Manager – who could see clearly the car's competition potential. Its overall proportions and the size of its engine bay made it an ideal candidate, there being no need to resort to twisting the angle of a high-performance engine, just to get it under the bonnet – as had been the case when fitting the Lotus twin cam engine into the Escort.

While Henry Ford's notion of creating a unified Ford of Europe was intended to break down barriers (technical, as well as production, financial and national borders), it also made sense to establish a Competitions Department in Germany, based on the facilities that had been created at Boreham in 1963 and hence merging the talents of the two teams. It all began, as ever, with Walter Hayes looking for a suitable candidate to run the German team. Among those approached were race driver Hubert Hahne, Porsche team leader Rico Steinmann, and motorsport expert Jochen Springer. Although initial overtures to Jochen Neerpasch were turned down, personal influences and a brace of racing fatalities involving friends changed his mind. Neerpasch's racing career had started with drives in a Porsche Carrera in 1964, and he had gone on to compete in cars such as the Shelby Mustang, Elan and John Wyer's potent GT40s. It was for Porsche that he did most of his work, entering a total of twenty-four races during the mid-1960s. A serious accident at Spa, however, had fundamentally changed his attitude to the sport.

In the event, Walter's choice proved to be a wise one and Neerpasch revealed himself to be an excellent team manager. Ford's German Competitions Department came into being in early January 1968.

'Someone called Bob Stephenson came over to see me at Warley and we got talking about Germany and he asked me why Ford Germany was not involved with motor sport,' said Walter Hayes recently, explaining the background to how Boreham's equivalent in Cologne came to be established. 'When I was made Vice-President of Ford Europe in 1967 I went over to Cologne and put Germany into motor sport. There was no point in duplication, so Germany went motor racing and Ford in Britain went rallying.'

FOUR-WHEEL DRIVE

It was only natural, that there would be an element of friendly rivalry between the two competitions camps. To steal a march on their Teutonic counterparts and to coincide with the Capri's introduction, Ford UK planned to enter a Capri with four-wheel-drive transmission in a rallycross event at Croft, Co Durham, in February 1969, an event that had a TV audience of millions. It was a simple yet audacious plan to give the car a strong competitions career kick-off.

A posed shot of a four-wheel-drive 3000GT Capri, one of at least seventeen built by Harry Ferguson Research for testing, evaluation and competition. Within days of the Capri's launch Roger Clark won a televised rallycross event at Croft in one of the earliest converted cars.

In truth, the notion to go four-wheel-drive with the Capri was not that outrageous, for the 1960s had seen an energetic programme campaigned by Harry Ferguson Research Ltd (HFR) to convince major companies to manufacture cars with this ultra-safe form of transmission allied to anti-skid braking. The first four-wheel-drive production car was, of course, the Jensen FF, the Italian-styled Grand Tourer that was introduced in 1966 alongside its two-wheel-drive sister, the Jensen Interceptor. With its 6.2-litre Chrysler V8 engine, the FF proved a profoundly safe car in most conditions. And while HF Research was hugely pleased and proud of the FF's success, it never the less nurtured a desire to see its transmission system fitted to volume-manufactured models. In 1968 a Ford Mustang was converted to four-wheel drive using a split-drive transmission arrangement similar to that fitted on the Jensen FF; many convincing demonstrations were given and much interest created. However, the same snag surfaced time after time: HF Research was only interested in prototype development, not volume manufacture. Sadly, no volume manufacturer had been sufficiently convinced that 4WD should be fitted to mass-produced saloons, arguing that the buying public would not shoulder the inevitable extra cost.

This situation changed when GKN made the decision to purchase the manufacturing

Powered by the Capri's 2,994cc V6 engine, drive was taken through a five-speed ZF gearbox to an HFR 4WD transfer box, which in turn connected to the front and rear differentials, with torque split 37/63, front to rear.

rights to the four-wheel-drive transmission system developed by HF Research. GKN immediately began a high-profile promotion campaign which resulted in small quantities of semi-prototype conversions being undertaken: two Triumph Stags; a Michigan State police car; and twenty Zephyr Estate cars for the British police. News of these four-wheel-drive exploits spread throughout the motor industry. The value of 4WD capabilities made good sense, even if the additional cost to the market price of a family saloon did not appear to the buying public. Henry Taylor, who counted among his friends the directors of GKN and the team of HF Research Ltd at Toll Bar End in Coventry, provided the link which got the 4WD Capri programme off to a promising start.

While it is true to say that a demonstrator Capri was fitted with a BDA engine for the press to drive in Cyprus, Rod Mansfield views this as nothing more than a Walter Hayes 'kite-flying exercise' to measure reaction; in other words, it was never a serious production consideration. Meanwhile, Weslake Engineering in Rye, East Sussex – the world-renowned gas-flow specialists – had been working on the V6 unit to improve its performance.

During the latter days of 1968, three Capris were converted by HF Research into full mud-plugging rallycross machines with 3-litre engines and all-wheel-drive transmission, two of them being used for demonstrating to members of Ford's management hierarchy and the dealership chain. The big moment came on 8 February 1969 when Roger Clark drove his 4WD Capri to victory in a very muddy rallycross event at Croft, the success being televized on ITV's popular 'World of Sport'. However, once the event was over the 4WD Capri programme was put on the back burner until the following year as the Boreham boys had something else on their minds – the 1970 World Cup Rally!

Ford did return to campaigning 4WD Capris in the winter of 1970/1, when a team of three cars was entered in events at Cadwell Park and Lydden Hill, the tiny race-circuit near Canterbury in Kent. Driven by Rod Chapman, and Roger Clark and his

ROGER CLARK

Roger Clark

Despite a galaxy of foreign rally stars – and in particular those from Scandinavia – in most people's minds it is Roger Clark who stands in the forefront of works Ford drivers. However, his value to the Ford team was not just as an outstanding driver. It was Clark's ability to undertake test trials – putting cars through their paces at the Bagshot proving ground, getting them into quite extraordinary situations and then recovering from them, only to step out of the car minutes later to discuss, quite dispassionately, suspension settings – which was also of great value.

Roger Clark was born in Leicestershire in 1939. At the time, the Clark family ran a fleet of buses from premises in Narborough. With the war over, Roger's father began to build up a garage business which Roger joined upon leaving school.

Clark's competition career began with an Elva-modified Ford Ten van. This was replaced in 1961 (the year which also saw the start of the legendary Clark/Jim Porter duo) when he bought a Mini Cooper through the family firm. Clark then took second place in the International Scottish Rally in 1963. This year also saw Clark's first works drive, for Reliant, in the Alpine. Next came a drive with Triumph in the Liège–Sofia–Liège and then on to Rover in 1964 to pilot the newly launched Rover 2000. He finished sixth overall and first in the Touring Car category in the tough Monte Carlo Rally, enduring quite appalling weather conditions and driving what can hardly be considered the most competitive of machines.

Despite his outings in the Rover, Clark resorted to his own transport (the company's Cortina GT demonstrator) when he won the Scottish International in 1964 and 1965. He also won the new London-Gulf Rally in 1965 and came third that year in the Circuit of Ireland.

Meanwhile, not surprisingly, Clark was coming to the attention of the Ford Competition Team and was given a works Lotus Cortina in which he won the 1965 Welsh Rally. His first overseas victory was in the Shell 4000 in 1967. That year he also won the Scottish and took part in arguably one of the world's toughest rallies – the East African Safari.

The following year saw Roger begin his now well-documented career with the Escort. He was involved with much of its initial testing at MIRA, Bagshot and Boreham. Much of Clark's subsequent success can be attributed in part to the fact that his rally cars were prepared by one man, the very talented Norman Masters, who knew *exactly* how

Roger Clark testing at Boreham in 1971 driving his 4WD Capri powered by a 2,994cc V6 unit, fitted with Gurney-Weslake alloy cylinder heads and Lucas mechanical fuel injection. The CanAm-style air trumpets can be clearly seen protruding through the bonnet!

Clark wanted his car set up. The result was that Clark was able to match the skilled Scandinavians. Indeed, he is the only British driver to have won a World Championship Rally: the RAC in 1972 and 1976.

A quick glance at Ford's competition entry list is sufficient to prove the point: for twelve years from 1968, Clark won twenty international rallies driving what was probably the world's most successful rally car ever, the Escort, usually with the loyal Jim Porter as co-driver.

Of Clark, Stuart Turner once remarked, 'It's his awareness and confidence which makes him able to pace himself and only drive just fast enough to win. It must make life very frustrating for the opposition.'

After the Escorts came a couple of seasons driving Triumph TR8s, as well as the occasional drive in a Porsche and a season with a Metro 6R4, 'purely for fun', Clark is said to have remarked. But it was clear that the Escort years could never be repeated and today Roger is busy running his Porsche agency and his latest venture, a power-boat business.

Just to prove that Ford were serious about developing a 4WD road Capri this car is being tested on the rolling road specially installed at Boreham. Sadly, the project was grounded because of production and technical complexities.

brother Stan, these Capris (sponsored by the *Daily Express*, *Cars and Car Conversions* and the *Daily Telegraph*) won the Castrol-backed championship in fine style, often managing to defeat the opposition through sheer right of might. Indeed, for the driver of any rallycross Mini, Imp or Triumph, the sight of these monster Capris in their rear-view mirror (the Capris often started with a time handicap) must have been fair warning to move over! In truth, however, the HFR-modified cars were considered to be something of a handful at high speeds in such mud-caked conditions. Despite the antics of people such as Bill Meade – who used marine bilge pumps to direct jets of water on to the windscreen to keep the view ahead clear – staying on course was a matter of balancing power against steering. The technique was to set up the car well in advance of the next corner, although often as not this was not achieved, the result being an increasing amount of understeer despite the driver pouring on more lock as the corner arrived. That master of the understatement, Roger Clark, was to quip that these all-wheel-drive Capris were great cars, though not the easiest he'd driven despite plenty of traction!

Essential Modifications

The first generation of Weslake-developed V6 Capri engines used for rallycross boasted nothing more than gas-flowed cylinder heads matched to mild road/rally tuned sports camshafts, sufficient to produce a true 160bhp. Later, as the campaign was given momentum, modifications became somewhat more radical: an increased compression ratio of 11.2:1; larger inlet and exhaust valves; a wilder camshaft with 300-degree overlap; and, of course, the inevitable Tecalemit fuel-injection system. These engines were blue-printed and built up by the Boreham boys, Terry Hoyle and Brian Reeves; by this time power output had risen to a rather healthy 200+bhp.

However, engine-tuning was the easy part; conversion of the Capri bodyshell to accept the four-wheel-drive transmission was no quick engineering job. To begin with, the front-mounted differential was located in its own cast-aluminium casing fitted on the near side of the engine. The driveshaft for the off-side wheel actually passed through the sump, the front wheels being supported on Ford Taunus (Ford's only front-wheel-drive car) suspension legs, the upper locating points themselves being modified so that their height was increased by 1.75in (44mm). A new bell housing was cast to link the V6 engine and the five-speed ZF gearbox, the transfer case containing the HFR-developed differential and transfer drive, this bolting on the rear. Normal torque split was set at 37 per cent to the front and 63 per cent to the rear wheels, the drive being taken to the front and rear differentials by short prop shafts.

The original chassis rails which supported the engine were cut away and replaced by a new cradle fabricated from 1.5in (38mm) steel tubing. This accommodated the steering assembly and new engine mountings, relocated to clear the front driveshafts. To allow for the cradle's location in the Capri engine bay, considerable surgery had to be carried out in order to create sufficient space, while the transmission tunnel and scuttle also had to be modified to cover the enlarged bell housing, transfer casing and ZF gearbox. To cope with the additional traction and power, Bilstein dampers were fitted all round, located with uprated suspension bushes, while the brakes were given competition pads and linings. Some cars were fitted with anti-skid braking systems, although Roger Clark specifically asked that such a system was not fitted to his car! Wheels were 13 × 6in Minilites for dry use and 13 × 7in for slippery conditions, shod with Dunlop covers.

Too Expensive

In the event, the four-wheel-drive Capri's competition career was very short even though some courageous people, Rod Chapman among them, did go on campaigning the cars with mixed success. The problems, however, were a mixture of front-driveshaft reliability and GKN's decision to pull out of the four-wheel-drive market, feeling it not to be viable (even by 1971 no mass-manufacturer had put a 4WD car into production). As a production car, the 4WD Capri called for a degree of body modifications that could not easily be incorporated into the car once it had been taken from the production line. The cost of the mechanical parts added to the body surgery would have resulted in a retail price that far outstripped its market share.

GERMAN ENTERPRISE

Within twelve months of its establishment in 1968, the German half of Ford Europe's competitions activities was ready for business, the RS2600 being the tool in their armoury with which to do battle. The RS2600 was, as discussed previously, based on the German V6 motor, and although the prototypes had been built in Averley, the car was very much the product of Neerpasch's vision of the Capri's future race programme.

Even before the RS2600 had been developed, however, Ford Germany planned to go road rallying with the Capri, and to this end two 2300GT cars were prepared for the Internationale Rallye Lyon–Charbonnières in March 1969. The cars were based on 2,293cc engines, with gas-flowed cylinder head modifications by Weslake and three twin-choke Solex carburettors. With a 10:1 compression ratio, power was stated as being 170bhp at 6,500rpm, which was sufficient to give around 130mph (209km/h). The suspension featured Bilstein dampers all round, and there were 13 × 6in Minilite wheels on the front and 13 × 7in wheels on the rear. The two cars, painted grey and silver, finished fourth and seventh – not bad for their first time out.

Neerpasch entered three cars in an event open to sports racing cars, the Tour de France. Weslake continued to work magic with the 2300 engine, which by this stage boasted fuel injection and a slightly higher compression ratio, increasing power to 192bhp at 7,200rpm. Two cars failed to finish, one with dirt in its injection system and the other spinning off the road, leaving Jean François Piot to finish in sixth place over all in the third.

The next important event was the Corsican Rally, when the 2.3-litre engine gave way to the 2.6-litre unit, again featuring fuel injection and a slightly higher compression ratio that produced around 190bhp. Local conditions called for good torque characteristics and smart acceleration off the line.

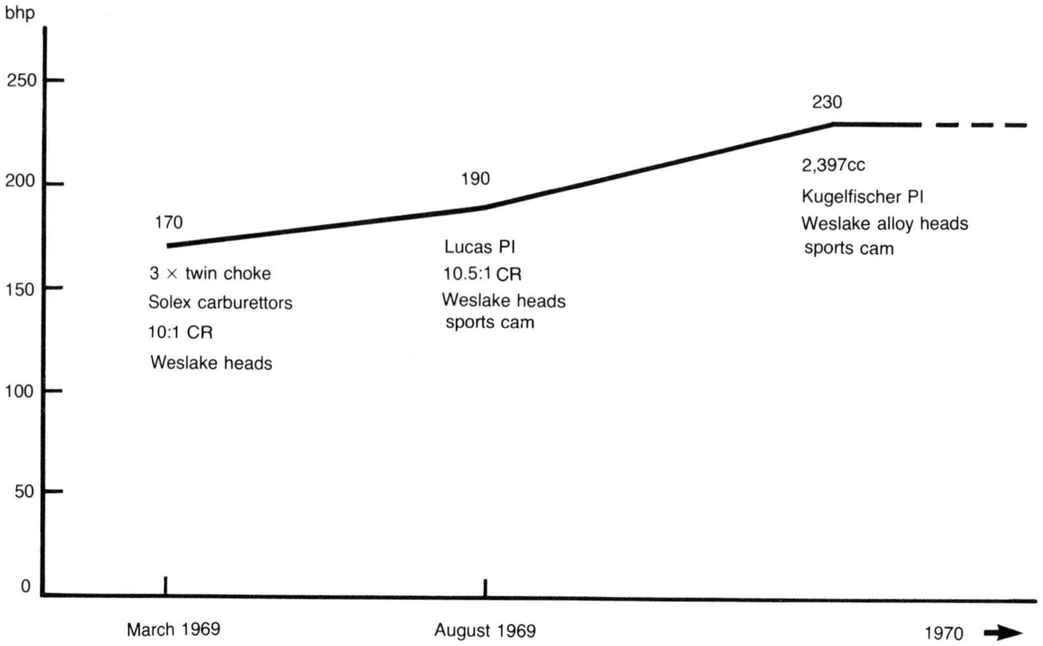

2300GT engine performance.

The car was driven by Jean François Piot and Jean Todt, and managed a creditable third overall. Of some twenty-three starts by the end of 1969 season, Capris could boast twenty-one wins, with Dieter Glemser winning the German racing championship.

Neerpasch had even bigger and better plans in store the following year, announcing that Capris would be taking part in the eleven-round European Touring Car Championship as well as the East African Safari Rally. More testing had been carried out on the 2300GT and, together with a promising pair of women drivers to boost the team, spirits were high. Walter Hayes had said 'Have what you want', and they were taking full advantage before he changed his mind!

The East African Safari Rally has always been considered the very toughest of events, while the necessary back-up support of equipment, repair vans and spotter aircraft also makes it hugely expensive. The benefits, however, are enormous, both in terms of lessons learnt and international publicity – which is why the Japanese now rate the event as being so important. After months of preparation and testing, three 2300GT Capris took off from the start line. Unfortunately, all three failed to finish – and in front of fifteen specially drafted Ford press people, too, with cameras ready! Robin Hillyar and Jock Aird suffered valve and suspension problems, Rauno Aaltonen and Peter Huth went out with engine-bearing troubles caused by a broken oil-feed pipe, and Dieter Glemser and Klaus Keiser could go no further when the gearbox/propeller shaft UJ broke. Of ninety-one entrants just nineteen finished – a measure of the Safari's ability to destroy both cars and drivers. Neerpasch's deputy, Michael Kranefus, also outlined problems with the Kugelfischer mechanical fuel-injection system which, apparently, had no altitude compensation valve, although this clearly did not affect Aaltenon, who had led the field during the early stages.

The spin-off for the German team of devoting so much time to the East African was that it resulted in precious little opportunity to make ready for the first round of the European Championship, to be held at Monza the following month. The race Capris (finished in silver and blue) had uprated brakes and suspension. The Weslake-developed engines were over-bored to 2,397cc, had Weslake-developed aluminium cylinder heads and were fitted with Kugelfischer fuel injection. Power output was rated at 300+bhp.

Three Capris were entered in the race. During the first laps it was the graceful-looking Alfa Romeos that showed the way, but gradually the Ford and BMW teams hauled them in. Ford then lost two of the Capris through ignition problems, leaving the third car to finish a very creditable second overall, a lap behind the leading Alfa Romeo – having been involved in a heavy shunt which badly damaged a door. The remainder of the European Championship, however, read like a bad dream: at the Austrian Championship none of the three Capris that were entered finished; a second place in Budapest; a fifth place in the Czechoslovakian round at Brno; a fifth place at Silverstone; and a seventh overall at Zandvoort. But the real disasters came when the Capris retired in full view of the paying public: all three went out at the prestigious six-hour race at Nürburgring, with the home crowd watching; two cars retired at Jarama; and three cars retired in the Tour de France – the list goes on. And the best results? These have to be at Monza and Budapest, with a new saloon-car record being set by Jochen Mass in the ADAC Bergpries Hill Climb Championship where he finished fourth in class, and fourth overall.

As the 1970 competition year drew to a close it was clear that something dramatic would have to be done if the Capri was to race successfully next season; too many people's reputations were on the line for it to go through another disastrous year. There would be no recriminations, nor any quick decisions that might be regretted later. The team would simply manage its way out of a problem in the manner Ford expected.

A 'wish list' was drawn up in Cologne to signpost the kind of car needed for the following year's round of racing. Key features included: an engine with a cylinder block that could be increased to 3.0 litres; the capability to produce at least 110bhp/litre reliably; and an overall fighting weight reduction to 1,984lb (900kg). By October 1970 the RS2600 had been homologated.

ASHCROFT'S ARRIVAL

The reliability problem was solved by sending over Boreham's skilled Peter Ashcroft. (Ashcroft had already gained an enviable reputation as an engineer, working his way up through the ranks; his claim to fame in 1969 was the development of the 'Ashcroft block', a technique of siamesing cylinder bores to increase capacity in engines up to 1,850cc for use in competition Escorts.) In the event, the no-nonsense engineer stayed for a full six months before he felt confident enough that things were progressing sufficiently well for him to return to Essex. Although Ashcroft spoke no German, he

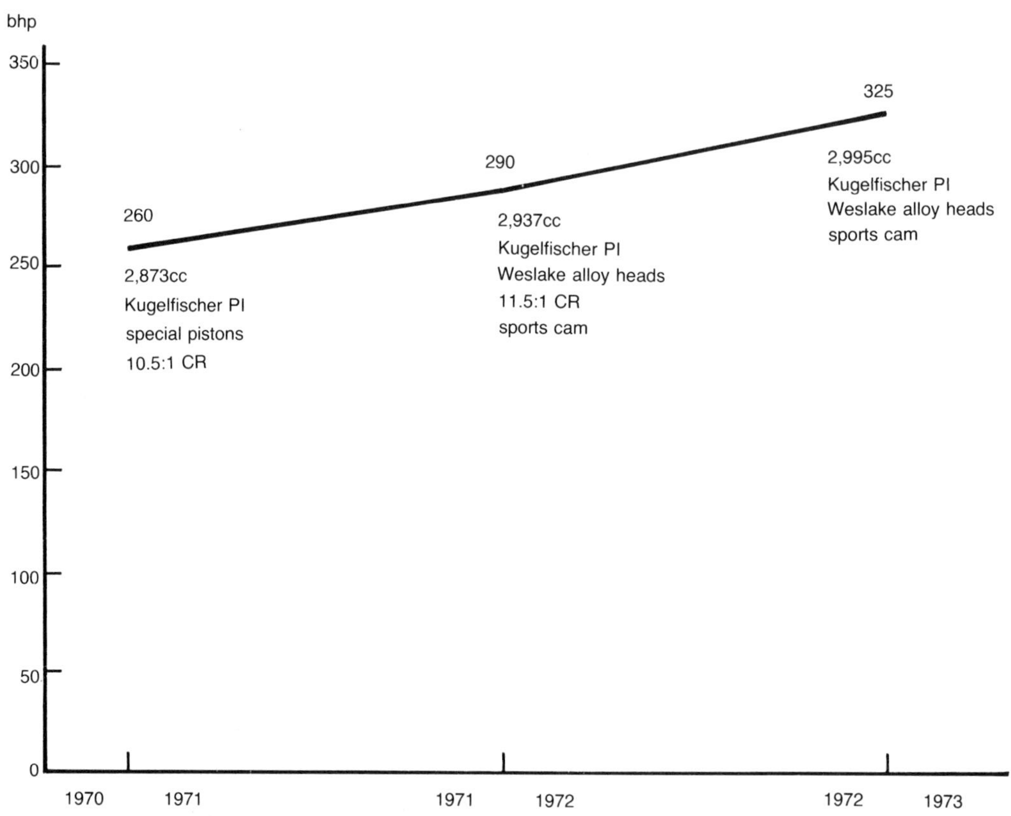

RS2600 engine performance.

managed to renew his friendship with ex-Mercedes Benz Development Engineer, Martin Braungart, whom he had met when Braungart had gone to work in the Boreham workshops. Then there was Otto Stulle, who had joined Ford from BMW and whose speciality was race-engine assembly. Unfortunately, the relationship between Stulle and Weslake Engineering was very cool, which hardly helped matters.

Upon his arrival at Cologne, Ashcroft immediately found reasons why – at least, in his opinion – the engines were proving troublesome under race conditions: the cylinder-block design allowed flexing under full load; while steel connecting rods, a new crankshaft and dry-sump lubrication were needed for reliability. But perhaps the most significant revelation was that the design of the original crankshaft throws in those sections which carried the connecting rods were arranged incorrectly, thereby resulting in unacceptable levels of vibration; under continuous high revs the engine would simply shake itself apart. Much to the amazement – and admiration – of his German colleagues, Ashcroft was happy to stretch out a hand and discuss the problem with Cosworth's Keith Duckworth on the telephone.

Ashcroft's theories over redesigning the cylinder block were totally vindicated in practice. Indeed, his ideas were incorporated into production 2.8-litre engines, the first units being fitted into federalized Capris and Mustangs, and later also into the Granada. A new steel crankshaft was produced in conjunction with Weslake, using stronger main-bearing caps to reduce flexing. A variety of pistons was also used so that compression ratios could be adapted to suit the prevailing race-circuit conditions, while bigger valves, camshaft and fuel-injection improvements, and a lighter flywheel all helped to increase power to around 280+bhp by the season's end. The engine revved safely to 7,500rpm and was more responsive.

PETER ASHCROFT

Peter was born in Walton-le-Dale, Lancashire, in 1928. Very much a Ford 'backroom boy', Peter's contribution to Ford's competition successes over the years has been considerable, totally belying his quiet, unassuming manner.

Like many people eager to start in motor sport, Ashcroft began racing in 1950 with a Cooper 500, competing in Formula 3 events. His reputation as a man with considerable expertise in engine tuning began to get round and he soon became in demand as a racing mechanic of some note. Such were his skills that he was able to earn a living from race-engine preparation, his knowledge and experience being behind many of the successful cars in the north of England during the mid-1950s.

However, it was very much a hand-to-mouth existence and in 1959 Ashcroft joined the Gilby Racing team run by the late Sid Greene, becoming the chief mechanic. During this period he contributed largely to the design and development of the 1,100cc Gilby-Climax sports racing car and later the Gilby Formula 1 car.

In 1962 Peter left the Gilby team to join Ford as a mechanic, although it was to be short-lived for he soon left to take up the post of chief engineer for the Peter Sellars Racing Team. However, only eighteen months later Peter rejoined Ford, this time as Engines Engineer and in May 1972 he was appointed Competitions Manager.

During his career with Ford, Peter's name has been linked with the design and development of the 1,950cc pushrod engines for the London–Mexico World Cup Rally, the development of the 2.9-litre V6 Capri engines and the 1.8-litre thick-wall 'Ashcroft Block' version of the legendary twin cam engine. Today, Peter Ashcroft heads up Ford's Competitions Department.

The opportunity was also taken at this time to relocate the engine so that it was lower and further back in the body. Initially, a special steel sump was fabricated and the oil tank located under a front wing, although this was later moved to the rear of the car in the interests of better weight distribution. An improved braking system called for aluminium hubs with large ventilated discs, the MacPherson suspension legs being located by a lower compression strut which prevented rearward movement of the front suspension assembly under heavy braking. At the rear there was a vestigial leaf spring, the suspension itself utilizing coil spring/damper units. The rear-hub assemblies also had to be changed to accommodate the new disc-brake units. To keep things firmly located, there were parallel arms and aluminium Watts linkages. Finally, the wheel-arches were flared to accept the increasingly wider road wheels, and a small front spoiler was added to improve aerodynamics at racing speeds.

It would have been good to relate that all this hard work paid off handsomely at the team's first time out at Monza in April 1971, but it was not to be for cylinder-head-gasket failures plagued the team right up until race day. Glemser led from the beginning and set a new class lap record, but the car's gasket gave out later and he had to retire, the other Capri suffering a broken valve spring.

In order to overcome the gasket problems, Ashcroft fitted Lechler gas-sealing rings inside the gasket wall, which were reset into the cylinder-block face. This cured the problem for good. In the Austrian race, Capris finished first, second and third, and set a new lap record. Of the seven remaining rounds of the championship, Capris won five, taking the German Touring Car Championships for drivers! What an improvement on the previous year!

FROM STRENGTH TO STRENGTH

In 1972 Capris performed even better. Improved reliability and a power output of almost 300bhp were the result of continued development by Weslake, Ashcroft and the German team. The units had been enlarged to 2,933cc and fitted with Weslake-developed alloy cylinder heads and re-profiled camshafts. Borg and Beck twin-plate clutches were called upon to transmit the power to the ZF five-speed gearbox and limited-slip final drives. Using a 3.22:1 ratio, as fitted for Le Mans, the Capri was capable of a reputable 161mph (259km/h)!

Gerry Birrell, the Scottish driver who competed in Capris for both Ford GB and Cologne. Sadly, he was killed while driving in the F2 event at Rouen.

(In fact, the rear-axle half-shafts were to stay unmodified, even when they had to handle the 600bhp Zakspeed turbo Capris.)

The suspension of these German race Capris used 15 × 10in diameter road wheels on the front and 15 × 12in on the rear (thus allowing for lower profile tyres), along with larger diameter brakes with greater space for improved cooling. The GRP lightweight doors skins, boot-lid and bonnet continued just as before, enthusiasts beginning to fit them to their road cars so that they could emulate the blue and silver racers in all but speed and verve.

The 1972 specification Capris proved more than a match for the competition, winning thirteen out of sixteen European Championship races, and finishing first overall in races including Hockenheim, Manthorp Park, Zandvoort, Nürburgring, Paul Ricard and Jarama. Birrell and Bourgoingie also managed a creditable tenth overall, with Glemser eighth overall and second in class in the arduous Le Mans 24-hour race. Such success in 1971 and 1972 had a fundamental effect in boosting the hitherto deflated egos of the competition team members in Cologne, who had been hugely saddened by the results of their Capris during that fateful year of 1970.

The only black cloud to emerge during the mid-1972 season was when both Martin Braungart and Jochen Neerpasch decided to leave Ford and join BMW. Michael Kranefus was promoted to Team Manager, replacing Neerpasch, and Gerd Knotzinger took over Kranefus's old slot. Otto Stulle moved over to FAVO, while Schutzbach was given the task of engine development. As Kranefus was to remark later, Neerpasch's decision did not endear himself to Walter Hayes, whose drive, determination and energy had sold the idea of competition to Ford's hierarchy.

Towards the end of the 1972 season, an interesting modification being developed by Weslake for Capri race engines came to light. The Rye-based company had found that the shortfall of using the same inlet manifold for both left- and right-hand cylinder banks caused fuel to spray back on partial throttle opening. Although Weslake's modification had no perceptible effect on power delivery, it did reduce fuel consumption noticeably. Weslake outlined the situation to Cologne, suggesting a workable if time-consuming cure. The notion was rejected. However, Brian Muir and John Miles did listen, making modifications to the manifolding to overcome the problems, their Wiggins Teape-backed Capri managing a second at Zandvoort. The car's second entry was at the Paul Ricard circuit, where Brian Muir set an amazing pace, overtaking double World Champion Jackie Stewart, setting a lap record of 2 minutes 13.9 seconds, and finishing first overall. The Cologne Capris came home in second and third places. The most noticeable difference between the cars, however, was the improved fuel consumption of the Muir/Miles Capri, which stopped just twice compared to the three stops made by the other two cars. Imagine the remarks! A complaint was lodged and the engine in the Wiggins Teape car was stripped for checking. That's racing for you. Capri drivers took the European, German and Belgian Championships, too.

BEATING THE COMPETITION

Kranefus and the German-based team knew that the following year, 1973, would be altogether tougher. The competition had not been idle and the other teams, especially BMW, would be putting up some sharp machinery. Ford would have to be equally clever if they were to maintain the momentum established in 1972.

In late 1972 Kranefus discussed the situation with Stewart Turner, Henry Taylor's replacement, suggesting that the way for-

MICHAEL KRANEFUS

Kranefus joined Ford in 1968 as Assistant Manager of Ford of Germany's newly formed competitions department. Within four years he was promoted to motor-sport manager, stepping into the breach upon the sudden resignation of Jochen Neerpasch, a position he would hold until he was made Ford of Europe's Motor Sport Director in 1976.

Kranefus's early years at Ford were exciting and rewarding, Capris dominating the European Touring Car scene with wins at Spa, the German Production Car Championship (which it achieved six times) and the European Touring Car Championship on three occasions. His responsibilities also included the highly successful (some might say, most successful) rally car, the Escort. The rally team was run by Peter Ashcroft, Ford winning the Rally Championship in 1979.

The job did have its down side, however, especially in 1973 when news came through that Ford was going to close FAVO, withdraw its support in the race Capri programme in Germany, and instead focus its efforts, albeit much reduced, on the Escort rally cars. For Kranefus it was a tough period.

Michael Kranefus

When Walter Hayes was invited to move to the USA by Henry Ford, he lost no time in bringing Kranefus over, too, appointing him Director of Special Vehicle Operations. Among Kranefus's many and varied tasks, he managed the development of the Ford Performance Parts programme, increasing sales from US$200,000 in 1982 to US$14 million six years on. He also controlled the Ford Motor Company's interests in motor sport – from Formula 1 to NASCAR, TransAm and drag racing.

As a youngster, Kranefus would hitch-hike from his home town of Westphalia to watch the top teams of the 1950s race at the Nürburgring, later going on to compete himself in an Escort. Never did he dream that one day he would be responsible for Ford's motor-sport interests world-wide.

ward was a new RS model with a rear spoiler sufficiently effective to overcome the rear-wheel lift problems that had caused wheel spin at Le Mans half-way through that year. Such a programme would, however, mean that some 250 cars would have to be built to comply with the homologation rules, and Kranefus needed instant solutions.

The gap left by Martin Braungart's departure was filled by Thomas Ammerschlager, who immediately set about making a comprehensive and detailed examination of the Capri's aerodynamics. Using the company's wind-tunnel facilities he evaluated wind-pattern formations around the wheelarch sections. The car, with its 12in-wide rear wheels, was found to have a drag factor of 0.45; squaring off the wheelarches and blending in the front chin spoiler so that it reached further round the car reduced this figure to just above 0.4. In order to reduce tyre and brake-disc temperatures, and to release air when the suspension was on full compression, slots were cut in either side of the wheelarches. Under the bonnet, the radiator was raked forward, creating valuable space which was filled with a new air duct that supplied fresh, cool air to the induction system. And the result of all this work? Equivalent to an all-important extra 20bhp in power at the rear wheels.

Weslake had also been hard at work with its ongoing development programme. An increase in bore size had brought the engine out to 2,995cc, while more gas-flow work on the cylinder heads, together with larger valves and a reprofiled camshaft, resulted in an engine that produced a healthy 320bhp at 7,800rpm with peak torque delivered at 7,600rpm. However, this represented the

The later 1973 version of the Ford-Weslake racing V6 tuned to produce around 320bhp developed from 2.9 litres. The unit was fitted with alloy cylinder heads and Kugelfischer fuel injection. But by this time BMW's CSLs were boasting at least 350bhp from 3.5 litres.

The 1973 season was dominated by the battle between BMW and the racing Capris. Giving away some 50bhp Jochen Mass, seen here at Silverstone, had his work cut out but managed to equal the lap record time set by Hans Joachim Stuck in the Bavarian coupé, finishing second.

virtual extent to which the engine could be tuned reliably. Weslake had achieved the goal it had been set.

The suspension system also caused some huge headaches for Ammerschlager and his team. Although monster 16in-wide wheels were tried, considerably more usual in 1973 were 12in-wide wheels at the front and 14in-wide wheels at the rear, the rim width off-sets growing ever closer to the springs and dampers. Rising rate springs were also fitted experimentally, but were only found to have a real bonus on banked tracks. The steering geometry was changed in an effort to reduce steering loads, partly brought about by those huge tyres. The real conundrum was that the increased ride stiffness which was introduced to overcome body roll when cornering resulted in the Capri lifting one wheel or, in severe conditions, even two wheels, which upset the car's delicate balance. If little progress was made during 1973 in suspension development, Ate at least carried out some beneficial work to improve braking with the use of aluminium callipers. Indeed, Ford and BMW worked to mutual advantage over suitable wheels, tyres and dampers. Significantly, BMW's CSLs – Ford's greatest rival during this period – boasted at least 40bhp more than the Cologne cars, and the in-line six-cylinder unit was enlarged from 3.2 to 3.5 litres during the 1973 season.

Safety was another area which was studied closely in Ammerschlager's programme, the team making full use of development work carried out in the States on roll-cage design and location. Starting at the front, close to the radiator, the cage ran back, picking up the front-suspension mountings and running through the cab to the rear-suspension locating points, the whole structure adding stiffness to stress points in the bodyshell. Such was the effectiveness of this new cage that Gerry Birrell stepped out from a badly dented Capri after a 160mph (257km/h) accident at the Austrian circuit, sustaining only a few bruised ribs and a lost watch! Thought had also been given to the use of fire-retardant material for the seat trim, reflecting an overall tightening-up in driver safety standards.

Ford signed up three star drivers for the 1973 season: Jackie Stewart, Jody Scheckter and Emerson Fittipaldi. While Fittipaldi never really felt happy behind the wheel of these brutes, Stewart spent much time testing with the Cologne team in an effort to perfect the car's handling.

The duel began at Monza in March, with fourteen Capris and nine BMWs appearing in the 25-car line-up on the grid. Despite leading for much of the race, the Stewart/Glemser car finally failed with a broken camshaft. Birrell and Fitzpatrick also went out with engine failure; the Mass/Scheckter car did finish, but a fan-belt replacement took up valuable time. With speeds approaching 170mph (274km/h), Stewart shared a new fastest lap time of 1 minute 38.3 seconds.

The following event was a four-hour race at the legendary Le Mans circuit, although, sadly, the Birrell/Heyer Capri failed to finish. There were further problems at both Nürburgring and Spa soon after, the latter venue seeing Jochen Mass in a Capri battle it out with Nikki Lauda in the Alpina BMW, the Capri finally retiring with a broken half-shaft. However, the next round at the Satzburgring in Austria went Ford's way, although the Birrell/Larrousse car failed to start and the disconsolate pair had to look on as Birrell and Fitzpatrick went on to a first over all in the other Capri.

Both companies fielded two entrants at the Nürburgring in early June. After a tough initial battle, the Stuck BMW went out, followed soon after by the Mass Capri with a failed main bearing bolt. So, it was left to Birrell and Fitzpatrick once more, the game Capri finishing sixth overall. Only a single Capri presence was made at the next event, Sweden's Manthorp Park, all effort instead being directed towards June's Le Mans 24-hour race where Ford would field a three-car team. Other teams were also unwilling to support the Swedish venue, this lack of competition allowing the Glemser/Mass car to go on to an unpressured win.

The Ford team at Le Mans was up against a pair of factory BMWs. By Sunday morning the Ford team had lost two cars, one through engine failure (the result of being over-revved), and the second with distributor trouble. This left the Glemser/Fitzpatrick car ahead of the remaining BMW, with things looking good. Then, just as Walter Hayes arrived with some of Ford's top executives, the sole Capri retired with crankshaft-bearing failure. Its sense of timing could not have been worse!

BMW'S BATMOBILE

It was after Le Mans that BMW pulled its master stroke. Martin Braungart had designed a boot-mounted tailplane aerofoil which had been perfected by some quick wind-tunnel testing (the same tunnel, incidentally, that Ammerschlager had used to improve the Capri's drag factor). From the outset, the BMWs proved to be markedly quicker, the new 'batmobile' wings making all the difference – especially when combined with the even more powerful Bavarian six-cylinder engine, which had been stretched to 3.5 litres!

Faced with such formidable opposition at the Nürburgring in July (BMW really had moved that quickly), the Ford team suffered major blows. First, Glemser went off the track while travelling at a reputed speed in excess of 150mph (240km/h); he suffered serious injuries and was out of racing for several months. Then Mass crashed his Capri after putting in some impressive lap times during practice. During the race itself, the Stewart/Fittipaldi car went out with an over-revved engine, showing that even the most experienced drivers could not counter the BMWs' new-found performance.

Round five of the European Championship was held at Spa. Again, the BMWs showed their form and, despite giving it their all, the Koinnigg/Heyer Capri retired with a broken rocker stud. The disease seemed to be catching, for the second Capri of Mass/Fitzpatrick also suffered the same fate, although energetic team work in the pits had the car going again on five cylinders and it rolled back on to the track, albeit noisily. Much against everyone's wildest dreams, the car finished, coming in second overall! There were, however, other serious penalties to pay during the race as a total of three divers were killed in separate incidents.

At the Zandvoort four-hour Trophy event, Ford fielded two cars. Mass drove with courage against the BMWs (which suffered from overheating tyres), until a half-shaft failure put the Capri out. This left the Fitzpatrick/Larrousse car which, despite misfiring due to ignition problems, came home third in the pack.

The seventh round was held at the Paul Ricard circuit where the dreaded timing problems emerged yet again. The Fitzpatrick/Larrousse car finished fifth on five cylinders, while the Mass/Stewart car retired with engine problems.

The end of the series saw the teams meeting at the Silverstone circuit. Ford entered three Capris, driven by Mass, Fitzpatrick and Glemser, while a fourth Capri was entered by Broadspeed and driven by Andy Rouse. It was to be a two-race day, although BMW's successes at the Paul Ricard circuit meant that the Bavarian team already had the title. In the first round Rouse went out with a broken crankshaft, while Glemser's Capri met Muir's BMW at Woodcote with the result that Glemser was disqualified. This left Mass and Fitzpatrick to finish in second and third places. Despite starting the second event with a hot engine, Jochen Mass entered into a huge battle with Quester in the BMW, the Capri of Fitzpatrick having retired with piston failure. Mass came home in second place over all and shared a lap record with Stuck of 1 minute 32.4 seconds, to round off the season.

MORE POWER

Despite the efforts of the Cologne team, many people – including Kranefus himself – were highly critical of the way the Capris had handled during the 1973 season. Ammerschlager admitted that there was a degree of rear-axle steering, and most agree that they were frightening cars to drive; indeed, it could be said that Jochen Mass achieved his results through courage, willpower and sheer brute strength alone! It was clear, however, that the team desperately needed more power as well as better handling if they were to match BMW's futuristic-looking CSLs in 1974. The answer, at least to the first half of the equation, lay in a forward-thinking decision Mike Kranefus had taken in 1972.

As already discussed, feelings over the development programme for the German-based V6 2600 engine had run high during the winter of 1972/3. The Cologne team (and Otto Stulle, in particular) thought that Weslake Engineering was struggling with its continuous development programme to extract ever-increasing power outputs and supply small batches of reliable race engines

The Cosworth tohc engine for 1974. Based on the 3.0-litre Essex engine, the cylinder head layout was designed by Chief Engineer Mike Hall. Called the GAA, the 3.4-litre engine utilized pent-roof combustion chambers and four valves per cylinder.

assembled to the same specification. The Germans needed the talents of Peter Ashcroft to rectify the quite major design snags with the 2600 motor. The solution was as radical as it was inspired: a different engine *and* a different tuner – the 3.0-litre V6 and Cosworth.

The new engine was known as the GAA (the reference given by Cosworth themselves), and work began on the first twenty-five units out of a planned 100 for the 1974 season, these all having to be built under European Saloon Car Group Regulations. However, when the Ford cylinder block was set up on the test bed it soon began to show its limitations when the power output was increased to 425bhp – hardly surprising as the casting was designed to accept only 140bhp! Under such conditions the weakest point was found to be where the main bearing bolts located into the cylinder block. Of 200 cylinder blocks checked at Ford's foundry in Dagenham, perhaps only three were suitable for racing. The long-term solution was to strengthen the block structure, which took both time and resources.

The team also looked at aerodynamics, and an opportunity to try out a Capri fitted with rear spoilers presented itself in late 1973 at Fuji in Japan. Of the two cars entered in the race, one retired through an over-revved engine while the second, driven by Glemser and Mass, went on to win on a fast track with high bankings that called for nerve and courage. A winged Capri was also driven to a first place in the Macau Grand Prix – incidentally, this was the last time a 3.0-litre RS2600 Capri was entered in a race. The rear spoilers had proved their worth.

Initial wind-tunnel testing of the RS3100 was undertaken by Ammerschlager to assess the most efficient shape for front and rear spoilers and wheelarch shapes. The result of this work revealed a Capri with a blanked-off front-grille aperture, and while a rear-mounted radiator was also tried this was later replaced by side-mounted units. The overall package produced a top speed of 170mph (274km/h) when powered by the 415bhp Cosworth engine.

The first track tests of the RS3100 took place at the Belgium Lommel circuit. The car was fitted with an 'old' Weslake engine, the colourful Toine Hezemans driving and Thomas Ammerschlager in charge of engineering. It was found that the height of the rear spoiler was critical: too much height – even an additional 2.5in (64mm) – had a detrimental effect, reducing speed to such an extent that lap times were up to 8 seconds slower!

The fully dressed GAA unit was also found to be some 25lb (11kg) heavier than the old Weslake unit, altering the weight distribution from 55/45 front to back to 57/43. The answer was to move most of the ancillaries to the rear of the car.

Development of the drivetrain resulted in

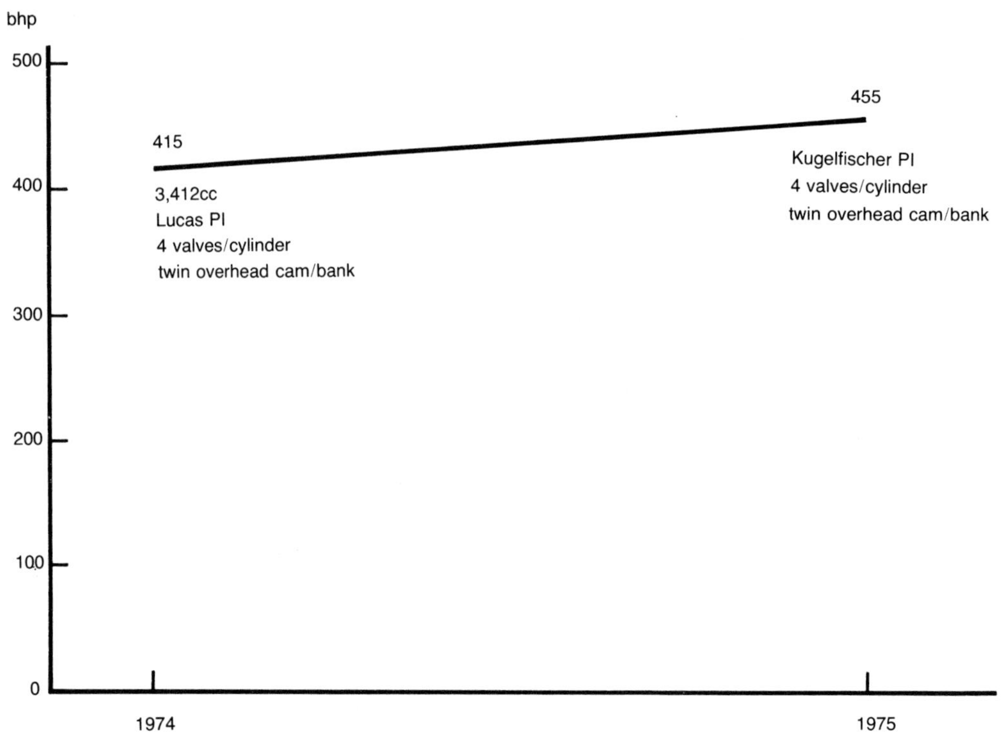

RS3100 engine performance.

the five-speed ZF gearbox being retained, but the original two-plate clutch was changed for a triple 7.2in (18.3cm) Borg and Beck unit, mounted inside a magnesium-alloy bell housing. Transmission-fluid temperatures had also come under review, both the gearbox and the differential having their own oil pumps and radiators, these being connected by aircraft-specification armoured hosing.

Criticism of the Capri's handling from many quarters, including the knowledgeable Frank Gardner of Camaro fame, led Cologne to carry out more work on suspension set-ups. New magnesium hub carriers were fitted back and front, which reduced unsprung weight and also resulted in the use of a single wheel-retaining nut, this reducing pit-stop tyre-changing times. Much of the redesign work was centred on the rear, which featured lower radius arms, an anti-roll bar and lateral watts linkage with alloy-cased Bilstein dampers. A single-leaf spring was retained, the lower spring-locating points being moved outwards as far as possible to increase roll stiffness. Later in the season titanium coil springs were substituted, although these were not found to be of any real benefit. Overall, spring rates were stiffened up markedly on those used the previous year.

Wheels, tyres and brakes were also updated and improved. Wheel diameter increased to 16in, with the front wheels 12.25in wide and the rear 15.75in wide, these fitted with 11.89in tyres and 11.5in 'boots' respectively. To stop the brute four-pot Ate callipers acted on ventilated discs all round, these powered by an electro-hydraulic assisted system which had been developed in conjunction with BMW. This design allowed brake-fluid pressure to increase to 2,352–2,499psi (160–70atm) by using an electric pump, the result being a faster-acting and more sensitive system. Significantly, this arrangement was later fitted as standard wear on the BMW 7 series road cars, proving that racing really does improve the breed! To reduce disc temperature, jets of water were fed from a washer bottle reservoir

The massive 230 × 600 15in racing tyres fitted to the front of the 1974 race season Capris hid 11.89/302mm ventilated Ate disc brakes. The rears were 11.5/292mm. The system operated a pressurized hydraulic system using an electric fuel pump, giving better speed and sensitivity than a vacuum system.

Toine Hezemans takes a photo call while testing at Lommel. An oil radiator was tried in the boot area but was found to be less effective than coolers fitted below the rear skirt. While testing the Capri was fitted with a 2.9-litre RS2600 Weslake unit.

located under the passenger's seat; it may sound primitive but it was effective in dropping the temperature of the hard-worked front discs. Finally, in terms of performance, the company claimed these Ford flyers could achieve a 0–60mph (0–97km/h) time of 4.2 seconds and a maximum gallop of 174mph (280km/h).

CUT-BACKS

On the world stage, meanwhile, reaction to the oil crisis was beginning to take effect, and the German motor industry reacted swiftly to the fuel shortage by cutting back on its labour forces. Kranefus, with his engineers and clerical support team, had already signed up drivers for 1974 when he received an order to cut the budget, initially by 10 per cent and then by a further 25 per cent just four weeks later! It was a cruel blow and dictated that the race venue list be trimmed aggressively.

It came as no surprise, therefore, when it was decided that the team would miss the first round of the European challenge due to be held at Monza, and start the season instead at the Austrian Salzburgring circuit.

The RS3100 at the Lommel test track complete with rear spoiler. For 1974 Ford's aerodynamicists had developed improved air flow by flaring in the front apron spoiler round the wheelarch while the rear 'duck tail' reduced tilt, creating a Cd of 0.375.

Here, two Capris faced a lonely BMW, yet despite the Capris' hard work the BMW still proved to be the quicker car around the track by 0.3 seconds. In the event, both Capris failed to finish through engine problems, one unit suffering from an exploding block which blasted the casing in two.

A few days later the team was out again, this time at the German Championship event at the Nürburgring. Stommelen and Hezemans managed to redress the balance, finishing first and second. Four weeks later came the Nürburgring 1,000km race, where, once again, two cars were entered. The Glemser/Hezemans Capri came home in eleventh spot (and first in class, while the Mass/Lauda car was forced to retire when a rear wheel threatened to distance itself from the rear suspension. In June Stommelen was entered in the German Championship race at Hockenheim, where, despite having tyre and spark-plug problems, he still managed a creditable second place.

Next on the calendar was the six-hour race at the Nürburgring in July, where conditions proved ideal for an all-out confrontation between the Ford and BMW teams. Lauda and Mass were second-fastest in practice, closely followed by team-mates Glemser and Hezemans. However, no sooner had the race begun than Mass was back in the pits with fuel-injection problems. Once he had finally got going it was only to have an accident, which put him out of the race. In the other car Hezemans took over from Glemser (who had established a good lead) just as the weather changed, initially managing to sustain the car's position. But things took a downward turn when the differential began to fail, and the 28-minute pit stop required to change it put the Capri well back. The car finally came home in second slot, thanks to a brilliant piece of driving by the substituted Lauda in the final laps.

Next came entries in the Diepholz and Nürburgring events, where Stommelen finished third and first respectively. By this time the combined influences of the Energy Crisis and the reduced visibility of the Ford team were taking their toll on spectator interest in the sport. However, all was not completely lost, for in the four-hour race at Zandvoort in Holland, the Capri RS3100 achieved its first victory in the European Championship since BMW had fitted its cars with the bat-like rear fins in 1973. The two-car team was made up of Hezemans/Glemser and Mass/Stommelen. After an initial duel between the Capris and Frank Gardner's V8-powered Camaro, things looked to be going Ford's way when Hezemans was knocked severely from behind by a BMW CSL. The shunt caused fuel-starvation problems, and it took the pit team six laps to locate a damaged fuel-pump connection. Hezemans never made the time up. First place went to Mass and Stommelen, the second Capri finishing a game sixth overall – reason to celebrate for sure!

In early October the factory entered a lone Capri in the European Championship round at Jarama, the car taking the chequered flag! Finally, at the South African Kyalami circuit in November, the Capri of Mass and Hezemans won the Touring Car category in the tough nine-hour event, the car being fitted with Kugelfischer fuel injection when problems were experienced with the cold-running metering unit on the more usual Lucas system.

At the year's end news began to filter through that Ford was about to close FAVO with the loss of over 200 jobs, as well as the Competitions Department at Cologne. It had been a tough decision, but Walter Hayes could not avoid the inescapable truth that racing Capris was an expensive business and that demand for FAVO-built Escorts in the UK had dwindled dramatically.

Dieter Glemser, who raced and rallied Capris between 1969 and 1974. Reckoned by critics to be an accomplished all-round driver he went on to become one of Zakspeed's team managers during the 1980s.

7 Competition Years: 1977–82

The decision to close Averley and the German Motor Sport Centre had been tough for Hayes, but in the sheer economic climate of the period it made sense. Stuart Turner, who had been put in to run FAVO on Ray Horrocks' departure, couldn't disagree, even though 200 jobs were on the line. In Germany Michael Kranefus was forced to face up to the reality that it was cheaper to build rally cars in the UK – thereby maintaining some degree of Ford competitions visibility – than to continue producing racing cars at the Cologne centre. Track Capri preparation and competition was very expensive. But all was not doom as 1974 proved to be a remarkably good year for Erich Zakowski and Team Zakspeed. The company's Escort (sponsored by Castrol and Radio Luxemburg) won the European Touring Car Championship, never losing a class contest. In stark contrast to this success, the Capri was raced only once with factory backing at Kyalami in November, where, driven by Jochen Mass and Karl Ludwig, braking and engine problems caused the car to retire.

The effect of the international Energy

In 1974, the doom year for Ford's competition activities, the Capri raced only in a limited way, scoring its first win in the European Championship at Zandvoort in August. Here two Capris in works colours compete at Salzburgring in April. Sadly both retired with broken engines.

STUART TURNER

Stuart Turner

Born in Stoke-on-Trent, Staffordshire, Turner initially wanted to be a doctor, his boyhood days spent cutting up worms and dissecting them with amateur enthusiasm. Then one day his attitude changed when whatever he was investigating oozed red blood; overnight his mind was changed and he decided upon accountancy. Then came National Service and the chance to learn Russian.

Back in 'Civvy Street', Stuart competed in his first rally in a 1937 Rover 14, commanding operations from the back seat. From then on there was no stopping him; 1956 saw him in his first RAC rally, competing as navigator (a role he was to become well known for) in – of all things – a VW Beetle. But fame really came when Turner won the Autosport's Navigator's Trophy in 1957, 1958 and 1959. However, the pinnacle of his success in those heady days was his victory in the 1960 RAC Rally with Eric Carlsson. That year also saw Turner joining the team at *Motoring News* although, in the event, it was to prove a short interlude because Marcus Chambers, who headed up BMC's Competitions Department at Abingdon, was leaving his post and looking for a replacement. He recommended Stuart Turner, who took up the job in 1961.

Under Turner's motivation, planning and determination, the Mini Coopers and their drivers became legendary. But it took its toll and in 1967 Turner decided to leave, taking a job with Castrol. However, he had only just settled in when Walter Hayes telephoned again (he had first asked Turner to join Ford while he was still with BMC, but Turner had declined), offering him a job heading up Ford's Competitions Department; so in 1969 Turner went to work for Ford.

Just over a year after taking up the job of Competitions Manager, Walter Hayes created the job of Director of Motor Sport for Ford of Europe for Turner, although his time in this job was to be short-lived. His place was taken by Mike Kranefus, allowing Turner to take up the management of the AVO factory, the Competitions Department falling under the control of Peter Ashcroft. Then, in 1975, Turner moved again, this time to head up Ford's Public Relations Department. He retired in late 1991.

Crisis had a dramatic effect on the world stage of motor sport, although Zakspeed Escorts dominated the all-important German national racing championships throughout 1975, despite the fact that many events were cancelled. Initially supplied with parts from Broadspeed and engines from Brian Hart, Zakspeed's owner, Erich Zakowski (a German of Prussian descent), was forced to become more self-reliant on components made in house for his race team. The result of this was that Zakspeed became less successful; the middle of 1976 the team's cars had not completed a single race and, faced with huge rebuilding costs, withdrew from competition. However, the company battled on, and within two years it had developed a replacement for the Escort, a mean, dramatic-looking machine which was entered in the highly modified class of German Group 5 racing to good effect. This much lower and wider car looked like a Mk III Capri – just!

The background to Zakspeed's car can be traced back to work carried out on interior roll-cage development for the last of the 'big-banger' Capris, the 3.4-litre cars. The cage consisted of much more than just a loop of steel over the driver's head and was instead designed as an integral part of the body monocoque, the principle using a tubular structure which located on to all four suspension mounting points. The Group 5 Capri simply took this idea further. A complete body/chassis framework was created using 260ft (80m) of aluminium tubing of 40mm and 30mm diameter, with lengths of square-section tubing for chassis rails at the base of the framework. The whole spider's web weighed just 154lb (70kg). Aluminium was used for the floorpan, while vestigial metal sections from the Mk III Capri bodyshell were located around the main cockpit area, roof panel and rear sections to maintain a certain Capri-like appearance in silhouette.

KEVLAR CAR

The remainder of the body of Zakspeed's car was formed from Kevlar 49, a lightweight compound that was a compromise between GRP and Kevlar, and that was 45 per cent lighter than equivalent metal, panel for panel. Areas subjected to stress loads were made up as sandwiches consisting of Nomex paper bonded between two skins of Kevlar! The material was used for the detachable bonnet, front and rear wings, doors and front spoiler. The rear aerofoil angle was made adjustable and located on to the rear body above the tailgate, which allowed access to the myriad pumps and tanks for fuel, lubrication and the automatic fire-extinguisher system. Four electric fuel pumps were connected to a 22-gallon (100-litre) plastic tank, located ahead of the racing Escort's rear axle.

The front suspension utilized fabricated wide-angle wishbones to locate with the MacPherson struts, with alloy-cased Bilstein dampers and very stiff coil springs to handle the added downforce pressure. The rear axle was a Ford steel unit (to take the additional horsepower), featuring a ZF limited-slip differential with 90 per cent locking efficiency that was kept in place by parallel trailing links and alloy-cased Bilstein dampers, and a watts linkage. The hub carriers, which were designed to be interchangeable front to back, were made of aluminium. Brakes were Porsche units from the 917 race programme, using twin Girling callipers on the front that were cross-drilled and radially ventilated. Wheels were 16in diameter BBS alloys, 12.5in wide at the front and 15.75in wide at the rear. Initially the complete car weighed 1,716lb (778kg), which was 99lb (50kg) above the regulated weight, but further development reduced this to within the stated limits.

For competition in the 2.0-litre class, Zakspeed decided on the 1,427cc turbo-

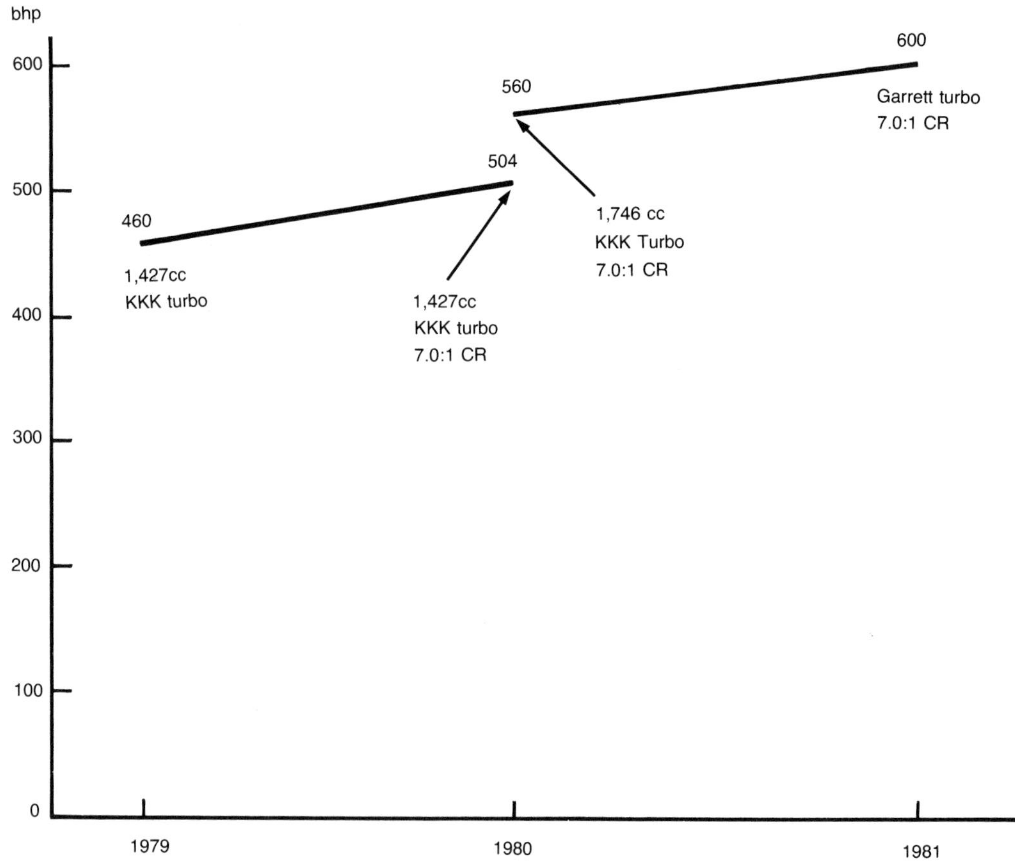

BDA engine performance.

charged version of Cosworth's 80.0 × 71.0mm BDA engine. By using the standard multiplication factor of 1.4:1, this engine had a capacity equivalent to 1,997cc, the unit producing a reputedly safe and reliable 380bhp at 9,000rpm. Both fuel injection and transistorized ignition were supplied by Bosch. Oil jets directed toward the inside surfaces of the pistons helped reduce the build-up of heat. The first batch of engines was assembled from 'kits' supplied direct from Cosworth, and were tested on new Schenk engine dynometers fitted in the Zakspeed workshops.

To align with the power and torque curves of the BDA engine, a Getrag five-speed gearbox that utilized ratios different to standard was used and located 1.6in (40mm) further rearward in the chassis, this calling for a deeper bell housing and modified input shaft. Drive was taken from a twin-plate Borg and Beck clutch to a single one-piece prop shaft.

Cooling for engine, gearbox and rear-axle oils was provided by Citroën radiators located in the convex curvature of the body ahead of the rear wheels. Maurice Gomm, a name long associated with motor sport and one-off prototype work, was responsible for fabricating the alloy tank for the dry sump lubrication. Finally, a special exhaust system was assembled from chrome-nickel alloy pipes, capable of handling the enormous heat generated by a turbo engine at maximum power.

The engineer Thomas Ammerschlager had stayed on at Zakspeed's Niederzissen headquarters after the demise of the Cosworth GAA-engined Capri series. He spent a lot of time using the wind-tunnel facilities at Aachen Technical High School, perfecting the overall shape of the latest generation of racers using a one-fifth scale model. The result was impressive. Development of the overhang of the front wing section created the desired downward effect at speed, balancing the high tail-down effect of the rear aerofoil and thereby creating a 50 per cent increase in downforce action overall! Matched against the 3.4-litre Cosworth-engined Capri, the Zakspeed creation comfortably circled the world-renowned Nürburgring in 7 minutes 44 seconds, an improvement of 25 seconds over the speeds of Capris four years earlier.

Initial tests on the car revealed problems with the mechanics: a piston failure due to machining problems; a broken Cosworth camshaft (unheard of in racing circles); and breakages in the distributor drive – all of which gave rise to concerns over the engine's reliability. However, concentrated effort throughout the remainder of the year cured these early teething troubles. The car made its race début at the German Grand Prix weekend at the Hockenheim stadium in late July 1978, and was driven by Hans Heyer. Although it failed to win, its performance was sufficient to demonstrate that the team at last had a car which would take over from the earlier Capris and Escorts in a bid to outstrip the all-conquering BMW 320 turbos.

The Capri of Hezemans and Glemser at the Salzburgring (the second car was driven by Mass and Lauda). The additional rear body skirt hides oil radiators doing their best to cool the lubricants in the gearbox, differential and the all-new Cosworth engine.

The extra-wide BBS 19 × 13in alloy wheels fitted to the 1978 1.4-litre Zakspeed racer. Behind the body panel lies a Citroën radiator (duplicated on the opposite side of the car), while inside the wheelarch are radiators for the gearbox and final drive lubricant.

PUT TO THE TEST

A move into new premises at Niederzissen near the Nürburgring circuit in 1977 gave Zakspeed the capacity and the capability to build small production runs of special Fords (which would include the Zakspeed Turbo Capris in 1981–2); it also helped boost the company's relationship with Ford Germany. Moreover, as the Capri Turbo race programme got under way, it gave Erich Zakowski the confidence to enter a 1.5-litre car at Hockenheim in September 1979 against the invincible Porsche 935 twin

The 1.4-litre Zakspeed Silhouette racer in the workshops. On the shelf, just visible through the rear spoiler, is the model used for wind tunnel testing. The German team spent considerable time using the wind tunnel equipment at Aachen Technical College developing the most aerodynamic shape.

turbos. The circuit is renowned for its long, straight sections where sustained high-speed running capabilities are of paramount importance. The car, driven by Hans Heyer, finished third over all, despite some problems.

As the 1979 season drew to a close it was clear that team Zakspeed had undertaken a continued development programme on the little BDA engine to increase its horsepower. One dial inside the cabin allowed the driver to select the desired turbo-charger boost of 14.5–22psi (1.0–1.5 bar), while another control adjusted front/rear brake balance. But the main difference over the previous year was to use a KKK turbo unit that was one size larger, along with a Garrett AiResearch blow-off valve reset to a higher pressure. Two huge intercooler radiators were mounted side by side in the nose section to reduce charged air temperatures, these feeding into the Kugelfischer fuel-injection system. This, too, had been the subject of continuous improvement, uprated

Engine bay of the Silhouette racer clearly showing the tubular body/chassis structure on to which was fitted the Kevlar body sandwich panels. With its KKK turbo-charger unit, the 1.4-litre Cosworth-based BDA engine produced a healthy 460bhp at 9,000rpm, sufficient to give the car a top speed of 174mph (280km/h).

ZAKSPEED TURBO CAPRI (GROUP 5)

LAYOUT AND CHASSIS
Alloy tube structure with alloy sheet floorpan bonded to body 'birdcage'. Kevlar 49 body panels. Stress body panels made from Nomex paper bonded between Kevlar 49 – reinforced skins

ENGINE

Type	Based on Cosworth BDA
Block material	Cast iron
Cylinders	V6
Bore and stroke	80 × 71mm
Capacity	1,427cc
Valves	ohv
Carburettor	Bosch Kugelfischer fuel injection
Max. power	380bhp @ 9,000rpm
Max. torque	438lb/ft @ 7,600rpm

TRANSMISSION

Gearbox	5-speed Getrag (mounted 15.8in to standard with special elongated alloy bellhousing)
Final drive	ZF differential with 90% limited slip

SUSPENSION AND STEERING

Front	Alloy wishbones. Cast magnesium hub carrier. Titanium concentric coil springs. Alloy Bilstein gas-filled dampers. Cast steel stub axle and damper tube.
Rear	Alloy rear axle casing (1980+ spec), radius locating arms and Watts linkage. Alloy Bilstein gas-filled dampers. Titanium concentric coil springs
Tyres	Goodyear 10.0/225 × 16 (front); 12.5/225 × 19 (rear)
Wheels	BBS-type alloy wheels, 10.5 × 16in (front) and 13 × 19in (rear)
Rim width	10.5in (front); 13in (rear)

BRAKES

Type	Ate discs all round with provision for water cooling. Fully ventilated and cross drilled. Twin pot callipers in front, single pot at rear.
Size	11.9in

PERFORMANCE

Top speed	174mph+ (280km/h), depending on rear axle ratio

cams being fitted to the metering unit to keep pace with the increase in power, which at this stage was reckoned to be 450–460bhp at 9,000rpm. Other changes included a move to steel wheel hubs with magnesium carriers, together with a strengthened lightweight alloy rear axle. Also, the front brakes were changed to the single-calliper Ate-type with four-pot callipers. The culmination of all this development was the Zakspeed car winning the smallest class of the German Championship.

It was in 1980 that a 87.4 × 72.75mm 1.74-litre version of the Cosworth BDA unit was introduced, Zakspeed then being able to race its Capris in the 'big car' class (using the turbo multiplication factor, the unit had an equivalent of 2,443cc). On a boost level of 22psi (1.5bar), the engine started the season producing 560bhp. No alterations were considered necessary to the chassis/monocoque to handle this additional power, although changes to the shape of the rear of the body were made. Experiments were also carried out during the season using ground-effect techniques. Three cars were built during the winter of 1979/80, by which time the 1.4-litre machines had notched up a respectable twelve pole positions and nine wins from fourteen race entries.

For the 1980 season it was planned that the 1.4- and 1.7-litre cars would enter the thirteen-round German Championship series starting in March and finishing in September. Karl Ludwig won at Hockenheim in April in the 1.7-litre car, marking the Capri's first outright win in Group 5. The victory was not without incident, however, as Ludwig managed to collide with the leading Porsche 935 during a risky overtaking manoeuvre, yet still crossed the line ahead! By September the team had notched up a total of six wins, but Ludwig was stripped of his points from the first two events as these were shrouded in controversy over the size and shape of the Ammerschlager-designed rear wing.

The 1980 1.4-litre car in its multi-blue D&W Auto Sport livery. By the winter of 1979/80 the 1.4-litre engined car had notched up nine wins and twelve pole positions from a total of fourteen race entries.

The Miller Lite-sponsored IMSA Mustang in 1980. Water Hayes invited Michael Kranefus to join him in the States, appointing him as Competitions Manager. The Mustangs used the Capri-type multi-tube body/chassis unit built by team Zakspeed in Germany.

During mid-season the 1.7-litre engine was comfortably delivering a shattering 600bhp. Experiments had been carried out on the dynometer, fitting twin KKK turbos to both the 1.4-and the 1.7-litre engines, but with no improvement. Indeed, the only difference between the two engines was the size of the turbocharger itself, the bigger unit rating a turbo one size larger. Also there were minor differences introduced in the specifications for the Getrag gearboxes. A measure of how the 1.7-litre car was performing by this stage can be gauged from a timed lap at Nürburgring: 7 minutes 33.2 seconds, compared to 8 minutes 9 seconds for a 450bhp Capri in 1974 – now that's what I call progress!

After the decision was made to ban the big rear wing from racing, Ammerschlager quickly developed a new design to improve the car's ground-effect performance. Following modification to the chassis monocoque and body panels, a funnel was installed which started at the bulkhead section, gradually broadening out under the passenger's footwell to emerge, full width, at the rear of the car. Fixed skirts were also employed which, despite losing effect as the race progressed and the skirts were chafed away, still proved beneficial at the start. These Zakspeed/Ford racers were extremely fast, almost delicate machines which proved that the team could successfully remain at the forefront of racing technology. Sadly, they would have just one more year in Group 5 before things changed yet again.

In 1981 the 1.4-litre Capri Silhouette was showing 500+bhp on the dynometer. The team comprised Niedzwiedz, Hammelmann and Ludwig, joined by ex-ATS Grand Prix team driver, Manfred Winkelhock, who would campaign the bigger engined 1.7-litre car. Weighing some 37lb (17kg) less than the cars of the previous year, these exciting machines boasted 600bhp from the BDA-derived engine, the ground-effect aerodynamics no longer being the add-on feature of 1980 but instead an integral part of the monocoque. Again, a measure of the increasing performance of these cars can be gained from the lap times captured at the Nürburgring, Winkelhock managing 7 minutes 22.4 seconds only eighteen months after Ludwig's flying circuit. In May Winkelhock did even better, returning an impressive 7 minutes 18.4 seconds while practising for the Nürburgring 1,000km race; unfortunately, however, the strain proved too much and the car never made the start grid. A memorable finale to the German Championship came as Ludwig, in one of two 1.4-litre racers, took the over-all title, having achieved a commendable four victories from four starts during the season. Winkelhock, meanwhile, finished third over all.

Towards the end of the season Ford Germany outlined its plans to Erich Zakowski, explaining that since the German Championship would shift emphasis to Group C, Zakspeed were to support a C100 racer driven by Klaus Ludgwig in both German and World Championship events. However, while Zakspeed's priority was firmly directed towards the new car, the Capri Silhouette coupé continued to make appearances, driven by Klaus Niedzweidz. It was powered by the Cosworth-developed aluminium BDT engine, which was being evaluated for the exciting Escort RS1700T saloon back at Boreham.

An invitation from Henry Ford II to Walter Hayes to take up a post in the USA at this time was accepted with alacrity. No sooner had Hayes become established than he arranged for Michael Kranefus to be brought over to take on the awesome task of managing Ford's motor-sport programme world-wide. The job also demanded that Kranefus become Managing Director of SVO (Special Vehicle Operations), Ford US's equivalent of SVE (Special Vehicle Engineering) in the UK.

SILHOUETTE STATESIDE

With Miller Lite Beer sponsorship, Zakspeed took their talents to Detroit to help develop a Mustang racer, which in reality was little more than a rebodied Capri Silhouette, retaining the ground-effects principle so successfully developed in Germany. The car featured the same engine specification, albeit with a Garrett AiResearch turbo in place of the Michael May-influenced KKK unit. Power output was not affected, the unit continuing to develop a healthy 600bhp, but the rear wheels were changed to 16 × 14.5in in recognition of the more serpentine US circuits. The Zakspeed Capri won in fine fashion at Brainerd Raceway on its fifth outing, beating the Porsche 935 of John Fitzpatrick.

'When I went to work in Detroit in 1979 I said Ford US should go back into motor sport,' Hayes remarked candidly. 'To which Henry Ford simply said, "Do what you think". So I arranged that Erick Zakowski build me a Mustang with a Capri underbody, and that started Ford US back into motor racing.'

Kranefus organized a quite impressive shopping list of Ford entries into motorsport activities in the States, from circuit racing to NASCA, stock eventism and drag racing. To compliment the work being done by Rod Mansfield at Ford UK's SVE, SVO developed its own uprated version of the Mustang, which had clearly benefited in promotion terms from Zakspeed's racing activities – a 2.3-litre Mustang Turbo.

Meanwhile, Bob Lutz had been appointed Chairman of Ford Europe, and he in turn promoted author and PR expert, Karl Ludvigsen, to head up its Public Affairs Department. The task of this highly desirable job included handling Ford's European motorsport activities. By 1983, however, Lutz had gone to the States, and Ludvigsen had also left; Walter Hayes was back! Stuart Turner, the loyal and professional motor-sport expert, was quickly hoisted aboard to sort things out. Within weeks he had announced the demise of the Group C C100 sports car

FORD CAPRI ZAKSPEED TURBO (1981)	
LAYOUT AND CHASSIS	
Two-door coupé/monocoque construction	
ENGINE	
Type	Cologne
Block material	Cast iron
Head material	Cast iron
Cylinders	V6
Cooling	n/a
Bore and stroke	93.0 × 68.5mm
Capacity	2,792cc
Valves	ohv
Compression ratio	9.2:1
Carburettor	Solex Garrett AiResearch turbo-charger
Max. power	188bhp @ 5,500rpm
Max. torque	206lb/ft @ 4,500rpm
Fuel capacity	12.8 gallons (58 litres)
TRANSMISSION	
Gearbox	4-speed
Ratios	3.163:1, 1.95:1, 1.412:1, 1.00:1
Final drive	3.09:1
SUSPENSION AND STEERING	
Front	MacPherson struts
Rear	Semi-elliptic springs
Steering	Rack and pinion
Tyres	235/60 VR × 13
Wheels	Steel
Rim width	6.5in
BRAKES	
Type	Hydraulic disc/drum
Size	10.36in ventilated disc, 9.0in drum
DIMENSIONS (in/mm)	
Track: front	53/1,346
rear	54/1,372
Wheelbase	99/2,515
Overall length	171/4,343
Overall width	67/1,702
Overall height	51/1,295
Unladen weight	2,644lb/1,199kg
PERFORMANCE	
Top speed	133mph (214km/h)
0–62mph	8.0sec

A 3-litre Cosworth DFV V8 engine fitted into the Capri of Colin Hawker. Introduced in 1967, this was Cosworth's first ever F1 engine featuring four valves/cylinder and the first Cosworth-designed cylinder block.

Interior of the Cosworth DFV-engined Capri showing the large transmission tunnel necessary to cover the ZF gearbox, which is mounted well back in the chassis frame.

and the Escort 1700T rally car. Sometimes managers have to make tough decisions.

Now without Ford backing, Zakowski signed a sponsorship deal with West Cigarettes, realizing his life's ambition to enter F1. The single-seater was powered by the same Cosworth-based 1.5-litre engine used in the Capri Silhouette racers. Despite shunts and heartaches through the 1985–6 season, the car began to prove its worth. Then, just as things were looking good, Zakowski was entrusted with running the BMW Formula Junior M3 racing team for 1987. By then, the Capri had reached the end of its production life.

BRITISH SUCCESS

The Capri's racing career in Britain took on a much lower, mainly private entry, profile, Ford's directive to Boreham being to develop the Escort for international rallying where, arguably, it became the most successful rally car ever. In those days (the late 1960s and early 1970s) interest at home focused on international events, such as the Monte Carlo and East African Safari rallies, in which the name of Roger Clark and the Escort became synonymous. As we have seen, Walter Hayes and Ford's management were happy to let the Germans concentrate on radically modified track cars, since Capris were sold abroad (so they said) on racing results.

One of the earliest British Group II enthusiasts to campaign a Capri was Holman Blackburn, whose family owned a garage in Chiddingfold, Surrey. He started in 1970 with a 3000GT, the car being powered by a 180bhp engine tuned by Weslake, with modified suspension and 7in Minilite alloy wheels. Not content with simply limiting his activities to the UK, Blackburn entered the car in the Spa 24-hour race and in two races at the Nürburgring, one an 86-hour event, and the other lasting 36 hours. In both of the Nürburgring races he finished first in class, while at Spa he came home nineteenth overall, coming home seventh and fourth at the two 'ring' events, where he also achieved fastest lap during the second time out. In the same year Ford held the first of its celebrity races for Capri 3000GTs at Brands Hatch, an event that was to be repeated in 1972.

Although 1971 did not prove to be a good year for Blackburn, the following year he campaigned a new car to better effect. Powered by a 3.1-litre engine modified by Mathwall and fitted with triple carburettors, the car produced around 260bhp. The result was pretty competitive, with Blackburn gaining a class win at Thruxton. At Zandvoort he came home sixth over all in the European Championship event, and later in the season he was fifth on home soil at Silverstone.

It was also in 1972 that Group I production saloon-car racing was started, well-known racing names – Dave Matthews and Dave Brodie – taking part in Ford-supplied Capris. These cars were fitted with slightly modified engines tuned by Broadspeed and Racing Services, which produced around 160bhp each. Both featured lowered suspension, and 5.5in-wide (14cm-wide) wheels fitted with low-profile tyres and much-needed limited-slip differentials to take care of the handling. The highly experienced drivers gave the crowds their money's worth, winning eight victories each, though sadly this was not sufficient to win the Championship. Soon, however, the Capris would be overshadowed by the grumble of the 5.7-litre V8-engined Chevrolet Camaros!

In the background, meanwhile, rallying exponent Peter Browning of the BRSCC (British Racing Sports Car Club) was hatching a new idea: the Avon Motor Tour of Britain. Ford decided to enter the event with Capris! Homologation for the Capri had been granted in April 1970 and covered the basic specification for production-assembly tolerances, sufficient to allow for blueprinting the engine. Later amendments included the use of rear disc brakes and a five-speed ZF-type gearbox, suitable for Group II saloon-car racing. Changes to the car's production specification made the following year were reflected through to homologation, which included an increase in cylinder-tract diameters, compression ratio changes, a 3.09:1 final drive, a change in second gear ratio and a revised camshaft timing. By mid-1972 a limited-slip differential, 5.5in-wide wheels and lower export specification suspension had been added to the list. The face-lift Capri was then homologated in July 1973, the month the Tour of Britain event was scheduled to take place.

Ford entered three cars driven by Roger Clark, Prince Michael of Kent and Dave Matthews. There were private entrants, too, Gordon Spice and Adrian Boyd among them. Clark suffered a seat failure, of all things, during the first section, and later a distributor-drive breakage which put him back to twenty-fourth place over all. Matthews, meanwhile, managed a creditable fifth place, Prince Michael coming home sixteenth. In fact, the privateers did rather better: Spice came in second, having spun almost at the end to kill a very possible first position; Boyd managed fourth; Blackburn seventh; Mike Crabtree eighth; and Andy Dawson came home tenth. And the winner? A certain James Hunt in a 5.7-litre Chevrolet Camaro! The Capri campaigned by Prince Michael of Kent was then sent off to Spa for the 24-hour event, where it finished thirteenth over all with drivers Nigel Clarkson and knowledgeable Ford author, Jeremy Walton. The car was then passed on to Tom Walkinshaw, who used it in Group I saloon events. Walkinshaw spent the season battling against an Opel Commodore GS/E 2.8 and the BMW 3.0CSi of Tony Lanfranchi, coming out as the winner of the Championship.

Ford UK's last involvement with the Capri in racing was to prepare two cars for the Spa 24-hour event in July 1974. Built at Boreham, the Capri IIs complied with the newly introduced Group 'one and three quarter' rules. These precluded radical body and engine alterations, and were the result of some nasty accidents that had taken place at Spa during the previous two years involving Group II cars. The first of the two cars was driven by Tom Walkinshaw and John Fitzpatrick, sponsored by Shellsport and finished in black. The second car, sponsored by BP Belgium and finished in yellow, was driven by Claude Bourgiognie and Yvette Fontaine, but sadly failed to finish. The Shellsport Capri took the lead at the beginning, before being overtaken by a Belgian-entered Mustang. The Walkinshaw/ Fitzpatrick car went in front again until trouble hit, the exhaust system causing a 26-minute recess in the pits for welding repairs. Unfortunately, the car's time back on the track was short-lived, for a half-shaft failure soon after put it out of the event.

A futuristic-looking all-black Capri II GT was built for Dave Brodie to take on the likes of GM's Australian V8-powered Firenzas and Ventoras in club events during 1974. The lightened body frame featured huge GRP wings. The car, powered by a 3.0-litre Weslake-tuned engine which was later replaced by a 3.4-litre Cosworth unit, made various outings during the season, but its performance never lived up to its spectacular appearance. At one point the car was taken over to Ford's Research Centre at Dunton so that the styling engineers could take a close look. Soon after, in the spring of 1975, the Capri II S was launched – and surprise, surprise, its appearance emulated that of Brodie's bruiser.

Meanwhile, Blackburn, the Chiddingfold-based Capri exponent, was also persisting with the Dagenham coupé, an outing at Spa in a triple-carburettor car with co-driver

Dave Brodie's black brute Capri racer based on a Mk II GT. The car was raced with a 3.0-litre Weslake engine and later a 3.4-litre Cosworth unit, taking on the V8-powered Vauxhall Firenzas and Ventoras. Sadly, it never performed the way its looks suggested.

The rear GRP section of Brodie's club racer removed to show the suspension and chassis layout. The car was later taken to Ford's Research Centre at Dunton. Clearly, the all-black finish must have made its impression, for the following year Ford introduced the Midnight Capri S type!

Ford UK's last involvement with the Capri in racing. One of two Mk II racers being prepared at Boreham for the Spa 24-hour event. Under the wide arches would go Minilite alloy wheels. This car was sponsored by Shell and driven by Tom Walkinshaw and John Fitzpatrick.

The second of the two Spa cars was finished in yellow. Sponsored by BP Belgium it was driven by Claude Bourgoignie and Yvette Fontain. The BP car began suffering troubles almost from the start and failed to finish while the Shell Capri went on gallantly – despite a long pit stop to repair the exhaust manifolds – until a broken half-shaft forced retirement.

Tom Walkinshaw fielding the GRP 1 Capri at Silverstone. Fitted with Bilstein suspension and a 175bhp tuned motor the car competed successfully against BMW 3.0CSi coupés and Opel Commodres GS/E 2.8s throughout the 1974 season to emerge class champion.

Mike Crabtree ending in failure as the engine expired when the car was leading the pack. Luckily, a sponsorship link with Hermetite, the engine-sealant specialists, was set up in 1973. Blackburn's improved financial status allowed him to buy the 1974 Capris raced by Walkinshaw and Bourgoigne at Spa, which he entered at the 1975 Coupe l'Avenir races with Crabtree, Walkinshaw and Fitzpatrick. Walkinshaw managed a lap record and two wins during the season, as well as a rather nasty shunt at Monza. Blackburn, meanwhile, came home in third place in the Spa 24-hour race. Walkinshaw then took over one of the two Capris and converted it for the following year's events, where he took on the likes of Andy Rouse in a Dolomite and Gordon Spice, also in a Capri.

Blackburn continued his development, going on to use fuel injection, water cooling for the braking system and 15in wheels. He travelled as far afield as South Africa to race and was still competing in 1980 with a Mk III Capri.

Gordon Spice got his just rewards when he won the 1978 Spa 24-hour race, the fast 8-mile (13km) road-circuit event of speed tests and endurance. It was a magnificent achievement for the well-known Capri connoisseur.

Gordon Spice, one of the most famous of all Capri campaigners, leads the field at Silverstone in 1977. Between 1975 and 1980 Spice was consistently better than perhaps any other Capri driver. Following several near misses he won the last ever Spa 24 Hours event in 1978.

Behind him (and a number of other Capri stalwarts) was the engine-preparation experience of Bourne-based Neil Brown (the same Bourne as of BRM fame), as well as Peter Clark and Dave Cook of CC Racing, based at Kirbymoorside in Yorkshire.

CAPRIS AT CROFT

In May 1978 the well-respected road tester and journalist John Miles spent a day testing with Gordon Spice and fellow Capri campaigner Chris Craft, the two having joined forces for the year under the sponsorship of *Autocar* magazine. Spice, who had been a loyal Capri driver for the previous five years, had invited the intrepid Miles to the windswept Croft circuit (the scene of Clark's famous début in the four-wheel-drive Capri) to witness the effects of trying out different suspension settings on the team's modified S-type 3.0-litre cars.

Even in 1978 it would have cost some £8,000 – and 500 man-hours – to turn the 3.0-litre S Capri into full race trim of RAC Group 1.5, capable of knocking some 20 seconds off the Croft lap times using a standard car. Engine modifications, which were limited, allowed for polishing the cylinder heads and fitting larger valves. A new camshaft was ground from a raw casting with

Holman 'Les' Blackburn in his radically modified Capri II at Brands Hatch in 1978. Blackburn's long association with racing Capris clearly helped in promoting his Chiddingfold-based Ford dealership. He went on to campaign a Mk III, too.

That man Spice again, this time in a Mk III car in 1979, prepared by the talented CC Racing of Kerbymoorside. At that time a similar modified Capri would have cost £16,000, together with another £3,000, without taxes, for engine tuning, which accounted for 550 man-hours.

specific lift and timing, special pistons gave an 11.0:1 compression ratio, and a 32mm 'high-altitude' twin choke carburettor was fitted. In this trim the engine was reckoned to produce around 220bhp at 6,500–7,000rpm.

The cars were set up very much as Craft and Spice preferred, and Miles found there were considerable handling differences between the two. He seemed more confident in Spice's multi-race winner, with its heavy steering yet softer rear springs, than in Craft's Capri as he found it easier to brake turning into a corner in Spice's car. After a day's testing – during which springs and anti-roll bars were changed frequently to achieve the best results – Craft and Spice managed a few 1 minute 15 second laps, two seconds faster than a Group I Capri had lapped Croft before. And Miles' final comment? He couldn't understand how the 32mm carburettors managed to consume fuel at the rate of 7mpg (40l/100km)!

CAPRI VERSUS ROVER

In 1980 sporting Capris found themselves up against Rover's new David Bache-designed Rover SDI in Group I. You may think that the Rover would not form the most elegant or ideal basis for a race saloon, but it did have the obvious advantage of a GM-based V8 engine which offered considerable opportunities for tuning. Indeed, even in 1980 the engine had been around for so long that there was plenty of knowledge available on how to extract quite indecent volumes of power effectively. As for the Capri, Neil Brown's 1980 specification V6s were producing around 255bhp at 7,000rpm.

Rover gave the contract for preparing and racing its huge hatchback to David Price Formula Racing. Although initial outings did not outstrip Ford's sporting coupé as some observers had predicted, Rovers did beat the Capris at Silverstone, where they were entered in the saloon-car race which supported the prestigious British Grand Prix. By way of compensation, however, Gordon Spice won the Capri's class title for that year.

Tom Walkinshaw Racing had been busy developing the Rover's suspension during that first year's racing, so Austin-Rover decided to move its Group I competition contract in 1981 to TWR's Oxfordshire-based operation, which would field a two-car team. In the Capri camp eleven cars began the season, the drivers including Andy Rouse, Jonathan Buncombe, Stuart Graham, Gordon Spice and Vince Woodman. It was perhaps not the most organized of seasons, with Rouse and Spice in opposition rather than in combination, while lack of cash in the CC Racing/Vince Woodman/Jonathan Buncombe alliance restricted Buncombe to only five events. Both Rovers and Capris managed pole positions on three occasions, the Capris coming home first four times in a row, twice with Rouse at the wheel. Then it was the turn of the SDIs, which saw the winner's flag on five consecutive occasions and took two class positions. It was that sort of year. However, the pundits were saying that the Capri's racing days were over.

Neil Brown was able to extract even more power from the 60-degree V6s for the 1982 season, adding a further 10bhp to his 1980 specification with the addition of the Weber 481DA carburettor. Spice and Rouse teamed up to make the best of their abilities, while Vince Woodman continued to use CC Racing for preparing his Capri. The Rover team had the benefit of extra horsepower (around 285–90bhp), yet this bonus was largely offset by the bigger body and added weight penalty. Woodman was convinced the Capri *did* have life left, and he spent the season battling against Rover opponent and off-course friend, Jeff Allam. Although Woodman and Allam may have been happy to arrive in the same car, their on-track duels were the stuff of legends. By the end of the season Woodman had taken four outright wins and so had Allam; Allam had set four pole-position times and so had his Capri-driving arch-rival. It wasn't as closely matched as it appears, however, with 44-year-old Woodman taking just four fastest laps and establishing three lap records, the twenty-eight-year-old Rover racer taking five fastest laps and four lap records. At the Grand Prix support race at Silverstone, the points the two men had accrued were even, so the following day the organizers had to take into account all points scored to find a winner. The results were: Rover, six; Capri, five. One of the contributing victories was that of Gordon Spice, who had otherwise had a rather disappointing year when compared to previous seasons.

In 1985 Capri 2.8is finished first, third, fourth, fifth and eighth in the 24-hour production race at Snetterton (beating the Mercedes 2.3/16 by two laps) and also won the BTRDA Rally Championship.

So much for the Capri's halcyon days of racing. But, as every Ford fan and race enthusiast knows, the Capri continues to be campaigned well into the mid-1990s, providing stiff opposition and enormous crowd entertainment.

8 Variations on a Theme

Viewed thirty years on, the 1960s were clearly the halcyon days of the demon tweakers, the bolt-on goody merchants who sold polished cylinder heads, multiple carburettors and special exhaust systems to the likes of Ford Anglia- and Mini-owners. Even stick-on 'go faster' tape was reckoned to add a few extra miles per hour according to the wags in the public bar! Companies such as Downton, Nerus, Derrington and Oselli marketed a whole range of parts for the home-tuner. Alternatively, they offered tuning stages in various forms and packages which could be fitted in their workshops. The more you spent, the quicker you went. Willment, for example, marketed a conversion package for the Cortina GT which turned it into a Lotus Cortina eater!

Engine swapping – fitting a larger engine made by the same manufacturer – also became popular, and Ford enthusiasts were in their element as they selected from a multitude of engines, gearboxes and back axles from the Anglia, Classic and Cortina ranges. A trip to the breaker's yard could result in a bigger engine and a set of disc brakes – instant performance at a bargain-basement price!

So, what was it that changed the shape of the tuning market for good? Certainly, the international Energy Crisis had a marked effect, reducing racing and rallying activities on the international scene, and causing petrol prices to rocket. Meanwhile, manufacturers – with Ford leading the field – continued to offer GT versions of their products, these boasting improved performance, as well as extra instruments and special seats all as standard. The Capri is an ideal example of this marketing policy, the marque offering a wide range of engine options and trim packs to suit most pockets.

EARLY TURBO-CHARGERS

It was around the time of the Capri's launch that the world began to hear of the benefits of turbo-charging. Supercharging had, of course, been around for many years, initially gaining popularity in the 1930s when many companies used it on their racing cars to improve performance. Generally, superchargers were mechanically driven and located between the carburettor and the inlet manifold, the increased air volume being blown through the carburettor. (A good example is the 'blower' Bentley, with its supercharger hung on the front end of the crankshaft.) With the turbo-charger there is no such mechanical drive as it is driven simply by exhaust-gas pressure which turns tiny turbine vanes at very high revolutions; a second turbine fan mounted on the same shaft blows air into the induction system.

One of the first people to use turbochargers on Capris was Michael May, a Swedish engineer whose career had included becoming European Formula Junior Champion, working with Daimler-Benz and Ferrari on fuel-injection projects, and helping with the turbo-charger installations in the BMW and Alfa Romeo Group 5 race cars. In 1969 Ford Germany approved May's turbo-charger kit for the V6 engine, and the largest Ford dealer in West Germany, Schwabengarage of Stuttgart, took over installation and sale of the May kits. As with most turbo installations, the price was hardly cheap – a modified 2.3-litre Capri cost some £1,222, complete with suspension and braking modifications to handle the additional power. The result of this expenditure, however, was that an otherwise tame Capri was turned into a speedy motor car, the engine producing 180bhp at 5,800rpm (at which point a centrifugal governor cut the ignition), sufficient to give a 0–60mph (0–97km/h) of 7.8 seconds and a maximum speed of 120mph (193km/h).

It is also interesting to note here that May then went on to 'experiment' with the Ford V6 engine to find out what it could really produce. The result was 240bhp at 6,000rpm and over 300bhp with a highly modified unit that featured uprated camshaft and cylinder heads. A race Capri fitted with this engine finished fourth in a race at Hockenheim in October 1969, proving that it was almost as quick as the most powerful Camaros and Falcons! However, with the engine tuned to produce this sort of output May experienced problems with cylinder-head gasket failures – similar to the difficulties which faced Weslake, Cosworth and Ashworth when they began developing the Ford V6 engine for racing.

By 1972 the world had moved on a pace, and many of the well-known tuners were hard at work producing their own kits for making Capris really fly. One example is Jeff Uren, who had been working in conjunction with Weslake over modified Fords, the 3-litre Capri being marketed as the Comanche 190. Lumo and Vita were there too, but one of the legendary names in the Ford tuning business was Allards (remember the Anglia Allardette powered by the 1,340cc Classic engine?) Allards offered an uprated version of the 3.0-litre Capri fitted with the Allard-Wade supercharger, Allards itself having the world distribution rights for the Roots-style Wade blower suitable for 2–3-litre engines.

The boosted Capri 3000GT was tested by the motor-noters at *Motor* magazine in March 1972, and turned out to be an exciting car – even if the excitement was simply limited to getting the beast going, since stopping it relied on standard brakes, these having a tendency to smoke after hard use! Producing around 190bhp (though the actual figure was not quoted) the car's 0–60mph (0–97km/h) time bettered the German May Turbo car by 0.4 seconds, with a 0–100mph (0–161km/h) gallop of 17.5 seconds. This version of the Capri from Richmond in South London was certainly no slouch. The cost of a new Capri from Allards, complete with the full conversion (which included modified cylinder heads fitted with Weslake cylinder-head gaskets, uprated suspension, and GRP front spoiler and bonnet) was £1,978; alternatively, a customer could have his or her own car modified in the Allards workshops for £415.

BROAD'S BRUTE

Just over a year later, *Autocar* magazine tested a Broadspeed-modified Capri fitted with a Holset 3LD turbo-charger. This was a rather unusual conversion as the car had been fitted with an additional ignition key on its floor-mounted console (which also housed a clock and the boost gauge), this allowing the driver to switch the turbo in or out depending on conditions or temperament.

Ralph Broad, whose name needs no introduction to Ford fans, decided that such radical power-unit alterations demanded that the conversion – marketed under the title 'Turbo Bullitt' – would only be offered

RALPH BROAD

From the age of six, Ralph Broad worked in his father's garage in Stratford Road, Birmingham (one of the first Ford dealerships in the UK). Mornings and evenings were spent working on cars, Ralph managing to squeeze in some schooling whenever he could. Broad senior was a hard task-master and demanded the best of his car-mad offspring (damaged bodywork had to be beaten out to primer-quality finish; no lead loading was allowed), though young Ralph still managed to gain sufficient education to put him into grammar school. Sadly, Ralph's father was taken critically ill when he was only thirteen, forcing him to leave school and take over running the business.

In the early 1950s one of Ralph's neighbours bought a Jaguar and began motor racing, Ralph acting as mechanic. Very soon Ralph was spending more time on race preparation than on running his garage, so he decided to buy an Austin A90 and go racing himself. The car was later replaced by an 850 Mini, which became highly successful in most areas of motor sport. In 1961 Team Broadspeed was formed. Word got round, and Stuart Turner (who headed up BMC's Competitions Department) asked Ralph to run a team of works Mini Coopers in European events.

Towards the end of 1964 Broad severed links with BMC, accepting an offer from Henry Taylor to race 1,000cc Anglias. Sadly, Peter Proctor was badly burned in an accident while driving a Broadspeed Anglia, Ralph almost giving up racing because of it. But, deciding instead to campaign for better fire protection, Broad went on to race 1,300cc Anglias, 1,300cc and twin-cam and BDA Escorts, finishing second in the championship year after year.

In 1972 Broad transferred back to Leyland, this time preparing the delightful Dolomite Sprint, winning the championship four years later. Then came the XJ6 Coupé Jaguar 'big cat', but although Broadspeed spent much time in perfecting the car, poor reliability – caused by a huge weight penalty – resulted in many failures. As time went on, however, Ralph spent less time in race development, instead putting more effort into prototype building for large manufacturers, as well as marketing tuning conversions for popular makes (including the Capri) and in running a body-building company which specialized in commercial vehicles. In the background, however, was Ralph's engineering-trained son, ready to step in so that his father could retire to sunny Portugal.

as a complete package undertaken by the company's Southam, Warwickshire, workshop, with no option for customers to buy the parts and fit them privately. A quick reference to the work involved in turning a standard 3.0-litre Capri into a BMW-beater reveals why this was the case.

To begin with, the 3.0-litre engine was stripped and blue-printed, Broad maintaining that the basis for any high-performance engine was a unit assembled to the proper tolerances. Piston heights were equalized, with inlet and exhaust tracts matched to manifolds. Combustion chambers were reworked to balance the capacity and reduce the compression ratio from 8.9:1 to 8.2:1. The turbo unit itself was mounted between the engine and the radiator, thus resulting in the removal of the standard fan and the use instead of an electrically driven unit. The turbo itself was fed from reverse-mounted exhaust manifolds, the larger-than-standard exit pipe dividing into two and emerging from beneath the rear skirt.

Considerable thought had also been given to the problem of throttle response lag. Broad's solution to this unsatisfactory characteristic was to fit an air-feedback loop, so that when the turbo was not needed air was fed back into the unit via an air-control valve, thereby keeping the turbo shaft spinning. A sensing device was used to shut off the loop when the throttle was opened. To complete the gadget, a solenoid, operated by the second floor-mounted ignition switch, stopped the sensing device from functioning, thereby removing the turbo effect when it was not required.

Pressurized air from the turbo was fed via trunking to a plenum box which totally encapsulated the carburettor, thereby creating an artificially high atmospheric pressure around the carburettor and float chamber. Fuel to the carburettor was supplied by a Bosch recirculating electric fuel pump mounted in the boot.

The result of all this work was an increase from 138bhp DIN at 5,000rpm measured at the back wheels (equivalent to 149bhp on the bench) to a very respectable 218bhp at 5,500rpm, and an increase to 225lb/ft of torque at 3,500rpm. To handle this power increase, 10.5in (27cm) disc brakes were fitted to the front and four-pot calliper cylinders with harder linings to the rear. Spring rates were increased all round with Armstrong dampers and a softer front anti-roll bar. Other changes to the suspension included improved castor and camber angles, while a modified steering rack with specially fabricated steering arms was fitted to overcome the car's natural tendency to 'bump steer'. The wheels were changed to 14in diameter fitted with 195/70 VR tyres, which increased the standard gearing from 21.6 miles (34.8km) to 24.3 miles (39.1km) per 1,000 revs in top gear. Finally, to reduce front end lift at high speed – usually about 2in (50mm) at 120mph (193km) – a special chin spoiler was added.

Broad's conversion created a true 140mph (225km/h) Capri. Making full use of the turbo, the car really came into its own at 2,800–3,400rpm, when (as the motor-noters remarked) it was as though a second engine had mysteriously been coupled in. The faster the speed, the less pronounced the turbo lag, so that above 4,000rpm there was virtually no lag at all. In contrast, spirited take-offs and low-speed acceleration did show up the modified car's turbo-lag shortfalls (despite Broad's closed loop system) when measured against the standard 3.0-litre Capri. That said, a 0–60mph (0–97km/h) time of 7.0 seconds can hardly be called slow, and *Autocar* testers were of the opinion that in view of its benefits the cost of the conversion (£1,355 plus VAT) was not excessive.

THE CAPRI PERANA

If the turbo market was still in its infancy at this time, then the notion of realizing large increases in performance through fitting large engines certainly was not. However, in the case of the Capri Perana the idea was somewhat more radical than simply swapping the engine for a larger version of the same unit. An article that appeared in *Motor Sport* in 1971 gave a brief description of the background to these exciting machines.

Perana Cars was run by Basil Green Motors, based in Johannesburg, South Africa. The company specialized in uprating Fords, fitting V6 engines into Cortinas in a similar fashion to Jeff Uren's Race-Proved set-up in the UK. However, Perana went one stage further, spending considerable time and effort in successfully developing a V8-engined Capri using a 5.0-litre Mustang engine supplied by Ford SA. Early tests of the prototype Perana Capri V8 certainly impressed Jackie Stewart, who drove the car at Kyalami as part of a new-tyre demonstration arranged by Dunlop. Ford SA was also impressed, so much so that an agreement was given for Perana Cars to assemble some 800 units. The Peranas were backed by Ford SA (based in Port Elizabeth) and marketed through its country-wide dealer chain.

Perana V8 Capris began life as 3000Es

and were sent up to Johannesburg for modification. In a workshop described as being almost like a mini replica of Ford Advanced Vehicle Operations, the V6 engines and drivetrain were stripped out, and the bodies modified to accept the larger 302cu. in V8 Detroit unit complete with close-ratio gearbox, which gave 62mph (100km/h) in first, 85mph (137km/h) in second and 112mph (180km/h) in third.

The engines were given an uprated Stage 2 camshaft before fitting, along with stronger valve springs (which allowed the unit to rev safely to 7,000rpm) and a four-barrel Holley carburettor mounted on an aluminium inlet manifold – all of which reputedly increased power to a healthy 239bhp. To handle the increase in power and torque, a Basil Green-developed Borg Warner limited-slip differential rear axle was fitted, with a 3.08:1 final drive, producing 22mph (35km/h) at 1,000rpm. The steering rack was also changed and the spring rates uprated. Not surprisingly, a few cars were fitted with the Borg Warner C4 automatic transmission.

Inside, the instruments were altered to take account of the different engine characteristics and speed capability, and many other jobs were undertaken to make the conversion professional. Indeed, according to *Motor Sport*'s journalist such was the sales success of the Perana that it quite outstripped any similar conversion marketed by a British firm.

In an all-too-short morning's test the intrepid *Motor Sport* tester found the Perana exciting, if something of a handful (the particular car under evaluation had a soft front spring!). Tipping the scales at 2,390lb (1,084kg) – only 14lb (6.4kg) heavier than the V6 version – the addition of the extra two cylinders hardly added a weight penalty. Also, the V8 was mounted well back in newly fabricated chassis rails, giving a reasonable weight distribution of 53/47 front to back. And if things did get out of hand, there was always sufficient power to correct the inherent understeer characteristic of the V8 Capri; the technique was simply to 'squirt the back round to balance things up'. To give you an idea of how the car performed, a South African magazine recorded an im-

FORD CAPRI PERANA V8 (1970)

LAYOUT AND CHASSIS
Two-door coupé/monocoque construction

ENGINE	
Type	Cleveland
Block material	Cast iron
Head material	Cast iron
Cylinders	V8
Cooling	n/a
Bore and stroke	101.6 × 76.2mm
Capacity	4,942cc
Valves	ohv
Compression ratio	9.2:1
Carburettor	Holley four-barrel
Max. power	240bhp @ 6,500rpm
Max. torque	300lb/ft @ 2,600rpm
Fuel capacity	12.8 gallons (58 litres)
TRANSMISSION	
Gearbox	4-speed
Ratios	2.32:1, 1.69:1, 1.29:1, 1.00:1
Final drive	3.08:1
SUSPENSION AND STEERING	
Front	MacPherson struts
Rear	Semi-elliptic springs
Steering	Rack and pinion
Tyres	185/70 VR × 13
Wheels	Steel
Rim width	5in
BRAKES	
Type	Hydraulic disc/drum
Size	243mm disc, 9 × 2.3in drum
DIMENSIONS (in/mm)	
Track: front	53/1,346
rear	52/1,321
Wheelbase	100.8/2,560
Overall length	168.5/4,280
Overall width	64.8/1,646
Overall height	50.7/1,288
Unladen weight	2,390lb/1,084kg
PERFORMANCE	
Top speed	143mph (230km/h)
0–62mph	7.2sec

pressive 0–60mph (0–97km/h) time of 6.1 seconds and a maximum speed of 143mph (230km/h)! The Perana did, however, take courage to drive fast, particularly as the brakes were the standard out-of-the-box Capri type with hard pads and linings.

To complete the picture, Perana Capris also prepared a car for Bobby Althorp, who scored some impressive results, while other Peranas were raced to good effect by top South African drivers such as Peter Gough and Basil van Rooyen in events which often supported Grand Prix races. Of those Peranas that did reach the UK, all were privately imported. Ford UK looked at the project but discounted it on the grounds that the Type Approval process was too costly and would not have been viable for the projected sales volume.

MK III BULLITT

By 1978 many of the established tuning firms were offering turbo-charging in both after-market bolt-on kits and as professional conversions. Among them was Janspeed Engineering Limited of Salisbury, the remarkable Jan Odor (who started life as a protégé of Downton's Daniel Richmond) smoothly making the transition from offering uprated cylinder heads and camshafts to turbo-charging specialist.

Broadspeed had also come on, and was offering the Capri Bullitt conversion on the Mk III version, which included engine modifications, an uprated clutch, and oil-cooler, electric-fan, suspension and brake improvements (including 195/70 VR tyres), as well as a change to electronic ignition. The cost was £2,600, this including fitting. As with previous Broadspeed turbo-charged Capris, changes were made to the suspension – uprated dampers, front suspension geometry alterations, rear spring trailing links and solid suspension bushes – to cope with the 200+bhp. The car tested by *Autocar* in 1978, however, did not feature a limited-slip differential, and there were traces of rear-wheel steering during gear changes under hard acceleration. But the journalist was charitable enough to say that Broad had deliberately compromised over suspension and tyres rather than create an impossibly harsh ride.

Perhaps as a reflection of the gradual increase in weight during the Capri's career, performance of the Capri Mk III Bullitt showed itself to be slower than the earlier car, with a 0–60mph (0–97km/h) time of 7.4 seconds (top speed was not recorded). Over all, however, the Bullitt continued to provide outstanding performance, with an acceptable compromise made between performance and handling.

ZAKSPEED CONVERSIONS

Ford's acceptance of Capri turbo-charging came in July 1981, when Zakspeed-converted Capris were marketed (although sadly only through the German RS dealership chain), the cars being available until September of the following year. Indeed, the name of Michael May crops up again, for in addition to some creditable work on the high-compression version of Jaguar's legendary XJ12 engine, it was May's teaching that brought Ford round to the bonuses of low-boost turbo systems.

Initially, the turbo-charging programme for these special cars involved utilizing the German 2.3-litre V6 (Ford also planned to fit these engines in the XR4i and the Capri developed by SVE). That was until it was discovered that the 2.8-litre unit was about to be introduced; Ford felt they could not charge a premium price for a 2.3-litre Capri which would not significantly out-perform its 2.8-litre rival!

Virtually complete 3.0-litre S-type Capris

The immaculate presentation of Derek Spiers' rare Zakspeed turbo, showing the flared front wheelarch and recessed bumper. The wheels are 6.5in FAVO-type alloys though there was an option of 7.5in. The brakes are 10.5in ventilated discs. The suspension utilizes gas dampers and an RS anti-roll bar.

An under-bonnet view from the driver's side showing the dual circuit brake servo and power steering pump. Zakspeed turbo Capris were available in left-hand drive form only.

were sent to Zakspeed's Niederzissen-based workshops, where the GRP body panels, wider wheelarches (glued into position), and front and rear spoilers were fitted. The cars were then sent back to Cologne for finishing, which included the installation of the German-modified turbo-charged engines.

At the heart of the conversion was the normally aspirated 135bhp Granada engine, with a Michael May-inspired KKK turbo-charger mounted to the side of the engine and feeding directly into the existing carburettor. Leaving the compression ratio as standard (9.2:1), the boost was purposely set at a mild 5.8psi (0.4 bar), the unit producing 188bhp at 5,500rpm with 206lb/ft of torque. However, production units utilized the Garrett AiResearch turbo unit which, like the KKK turbo-charged original, was fed directly into the carburettor with no intercooler. The crankshaft was nitrided for longer life and fitted with a damper to reduce vibration. A heavy-duty oil pump improved lubrication, and the head gaskets were changed to suit the higher power output.

Gear ratios and final drives were all left as

The front and rear spoilers on the Zakspeed Capri were unique to the model. Production of these cars involved unfinished cars being sent from Cologne to Zakspeed – where the body kit was added – before being returned to Cologne for the installation of the turbo power unit.

Offside view of the engine bay showing the Garrett AiResearch turbo. The engine is a standard carburetted 2.8-litre unit, producing 188DIN at 5,500rpm resulting in a 0–62mph (0–99km/h) time of 8.0 seconds and a maximum speed of 133mph (214km/h).

The Zakspeed turbo used similar interior trim to the Escort RS1600i – grey velour, not the Recaro-type seats used in the 2.8i Capri developed by SVE.

standard for the 3.0-litre Capri, with the option of either 6.5in (16.5cm) or 7.5in (19cm) wide 13in (33cm) diameter FAVO-type spoked alloy wheels with 235/60 VR Phoenix tyres. Brakes were also left unaltered. The interior was, however, given an improved level of trim, similar to the grey velour and special seats seen in the sporty Escort RS1600i homologation special shortly after. As supplies of the 2.8i Capri began to reach Germany, the benefits of the SVE-developed coupé (such as ventilated disc brakes and improved suspension layout, but not the later five-speed gearbox) were reflected through to the Zakspeed cars.

Overall, these Zakspeed-converted turbo Capris were exciting cars, although there is a school of thought that insists that Ford Germany was anxious to restrict the turbo-charging effect, such was the company's concern over the inherent weaknesses of the 2.8 engine! Even so, the car proved to be quick, with a 0–60mph (0–97km/h) time of 8 seconds and a maximum speed of 134mph (216km/h). Today these cars are particularly rare as only around 200 were built.

TECHNIC'S TURBOS

In the UK, Ford's first experience with turbo-charging their products came in the early 1980s when the company co-operated with Geoff Kershaw. Kershaw was a former Garrett AiResearch engineer (where he worked on the Saab Turbo programme) who left to set up his own company, Turbo Technics, based in Northampton. The object of their joint collaboration was the Escort XR3 and XR3i. Tests and evaluations were carried out, with Kershaw later selling the tooling and jigs for this conversion to Ford, who used them to develop the thrilling Escort RS Turbo, with its 125mph+ (200km/h+) performance. Turbo Technics, meanwhile, continued to offer Escort turbo conversions with outputs of 130–170bhp.

Turbo Technics then turned its attention to the Capri, and began offering conversions that ranged from the standard 200bhp version to a 'Total Performance Package' 230bhp model using a higher boost pressure that was selectable while driving. (The company also offered a 280bhp version, although very few were sold.) Such was the engineering integrity of these conversions that they proved very popular with enthusiasts – so popular, in fact, that Ford agreed to offer the 200bhp Turbo Technics Capri through Ford dealerships from June 1986.

The Technics conversions were very neatly executed. On early versions the plenum chamber was turned through 180 degrees to make pipe connections from the turbo straightforward. On later models, however, the plumbing was rearranged, which did away with this alteration. To improve timing and detonation control, the electronic ignition was given a modified advanced curve which took into account vacuum advance/pressure retard considerations. The Garrett AiResearch T03 turbo unit was mounted on a special cast manifold on the nearside of the cylinder block, both high-nickel-content exhaust manifolds being linked by a balance pipe. Charged air from the turbo then passed through an intercooler – which dropped temperatures by as much as 122°F (50°C) – before being fed into the plenum chamber. To improve lubrication (and reduce temperatures) a 30 per cent larger oil pump was fitted with a dedicated feed to the turbo unit.

Included in the £1,395 price-tag for the 200bhp version were uprated brake pads, brake shoes and suspension bushes, although the car's performance really demanded the additional brake and suspension alterations the company fitted as standard to the 230bhp version in order to keep handling under control. As a package it is easy to see the car's appeal: 0–60mph (0–97km/h) in 6.8 seconds; 0–100mph (0–161km/h) in 18.6 seconds; and 39mph (63km/h) available in first, 70mph (113km/h) in second, 110mph (177km/h) in third, 132mph (212km/h) in fourth and 138mph (222km/h) in top, using a maximum pressure boost of 9.5psi (0.65 bar).

FORD CAPRI TURBO TECHNICS 2.8 INJECTION (1986)

LAYOUT AND CHASSIS	
Two-door coupé/monocoque construction	
ENGINE	
Type	Cologne
Block material	Cast iron
Head material	Cast iron
Cylinders	V6
Cooling	n/a
Bore and stroke	93.0 × 68.5mm
Capacity	2,792cc
Valves	ohv
Compression ratio	9.2:1
Carburettor	Bosch K Jetronic fuel injection Garrett AiResearch T03 turbo-charger
Max. power	200bhp @ 5,700rpm
Max. torque	235lb/ft @ 3,800rpm
Fuel capacity	12.8 gallons (58 litres)
TRANSMISSION	
Gearbox	5-speed
Ratios	3.36:1, 1.81:1, 1.26:1, 1.00:1, 0.82:1
Final drive	3.09:1
SUSPENSION AND STEERING	
Front	MacPherson struts
Rear	Semi-elliptic springs
Steering	Rack and pinion
Tyres	205/60 VR × 13
Wheels	Alloy
Rim width	7in
BRAKES	
Type	Hydraulic disc/drum
Size	249mm ventilated disc, 9 × 2.3in drum
DIMENSIONS (in/mm)	
Track: front	53/1,346
rear	52.5/1,334
Wheelbase	101/2,565
Overall length	171.35/4,352
Overall width	67/1,702
Overall height	51/1,295
Unladen weight	2,620lb/1,188kg
PERFORMANCE	
Top speed	138mph (222km/h)
0–62mph	6.8sec

CAPRI 2.8T

The most dramatic of converted Capris must be Tickford's 2.8T, that very special-looking Capri with the blanked-off grille aperture, wide wheelarches and leather interior. But let us start at the beginning.

The story of the Capri 2.8T really begins towards the end of the 1970s, when a company called Aston Martin Tickford Ltd (AMT) was set up specifically to handle the special-prototype/low-volume projects (such as the Ford RS200 programme) large companies find so difficult to undertake. By the mid-1980s, a complex series of company changes resulted in AMT becoming part of CH Industries, whose factory premises were based at Bedworth near Coventry.

The catalyst behind the Tickford Capri was the well-known and respected journalist, Lotus test driver and engineer, John Miles, who had spent much time perfecting the Capri's performance and handling. A dedicated Capri enthusiast, Miles was to write some knowing words for *Autocar* in 1981 on his vision of the ultimate Capri. It would be a car with all the practical virtues of the standard machine, yet with a top speed in excess of 140mph (225km/h), a mid-range performance that bettered anything else in its class, gains in handling and road-holding to match, plus reduced noise levels. It was a tall order, yet Miles clearly felt it was not only possible but marketable too.

The opportunity to put meat on the notional bones of this exciting project came over lunch, when Miles confronted Victor Gauntlet, chairman of Aston Martin (who still owned

Probably the most expensive production Capri ever, the 2.8T Tickford Capri, seen here in prototype form in late 1982 showing its body kit, blanked-off grille and special 7in × 13 cast alloy wheels.

Interior of the 1982 2.8T prototype. Customers got a leather/walnut dashboard and the choice of full leather trim and luxurious deep pile carpeting, as befitting a car with a £14,985 price-tag.

Tickford at this stage), and Bob Lutz, then chairman of Ford Europe. The aims were clear: to build a car that resembled an eight-tenths Aston Martin Vantage and that was a civilized 'muscle' car while still retaining the basic advantages of the Capri. Assurances were given on all sides that the car would become an official Ford model, but shortly after the project got under way Bob Lutz was promoted to Ford of America and – as far as Ford was concerned – the Capri Tickford was put on ice.

Miles and Gauntlet, were however, made of sterner stuff. An agreement was drawn up to build 250 of the Capri Tickfords in the Coventry factory where Jaguar's XJ-S Cabriolets were finished. The question which must be raised now is whether Tickford could really afford this commitment, for fundamental to making the car a reality was the highly expensive business of Type Approval, the cost of which the company had to bear. Thankfully – as far as 2.8T fans are concerned – common sense did not prevail!

Tickford persevered to the point where a prototype was built and displayed on the Aston Martin Tickford stand at Motorfair in October 1983, where its dramatic styling

A 1984 production 2.8T seen at the 1994 Club Capri International Day at Windsor. Owners of 2.8Ts say they handle and ride like no other Capri – the result of suspension development by race driver and automotive journalist, John Miles.

drew many admiring glances. There must also have been many sharp intakes of breath, however, as spectators wrestled mentally with the £14,985 price-tag.

What did the customer get for this pretty substantial sum of money? To begin with, the V6 engine was fitted with a turbocharger. Sadly, that was not the system developed by Michael May in conjunction with the RS division of Ford Motorsport in Germany (actually designed for a left-hand-drive car), but instead a Japanese IHI unit mounted laterally ahead of the engine that was similar in concept to the Broadspeed Bullitt layout. Alongside was a huge Garrett air/air intercooler. Power was increased to a commendable 205bhp at 5,000rpm, with torque increased equally impressively to 260lb/ft at 3,500rpm, all on a boost pressure of 8psi (0.55 bar). In view of the work carried out by other companies, it was perhaps surprising that the engine was left unaltered, with no effort to balance, blue-print or provide enhanced lubrication. The K-Jetronic fuel-injection system also remained unaltered, although the ignition system was changed to the AFT-type similar to that used in the Escort RS1600i.

The Capri 2.8T utilized the latest five-speed gearbox (which happened along from Ford at the right time), slightly modified to increase lubrication around the input and output shafts where loads were highest. Moving back further still, we find a Salisbury limited-slip differential with a 50 per cent locking factor and a final-drive ratio of 3.09:1, the unit being enclosed in a special aluminium casing to reduce temperatures.

As for the suspension, the front springs, geometry and dampers were left in production specification. At the rear, the springs and dampers were also left unchanged, with the exception of Prescolan spacers in the leaf-spring locating eyes. However, Miles and the team had opted for an A-frame location for the rear axle to overcome torque steer, while the original drums were replaced with 10.43in (26.5cm) disc brakes that had been developed by CC Racing Ltd of Kirbymoorside in Yorkshire for racing purposes.

The body-styling kit was specially designed for the Tickford Capri, partly to improve drag coefficient (reduced from 0.39 to 0.37) and partly to give the car special visual appeal. Miles estimated that front-end lift

Not all 2.8Ts had full leather-trimmed seats. This car has the 'standard' wool-covered squabs and back rests. Even so, the walnut dashboard and leather-covered steering-wheel and gearstick gaiter give the car a very elegant look.

had been reduced by an impressive 70 per cent, while rear-end balance had been created by reducing high-speed lift to almost nil. The complete panel set comprised a combined front bumper/spoiler moulding, wheelarch extensions and side-skirts, a rear bumper/skirt and rear tail spoiler, all manufactured from GRP to the very high standards one would expect from Aston Martin Tickford Ltd.

Inside, there were electrically operated tinted windows, a manual sun roof and walnut

The 2.8T used a front mounted IHI turbocharger set to give 7–8psi boost feeding the Bosch K-Jetronic fuel injection system. Power was rated at 205bhp at 5,000rpm, giving a 0–60mph (0–97km/h) time of 6.7 seconds and a top speed of 140mph (225km/h).

An eye-catching 2.8T Capri at speed during the Aston Martin Owners' Club rallysprint meeting organized at Goodwood in July 1987. It is a characteristic of the AMOC that owners are not afraid to compete their cars in motorsport events!

A Brands Hatch pace Capri fitted with the X-pack option, which included triple Weber carburettors, stage II cylinder head, bigger radiator and electric fuel pump. Suspension was uprated with Bilstein dampers, limited slip differential, ventilated front disc brakes and 7.5 × 13 alloy wheels, while the body was given flared wheelarch extensions. The 0–60mph (0–97km/h) time was 7.4 seconds with a 130mph (209km/h) top speed.

FORD CAPRI TICKFORD 2.8T (1984)

LAYOUT AND CHASSIS
Two-door coupé/monocoque construction

ENGINE	
Type	Cologne
Block material	Cast iron
Head material	Cast iron
Cylinders	V6
Cooling	n/a
Bore and stroke	93.0 × 68.5mm
Capacity	2,792cc
Valves	ohv
Compression ratio	9.2:1
Carburettor	Bosch K Jetronic fuel injection IHI turbo-charger
Max. power	205bhp @ 5,000rpm
Max. torque	260lb/ft @ 3,500rpm
Fuel capacity	12.8 gallons (58 litres)
TRANSMISSION	
Gearbox	5-speed
Ratios	3.36:1, 1.81:1, 1.26:1, 1.00:1, 0.82:1
Final drive	3.09:1
SUSPENSION AND STEERING	
Front	MacPherson struts
Rear	Semi-elliptic springs
Steering	Rack and pinion
Tyres	205/60 VR × 13
Wheels	Alloy
Rim width	7in
BRAKES	
Type	Hydraulic disc
Size	262mm ventilated disc, 265mm solid disc
DIMENSIONS (in/mm)	
Track: front	53/1,346
rear	52.5/1,334
Wheelbase	101/2,565
Overall length	171.35/4,352
Overall width	67/1,702
Overall height	51/1,295
Unladen weight	2,620lb/1,188kg
PERFORMANCE	
Top speed	140mph (225km/h)
0–62mph	6.7sec

dashboard fillets. There was also a burglar alarm, this being one of the first cars to have this gadget fitted as standard. Leather was used for the steering-wheel, map pocket and centre console. Full leather trim came as an optional extra, as did Wilton carpets and Pirelli P7 tyres. Colour schemes were available in red, white or black.

Most journalists lucky enough to drive a Tickford Capri said the car handled like no other Capri. Miles himself said that broken surfaces were handled in a much more compliant manner, while the car's ability to soak up B-road irregularities was most notable. High-speed straight-line stability, a direct result of the body-styling kit, was also improved dramatically.

Tickford had transformed the Capri into a true 140mph (225km/h) supercar with a 0–60mph (0–97km/h) sprint of just 6.7 seconds. Interestingly enough, the men from *Motor Sport* were less than anxious to call it a 'poor man's Porsche Turbo', although they did agree that its performance put it on a par with the 2.7-litre Porsche 911. Their greatest gripe was the perceptible turbo lag felt at low engine speeds in a high gear. There were also traces of resonance and vibration from the drivetrain under acceleration, though they did agree that the Pirelli tyres complimented the suspension set-up well, providing phenomenal cornering power!

Sadly, the Tickford Capri never did benefit from the backing of Ford's dealership chain, which in turn probably hampered sales – only around 100 were sold in total. Certainly, the car was pricy at £17,220 in 1986, especially when compared with the Sierra Cosworth two-door saloon at £15,950 and the standard Capri 2.8i at just £10,599. We should simply be glad that Gauntlet and Miles decided to go ahead with the project at all.

9 Buying and Restoration

The Capri – from the 1960s Classic Capri to the last off the line in late 1986 – has a particular attraction for the Ford fan. It's all about style and image – the self-same features that attracted buyers in the first place – yet with running costs more in keeping with those of a Cortina than a German or Italian exotic. Capris have now been elevated to classic status, their prices at least holding their own in today's economic climate. In short, they make a sensible choice for the collector/enthusiast.

However, a word of warning is in order here before we start to look at the nuances of purchasing a Capri. From the Classic Capri of the 1960s to the striking Brooklands version which marked the model's demise, little changed in the fundamental design culture: MacPherson strut suspension up front and a solid rear axle with leaf springs – simple and straightforward. The car had a conventional drivetrain layout, with no overhead camshafts or front-wheel-drive transmission systems. If you are looking for the sophistication of all-independent suspension set-ups and belt-driven camshafts with multi-valve cylinder heads, then the Capri is not for you.

CAPRI MK I TO MK III PRODUCTION DETAILS

Mode	Number of units	Production period
Capri Mk I:	1,172,900 units	Jan 1969 to Feb 1974
Capri Mk II:	403,612 units	Mar 1974 to Feb 1978
Capri Mk III:	324,045 units	Mar 1978 to Dec 1986

Initially, Capri manufacture was centred on Halewood and Cologne. In 1976 manufacture was moved to being located in Cologne only.

In 1970 Capri output peaked with 238,914 units produced.

Best UK sales (4,629) year for 2.8i: 1983.

Millionth Capri (RS2600) manufactured in August 1973 at Cologne plant.

Total RS2600 production: 4,000 units approx.

Total RS3100 production: 200 units approx.

Total 280 production: 1,038 units.

A 3-litre S-type Capri of 1978 vintage. Capris of all types are all about style and statement but not at all about sophistication. So if you're looking for multi-valve engines and all-independent suspension Capris are not for you.

It is equally important to remember that early Capris – especially the SB60 range – had little in the way of rot protection. No great thought was given at the design stage to eliminating rust traps, while undersealing was offered as a service through Ford agents before delivery, and was one many new owners simply didn't bother to take up! I am glad to say that as the Capri entered the 1980s, Ford, like most major manufacturers, began paying attention to rust-prevention processes during manufacture, the result being that Mk III cars have generally lasted better.

Another bonus for Capri enthusiasts is that servicing and restoration should pose few problems, at least for the foreseeable future. Parts for the later cars should still be available off the shelf, while owners' clubs offer an enormous field of opportunity to track down spares. Club days bring the usual collection of specialist dealers, while autojumbles provide another source of parts. Finally, there are always breaker's yards, though with the usual caveat that anything bought second hand should be inspected thoroughly before fitting.

Whatever the model of Capri you are thinking of buying, always aim to pay the most you can afford (leaving enough in the kitty for insurance). Remember, the larger the engine, the higher the running costs. During a year's motoring, a 2.0-litre S or Ghia model could prove much more economic for your purposes, yet still give the same level of trim and extras found on the

A concours car judge getting down to the job. One of the most fiercely fought activities in Capri Club International are concours events, for which owners spend many hours preparing.

3.0-litre versions. If you are under twenty-five years old it is as well to shop around for insurance quotations *before* you buy the car, just in case it proves prohibitive! Limited-mileage classic-car policies should also be considered.

It is as well to mention at this point that anyone really interested in Capris should join one of the clubs that specialize in these cars. There is much to be gained through going to meetings and chatting with knowledgeable members before buying a car, so that you can pick up tips and grasp the fundamental weaknesses of each model. You might even find someone who lives locally who will be willing to come along and check a car over with you. The Capri Club International also publishes information on what to look for when buying one of these cars. Indeed, there is so much detail on Capri technology available that there really is no excuse for anyone not having access to the right information; what follows here is very much a potted version of that information.

WHAT CAR?

Before discussing what to look for when buying a Capri, there are two main categories of prospective purchase (that is if you leave out cars that have been prepared for racing, or those bought for complete restoration projects). Let us start with the 'buying as new' car.

Despite the age of even the youngest Capri, it will still be possible to buy a good, clean example (as they say in the trade) off a garage forecourt. If bought from a reputable company, such a car should be original, with no signs of real wear in the interior trim, body or mechanics, and should also come with a warranty. The only considerations with such a car are: model type with associated engine size (to be considered for insurance purposes); price; overall condition; and what the warranty actually covers. It is, however, still important to check the body thoroughly to see if rust is beginning to gain a foothold; if it has, you may find yourself having to cope with major problems later on.

From this . . .

. . . to this. Beware of fakes. The car above is a 3-litre GXL while the car below being put through its paces is an RS3100, its rarity making it worth quite a lot more money on the classic car market.

Moving on to the second category, I shall assume that the car will be bought through the pages of one of the reputable magazines or even the columns of a club magazine. Whatever, it is important to say at this point that, as the values of classic cars have escalated, so too have the numbers of people trying to pass off fakes! The most obvious candidate for replication in the Capri market is a modified car being sold as an original RS. Here again, the clubs are an enormous fund of information and have lists of chassis numbers. They often even know the whereabouts of most 'original' limited-production models.

INSPECTING THE CAR

Assuming you have located the car you wish to buy, you then need to make arrangements to view it. Ideally, make the appointment for mid-morning or during the afternoon; people have been known to buy cars at night-time, only to regret their folly! Remember that you will be spending time under the car, so take along ramps, a jack (preferably a trolley jack), overalls and rags or domestic-type kitchen roll. Also take along a notepad to jot down any comments which may be used to bargain over a better price!

If the Capri you are considering is one of those that are worth faking, then the first thing to do is to make a note of the chassis number and compare it with the chassis identification table. If there is a query or the plate looks doubtful, walk smartly away!

Body Condition

Try to draw an over all impression of the car's condition. Does it look well cared for? Is the interior trim well worn? Are there any signs of accident damage? And are there any indications of hasty rust repairs? The oldest Capris – 109E or 116E of 1961–4 vintage – will obviously need the most rigorous inspection. That said, although the majority of these cars have now been relegated to the great Capri graveyard, there are still a few

When looking at a car begin by gaining an overall impression of its condition. Are there any indications of rust or accident damage? Does it look well cared for? You'd be lucky to find a Mk I X-Pack 1600 Automatic in this sort of condition.

The interior trim used on many Mk Is soon showed signs of wear if not looked after. With some Mk Is celebrating their quarter century it's hardly surprising they're looking a little tired.

left in remarkably good original condition.

Treating all Capris as one, start at the front, check for rust behind the headlamps, and look to see if it has taken hold in the sidelamp mouldings which form part of the wheelarch. Moving back to the front wings themselves (a weak point on all Capris), check both the tops of the wing sections and the inner to outer wing, seen by lifting the bonnet and inspecting closely.

All Capris were fitted with MacPherson strut front suspensions, so look at the mount-

Begin looking at the front of the car and inspecting the rear round the headlights. Tell-tale signs of bubbles indicate rust about to come through from inside the bonnet and wing panels.

Moving round to the side of the wings, see how signs of rust from the inside can begin to show on the outside surface, as on this Mk III 3.0-litre S. This will certainly mean a new wing soon.

ing points. Sometimes plates are welded on to repair these when an MOT failure looks imminent; such a job should be well executed and not bodged. It is worth mentioning that the Capri's front wings are not bolted on but are welded on instead, so wing replacement is hardly a weekend DIY job. While the bonnet is up, investigate the condition of the inner wings, the panels surrounding the radiator and the scuttle section.

Moving on, check the A-post and the base of the front screen, paying particular attention to the rear of the outer wing and the rear of the front wheelarch (a favourite rot section on Ford's products in the past). Severe rot in the A-post itself will cause the doors to drop; carry out a body-panel alignment check, and watch the way the door swings outwards from its aperture.

Door skins are next on the agenda. Moisture, especially on older Capris, will cause the skin to rot from the inside out, so small blisters apparent on the outside surface could indicate a major problem. Don't forget to look at the underside of the door frame, too, as moisture trapped in the bottom of the frame can cause rotting, especially if the drain holes are blocked.

Next come the well-known sill sections which, on a monocoque bodyshell like the Capri, form an integral part of the unit and therefore a major MOT check area. These should be inspected thoroughly on Capris of all ages. It may well be possible to effect repairs, but as on the door skins, bubbles that are apparent on the outer surfaces can indicate far worse problems on the inside. While you are looking at this part of the car, open the doors and lift the carpets to look at the floorpan. Damp carpets are *not* a good sign!

Moving to the rear wheelarch, check for rot around the circumference of the arch itself where the inner and outer body panels meet. Also have a quick glance at the inside of the fuel-filler neck. More advanced body rust is, however, more likely to occur on the inner wheelarch itself, which can be inspected from inside the boot. While the bootlid or tailgate is up, look carefully at the boot floor and the area around the rear light clusters. On three-door Capris, check the

The Rostyle road wheel, which was also seen on the popular 1600E Cortina. Look carefully for signs of rust bubbles caused by the accumulation of road dirt on the inside of the wheelarch. Also, check the suspension joints for wear and the brake discs for scoring.

condition of the tailgate, especially around the bottom edge. Finally, have a look at the rear apron under the bumper. Again, rot can start from the inside and work its way out, so beware of bubbles.

The Underside

The next stage is to check underneath the car. With the front of the car up on ramps (safely chocked in position, of course), it is possible to look at the condition of the front bumper mountings, the front cross-member and the rubber suspension bushes. Weak dampers and wear in the suspension bushes themselves will affect the car's handling. It is also important to look at the condition of the steering system (recirculatory ball box on SB60 cars and rack and pinion on later cars), checking for vital signs of lubrication leakage and the condition of the rubber rack gaiters. Evidence of fluid leakage should also be looked for on cars fitted with power steering. Before crawling out, it is worth looking for traces of oil leaks from the engine (perhaps caused by a faulty rocker box or sump gasket in need of replacement), indicated by oil on engine mountings and

Sills, door bottoms and door panels should be closely inspected. Sill panels are an MOT failure point if rust has taken a strong hold. Doors, however, can either be replaced or repaired by skilfully welding in sections carefully smoothed over with fibreglass.

Down below again and it is possible to see the condition of the rear skirt below the bumper line. Like the apron this panel is very often forgotten and neglected.

Vinyl roofs were poplar in the 1970s, echoing the days when cars had fabric roof coverings. Elegant when new they can begin to look tatty if the vinyl comes unstuck or is damaged.

With the bonnet lifted begin to make a close inspection of the headlamp supports and radiator surround. The adjustment screws can rust solid, making the headlight angle difficult to alter.

coolant pipes. Also, look for vestiges of leaks in the transmission; this is not difficult to cure, but just means that you will leave oil messages wherever you go! Finally, check the condition of the brake pipes, looking for rust in the tubes and examine wear in the flexible hoses.

You may wish to use the trolley jack to check the condition of the steering joints, wheel bearings and swivel joints (remember not to jack the car up using the base of the MacPherson strut as a lifting point). Play in these areas can affect handling and tyre wear. Also, check on the condition of the brake discs for scoring and uneven wear.

Next, drive the rear of the car on to the ramps and begin to look for rot in the spring hangers and the inner sill sections. You should be able to see if there are any signs of leaks from the differential, and should also try the universal joints on the prop shaft for play (nowadays, a replacement means a complete new prop shaft). Check the condition of the exhaust system, remembering that a replacement for a V6 is not cheap. Look at the condition of the brake pipes and locating brackets which, although they are MoT test points, may have deteriorated over the previous twelve months.

Wings on Capris are welded on so replacement is not a simple matter of removing bolts should it be necessary to replace the wing panel. This car has had a panel welded into the top of the MacPherson strut locating point. Check to make sure the job has been well carried out and is not just a 'bodge'.

The Engine

Mechanically speaking, Ford's engines have a good reputation for reliability and longevity. Even the problems with the overhead camshaft Pinto unit (caused through inadequate camshaft lobe lubrication) were sorted out long ago, although there was some resultant poor publicity in the motoring press at the time.

There really is only one way to check an engine properly and that is to run it until it

A favourite rust spot is the rear of the engine bay at the top of the scuttle where water can be trapped to do its worst. Serious rot can make the car a basket case since nothing short of a complete strip down will cure it.

If the engine looks like this there should be few problems! This is an early V4 (note the dynamo in the foreground) and, yes, the length of the fan belt on these engines did give problems.

is up on temperature so that the mechanical parts have reached their working tolerances and the oil is at its usual viscosity. An old engine will show signs of wear through noisy timing gear and a smoking exhaust, especially on over-run, worn valve guides that allow oil into the combustion chambers. The truth is, however, that modern lubricants allow engines to go on for well over 100,000 miles (161,000km) or more. Even if the engine is really worn, parts will still be readily available from Ford (or factors), so a rebuild will not be out of the question – although clearly this will have to be reflected in the price. Signs of wear in the 3.0-litre engine are piston slap and bottom-end rumble on cold start-up. The distributor driveshaft can shear if the engine has been neglected, while the fibre camshaft drive gears can also become damaged through old age.

Only the complexity of the injection system fitted to the 2.8i engine puts it out of the reach of the average mechanic. Problems of high-speed misfire, caused through a fault in the Bosch injection system, are about the worst that can happen if the engine has not been serviced regularly. Meanwhile, the carburettors on most Ford engines are pretty straightforward, although over-rich running could simply be due to a worn unit, calling for its replacement. Wear in the distributor skew gears can also result in uneven running.

Ford gearboxes are another item that motor-noters have praised over the years, and it was really only the somewhat agricultural 3.0-litre gearbox that came in for anything less than full marks. Gearboxes fitted to first-generation Consul Capris did not have synchromesh on first gear, while some cars had steering-column gear change – hardly sporting, and rather imprecise. With the introduction of the 2000E gearbox (first seen on the Corsair V4 2000E), changes were always smooth and the ratios better chosen for sports motoring.

In use, the gearboxes fitted to Capris from Mk I onwards (including 3.0-litre manual cars) should be smooth and precise with strong synchromesh action. However, wear can create a sloppy change, while weak second and third synchromesh cones can make downward changes difficult, the gearbox actually jumping out of gear in bad cases. Also, listen for noisy bearings – another give-away of a poor gearbox. Wear in the prop shaft (as discussed earlier) can cause backlash in the drivetrain, making it impossible to make smooth changes. Later Capris – especially the 3.0-litre Ghias – were fitted with the C3-type automatic transmission system which gave reliable service, although it did sap the engine of valuable horsepower. In all cases, however, spares are readily available for repair and rebuilt units can be bought from specialists.

Before shutting the bonnet it is worth casting an eye over the car's wiring, especially if it is an early model. For some reason competent mechanics can turn into ham-fisted electricians when faced with a soldering iron or multimeter, and tape joints and odd lengths of extra wire should be treated with suspicion! Seriously though, Ford's electrics – which are not Lucas – are no more fault-prone than the units used by other mainstream manufacturers, and parts are still readily available.

Moving to the interior of the car, first check on the inside of the sills and the condition of the B post. Here, too, signs of advanced rot from the inside can spell costly repairs.

The Interior

Sadly, some of the trim panels and carpets used on Capris were not that hard wearing, the result being that many (even carefully used examples) soon begin to look tatty. Typical of this are the vinyl seats in the Mk I cars, these tending to split their seams after hard use. The early Recaro seats fitted to S models also suffer from wear problems, the squab sides becoming worn and frayed through continued scuffing as driver and passengers get in and out. Seats on the later 2.8i cars had leather panels which largely overcame problems of wear.

Trim panels and carpets may now be looking their age, especially if they have been abused. And while it is true that replacements are available, experts agree there can sometimes be colour differences when old and new coverings are mismatched. The same experts also say that it is best to be careful when buying trim parts from autojumbles for the same reason. (If you are restoring the car and retrimming the whole of the interior, careful colour matching should

Typical interior trim used on Mk III cars. Experts suggest that buying trim panels at autojumbles can sometimes result in a colour mismatch while the side sections of the seat squabs, particularly on Recaro seats, can become worn; causing holes in bad examples making the interior look tatty.

not be a problem!) If you simply need to give the trim a good clean, use one of the excellent products that are available on the market for just this job. Before you finish with the interior, look for any evidence of leakage around the sun roof.

TEST DRIVING

As all cars have individual characters (this is true even of different examples of the same model and year) there is little point in trying to describe in detail how any one model will perform. Added to this, everyone's yardstick of what is good or bad handling and good or bad performance varies dramatically. However, a good measure of what to expect can be gained by reading the original road-test report. Also remember that more can be learned about a car's behaviour by driving it carefully, listening for ominous noises and feeling for any handling anomalies (does the steering pull to one side? Does the suspension wallow? Are the brakes spongy?), than by seeing how fast it goes!

A selection of special Capris seen at the Club Capri International Day at Windsor Castle in mid-1994. (a) A special-bodied pickup in canary yellow.

(b) A JBA Javelin GRP 'kit' car based on a Capri.

(c) A 1973 Capri convertible.

(d) A Crayford Capri, one of only thirty-one built.

A Mk I Capri 3.1-litre turbo with a brace of Cibie sport lamps and ultra-wide alloy wheels.

Whatever the model of Capri you are testing, the engine should start cleanly with no necessity to keep it turning over before it fires. Once it has reached its normal operating temperature, the gauge should stay static; any tendency to rise and fall with engine and road speed could indicate a blown head gasket. The sportier Capris have an oil-pressure gauge, so keep a watchful eye to see how this reacts on tick over when the engine is hot. Watch in the mirror for signs of smoke when applying the throttle after a period of over-run as this could indicate worn valve guides and/or cylinder bores. None of the Ford engines fitted to the Capri was afraid of hard work, although regular servicing was necessary to keep them at their best. Should you be lucky enough to find a low-mileage car with service papers, so much the better.

As discussed previously, suspension settings on the sporting versions of the Capri will give a noticeably hard ride – particularly over uneven surfaces – when compared to modern hatchback standards. If you are testing an S, a 2.8i or an RS car and it has a softish ride, then there is a strong chance that the dampers and springs need replacing.

Other characteristics which may be felt as the test progresses include vibration through the steering, an obvious sign that the wheels are out of balance. Another give-away is vibration through the brake pedal, which is a sure sign of warped discs. Neither

Under the bonnet lies a full house 3.1 turbo conversion based on the Essex V6. A comprehensive and well executed job.

of these problems are difficult to sort out once you know what is wrong. However, brakes that pull to one side could indicate a number of things, including a faulty slave cylinder.

As for the transmission and clutch operation, the Capri is notcably smooth in this department – as is the case with all latter-day Fords. There should be no snatch in transmission-drive take-up, while gear changes should be baulk-free during both upward and downward changes. Clutch take-up should also be smooth; check to see how much free travel there is before drive take-up to establish the condition of the clutch.

When the road test is over, lift the bonnet once more and check again for tell-tale leaks, then take another look underneath the car. Try to be objective, and make a note of any parts that need replacing so that you can relate the rough prices of these to the asking price. It is sometimes possible to negotiate a good deal once all the costs have been accounted for – you might get a better bargain than you had counted on!

Bibliography

Capri – Brooklands Gold Portfolio (Brooklands Press Ltd, nd).

Hayes, Walter *Henry – A Life of Henry Ford* (Weidenfeld & Nicolson, 1990).

Iacocca, Lee and Novak, William *Iacocca* (Sidgwick & Jackson, 1986).

Nye, Doug *British Cars of the Sixties* (Thomas Nelson & Sons Ltd, 1970).

Robson, Graham *The Works Escorts* (Haynes Publications, 1977).

Taylor, Mike *Sporting Fords – Cortina to Cosworth* (The Crowood Press, 1992).

Walton, Jeremy *Capri – Collector's Guide* (Motor Racing Publications, 1983).

Walton, Jeremy *Capri – The Development and Competition History of Europe's GT Car* (Haynes Publications, 1987).

Wood, Jonathan *Wheels of Misfortune* (Sidgwick & Jackson, 1988).

'Bye-bye Capri. Gone but never forgotten.'

Index